D1128604

Date: 6/16/16

GRA 741.5 DOC V.3
Ewing, Al,
Doctor Who : Conversion
the Eleventh Doctor.

PALM BEACH COUNTY
LIBRARY SYSTEM
3650 SUMMIT BLVD.
WEST PALM BEACH, FL 33406

DISCARDED

DOCTOR WHO

THE ELEVENTH DOCTOR

VOL 3: CONVERSION

"Amazing! It hit all the right notes, and got the Doctor perfect! 9/10"
COMIC BOOK CAST

"Mind-bending and impressive."
BENJAMIN HERMAN

"Balances out the serious with well-placed humor, slapstick included."
WHATCHA READING

"A fun read with some great characterization and a sense of adventure. 9 out of 10!"
COMICS VERSE

"An enjoyable romp."
FLICKERING MYTH

"9.5 out of 10!"
NERDS UNCHAINED

"Does a splendid job of capturing Matt Smith's expressions."
GEEK WITH CURVES

"The tone of the Eleventh Doctor is strong in this one."
WARPED FACTOR

"A fantastic Eleventh Doctor adventure! 9 out of 10!"
NEWSARAMA

"A great job creating a companion who can keep up with the Doctor. 10 out of 10!"
PROJECT FANDOM

"Nails the tone and spirit right out of the gate. 4 out of 5!"
COMIC BOOK RESOURCES

"A great continuation of a fabulous series. The character depth, dramatic arc and suspenseful flow make it a gripping read."
UNLEASH THE FANBOY

"Excellent script with great artwork. I've become a fan of Alice Obiefune – what a character she has become!"
TM STASH

"Compelling art."
BLEEDING COOL

"Well-written with great art!"
COMIC BASTARDS

TITAN COMICS

EDITOR
Andrew James

ASSISTANT EDITOR
Kirsten Murray

DESIGNER
Rob Williams

SENIOR EDITOR
Steve White

TITAN COMICS EDITORIAL
Lizzie Kaye, Tom Williams

PRODUCTION ASSISTANT
Peter James

PRODUCTION SUPERVISORS
Maria Pearson, Jackie Flook

PRODUCTION MANAGER
Obi Onuora

STUDIO MANAGER
Emma Smith

CIRCULATION MANAGER
Steve Tothill

**SENIOR MARKETING
& PRESS OFFICER**
Owen Johnson

MARKETING MANAGER
Ricky Claydon

ADVERTISING MANAGER
Michelle Fairlamb

PUBLISHING MANAGER
Darryl Tothill

PUBLISHING DIRECTOR
Chris Teather

OPERATIONS DIRECTOR
Leigh Baulch

EXECUTIVE DIRECTOR
Vivian Cheung

PUBLISHER
Nick Landau

BBC WORLDWIDE
**DIRECTOR OF
EDITORIAL GOVERNANCE**
Nicolas Brett

**DIRECTOR OF CONSUMERPRODUCTS
AND PUBLISHING**
Andrew Moultrie

HEAD OF UK PUBLISHING
Chris Kerwin

PUBLISHER
Mandy Thwaites

PUBLISHING CO-ORDINATOR
Eva Abramik

**DOCTOR WHO: THE ELEVENTH DOCTOR
VOL 3: CONVERSION**
HB ISBN: 9781782763031 SB ISBN: 9781782767435

Published by Titan Comics, a division of
Titan Publishing Group, Ltd. 144 Southwark Street,
London, SE1 0UP.

BBC, DOCTOR WHO (word marks, logos and devices) and TARDIS are trade marks
British Broadcasting Corporation and are used under license. BBC logo © BBC
Doctor Who logo © BBC 2009. TARDIS image © BBC 1963. Cybermen image © B
Pedler/Gerry Davis 1966.

With the exception of artwork used for review purposes, no portion of this book m
reproduced or transmitted in any form or by any means, without the express perm
of the publisher Titan Comics or the BBC.

Names, characters, places and incidents featured in this publication are either
product of the author's imagination or used fictitiously. Any resemblance to act
persons, living or dead (except for satirical purposes), is entirely coincidenta

A CIP catalogue record for this title is available from the British Library.
First edition: December 2015.

10 9 8 7 6 5 4 3 2 1

Printed in China. TC0663.

Titan Comics does not read or accept unsolicited DOCTOR WHO submissions of
stories or artwork.

Special thanks to
Steven Moffat, Brian Minchin, Matt Nicholls,
James Dudley, Edward Russell, Derek Ritchie,
Scott Handcock, Kirsty Mullan, Kate Bush,
Julia Nocciolino, Ed Casey, Marcus Wilson and
Richard Cookson for their invaluable assistance

DOCTOR WHO
THE ELEVENTH DOCTOR

VOL 3: CONVERSION

WRITERS:
AL EWING & ROB WILLIAMS

ARTISTS:
SIMON FRASER
BOO COOK
WARREN PLEECE

COLORISTS:
GARY CALDWELL
HI-FI

LETTERS: RICHARD STARKINGS
AND COMICRAFT'S
JIMMY BETANCOURT

 www.titan-comics.com

DOCTOR WHO

THE ELEVENTH DOCTOR

ALICE

Having lost her mother to illness and facing eviction from her landlord, former Library Assistant Alice Obiefune felt like her life was falling apart. Then she met the Doctor! Now she's determined to see all the beauty and strangeness of the universe as she travels with him in the TARDIS!

JONES

Initially a forgettable skiffle musician, Jones is destined to become a rock god! He was also Alice's mother's favorite musician. He changes his look as often as his underwear (*regularly*, thank you very much)! He's traveling with the Doctor in the hope it ignites his creative spark.

ARC

A shapeshifter, dubbed 'Autonomous Reasoning Cente by the rogue corporate scientis of SERVEYOUinc, ARC can shi form into anything it chooses Having found its own voice, AR now travels with the Doctor, enjoying the life of adventure while searching for the truth behind its mysterious origin..

PREVIOUSLY...

Alice first met the Doctor when she helped save London from a rainbow-colored alien dog.
The chameleonic Jones joined the crew when he snuck on board the TARDIS after a disastrous debut gig.
ARC boarded from a grim research base, where its probing attempts to communicate were terribly misunderstood.

Throughout their adventures, the malign SERVEYOUinc corporation lurked... personified by the tempting Talent Scout, who only wants to offer you... everything! The Doctor, in a moment of weakness, gave in to the Talent Scout's predations... and became CEO of SERVEYOUinc. It was a disaster! Alice, Jones and ARC saved the Doctor from himself. But can they learn to trust him again...?

When you've finished reading the collection, please email your thoughts to doctorwhocomic@titanemail.com

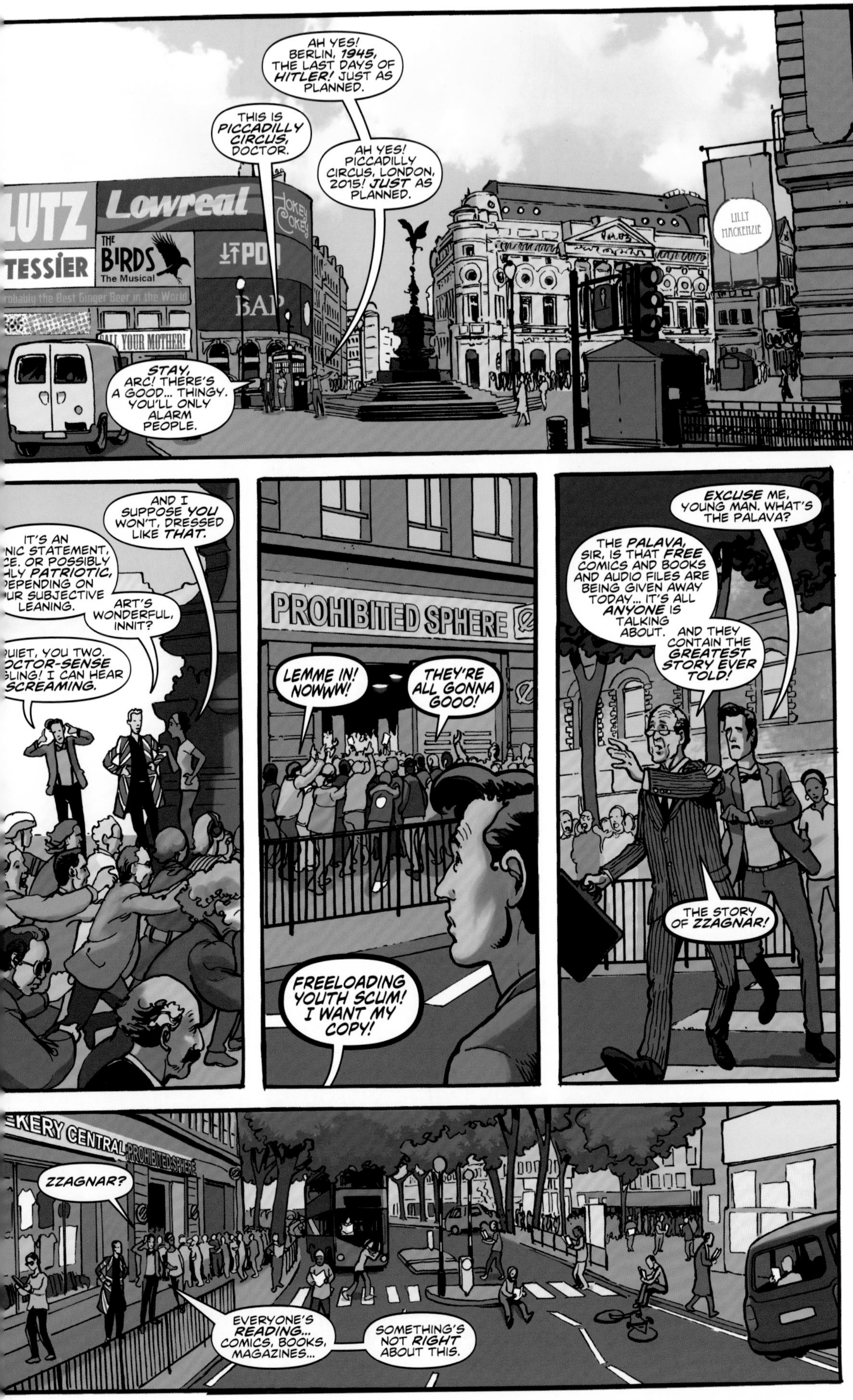
AH YES! BERLIN, 1945, THE LAST DAYS OF HITLER! JUST AS PLANNED.
THIS IS PICCADILLY CIRCUS, DOCTOR.
AH YES! PICCADILLY CIRCUS, LONDON, 2015! JUST AS PLANNED.
STAY, ARC! THERE'S A GOOD... THINGY. YOU'LL ONLY ALARM PEOPLE.
LUTZ
Lowreal
TESSIER
THE BIRDS The Musical
robably the Best Ginger Beer in the World
BAP
ALL YOUR MOTHER!
LILLY MACKENZIE
AND I SUPPOSE YOU WON'T, DRESSED LIKE THAT.
IT'S AN NIC STATEMENT, CE. OR POSSIBLY HLY PATRIOTIC, EPENDING ON UR SUBJECTIVE LEANING.
ART'S WONDERFUL, INNIT?
UIET, YOU TWO. OCTOR-SENSE GLING! I CAN HEAR SCREAMING.
PROHIBITED SPHERE
LEMME IN! NOWWW!
THEY'RE ALL GONNA GOOO!
FREELOADING YOUTH SCUM! I WANT MY COPY!
EXCUSE ME, YOUNG MAN. WHAT'S THE PALAVA?
THE PALAVA, SIR, IS THAT FREE COMICS AND BOOKS AND AUDIO FILES ARE BEING GIVEN AWAY TODAY... IT'S ALL ANYONE IS TALKING ABOUT.
AND THEY CONTAIN THE GREATEST STORY EVER TOLD!
THE STORY OF ZZAGNAR!
EKERY CENTRAL
PROHIBITED SPHERE
ZZAGNAR?
EVERYONE'S READING... COMICS, BOOKS, MAGAZINES...
SOMETHING'S NOT RIGHT ABOUT THIS.

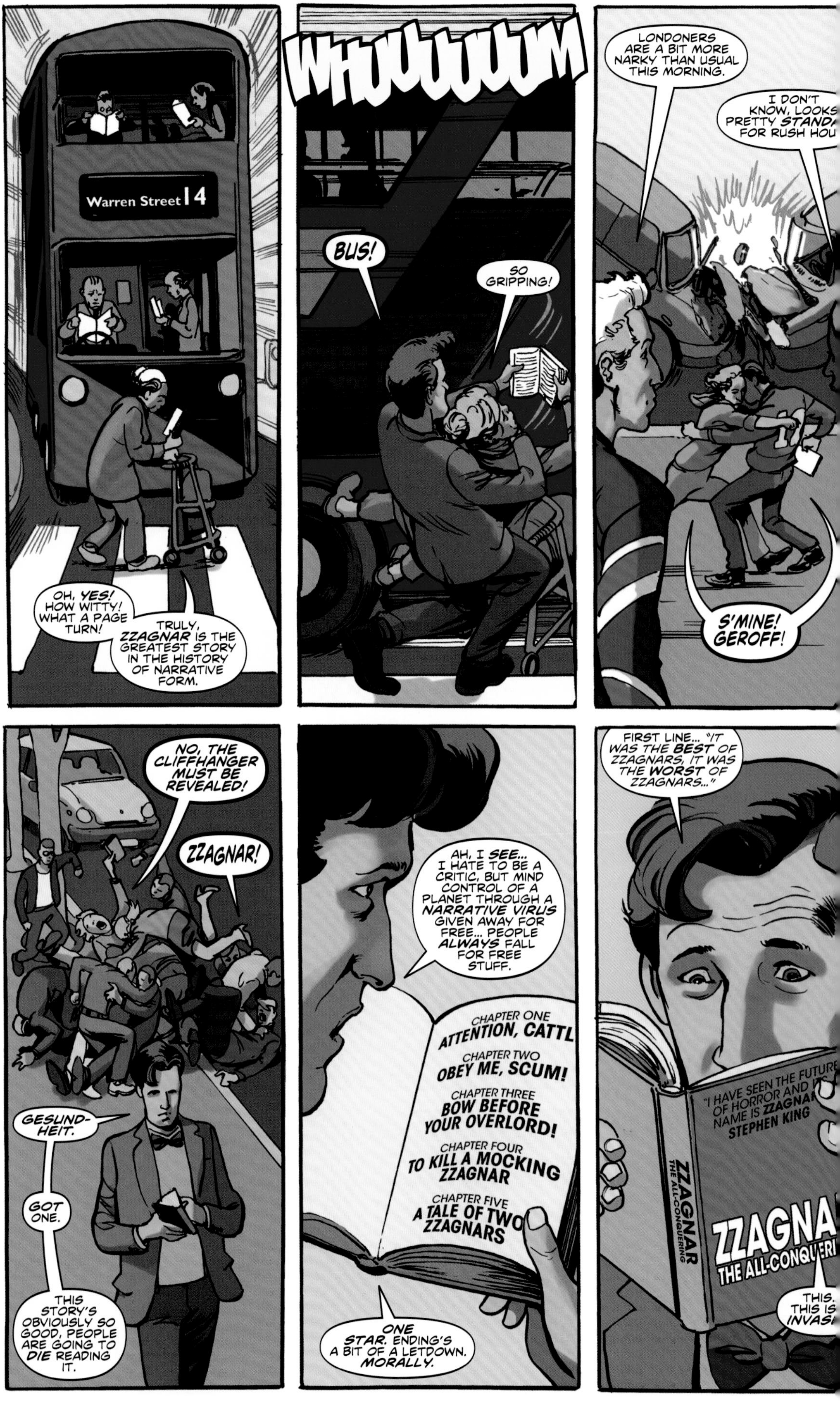

Warren Street 14
OH, YES! HOW WITTY! WHAT A PAGE TURN!
TRULY, ZZAGNAR IS THE GREATEST STORY IN THE HISTORY OF NARRATIVE FORM.
WHUUUUUUM
BUS!
SO GRIPPING!
LONDONERS ARE A BIT MORE NARKY THAN USUAL THIS MORNING.
I DON'T KNOW, LOOKS PRETTY STAND FOR RUSH HOU
S'MINE! GEROFF!
NO, THE CLIFFHANGER MUST BE REVEALED!
ZZAGNAR!
GESUNDHEIT.
GOT ONE.
THIS STORY'S OBVIOUSLY SO GOOD, PEOPLE ARE GOING TO DIE READING IT.
AH, I SEE... I HATE TO BE A CRITIC, BUT MIND CONTROL OF A PLANET THROUGH A NARRATIVE VIRUS GIVEN AWAY FOR FREE... PEOPLE ALWAYS FALL FOR FREE STUFF.
CHAPTER ONE
ATTENTION, CATTL
CHAPTER TWO
OBEY ME, SCUM!
CHAPTER THREE
BOW BEFORE YOUR OVERLORD!
CHAPTER FOUR
TO KILL A MOCKING ZZAGNAR
CHAPTER FIVE
A TALE OF TWO ZZAGNARS
ONE STAR. ENDING'S A BIT OF A LETDOWN. MORALLY.
FIRST LINE... "IT WAS THE BEST OF ZZAGNARS, IT WAS THE WORST OF ZZAGNARS..."
"I HAVE SEEN THE FUTURE OF HORROR AND IT NAME IS ZZAGNA
STEPHEN KING
ZZAGNAR THE ALL-CONQUERING
ZZAGNA
THE ALL-CONQU
THIS. THIS IS INVAS

ALL HAIL ZZAGNAR.

ALL HAIL ZZAGNAR.

ALL HAIL ZZAGNAR.

ALL HAIL ZZAGNAR.

L HAIL AGNAR.

ALL HAIL ZZAGNAR.

ALL HAIL ZZAGNAR.

QVC

ALICE! JONES! DON'T READ THE FREE BOOKS AND COMICS, WHATEVER YOU DO!

HE UBTS GNAR.

HE IS CRITICAL OF ZZAGNAR.

HE HAS POOR LITERARY TASTE AND THEREFORE MUST BE 'PULPED'.

WHOEVER'S DOING THIS IS A BIT TOUCHY ABOUT CRITICISM.

NOTICED THAT, YES.

S'THE ART OF CREATION, ALICE. THE AUTHOR HAS OPENED HIS SOUL TO US...

"THE PAST IS A DIFFERENT COUNTRY. ZZAGNAR DOES THINGS THERE. AND HERE. AND ANYWHERE HE PLEASES. SCUM."

IT'S A WINNING TURN OF PHRASE, I'LL GRANT YOU, JONES. BUT I'M NOT SURE THERE IS AN AUTHOR--

DOCTOR! THEY'RE GOING TO RIP US TO SHREDS! PAY ATTENTION!

I THINK THIS STORY AUTHORED ITSELF. 'ZZAGNAR' IS ALIVE -- HE'S THE VIRUS. A LIVING STORY...

DOCTOR! THE COMICS AND BOOKS ARE EVERYWHERE!

IT'S ALRIGHT, ALICE. THE TARDIS IS JUST DOWN SHAFTESBURY AVENUE IN...

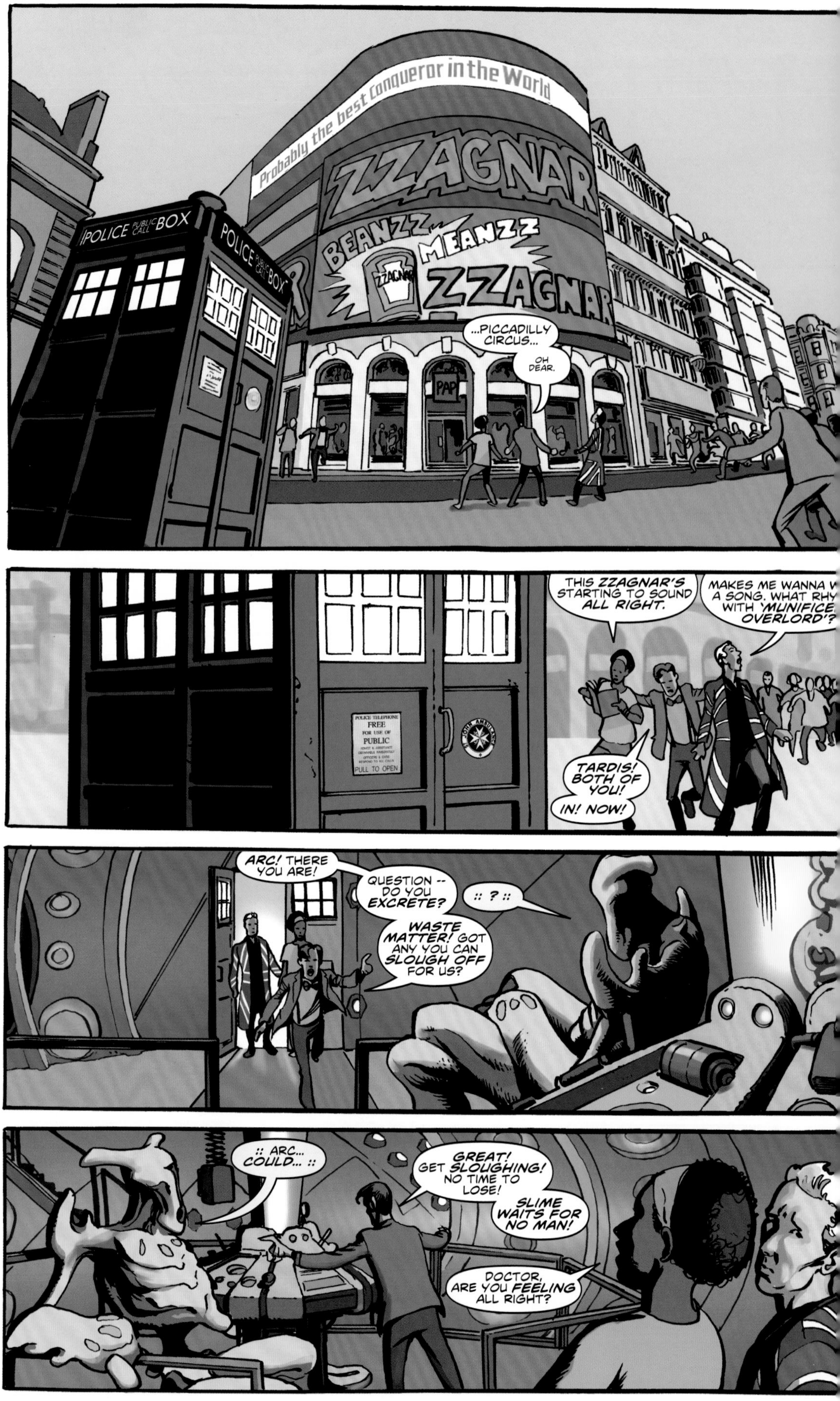
Probably the best Conqueror in the World
ZZAGNAR
BEANZZ MEANZZ ZZAGNAR
POLICE PUBLIC CALL BOX
...PICCADILLY CIRCUS...
OH DEAR.
PAP
THIS ZZAGNAR'S STARTING TO SOUND ALL RIGHT.
MAKES ME WANNA W A SONG. WHAT RHY WITH 'MUNIFICE OVERLORD'?
POLICE TELEPHONE FREE FOR USE OF PUBLIC
PULL TO OPEN
TARDIS! BOTH OF YOU!
IN! NOW!
ARC! THERE YOU ARE!
QUESTION -- DO YOU EXCRETE?
:: ? ::
WASTE MATTER! GOT ANY YOU CAN SLOUGH OFF FOR US?
:: ARC... COULD... ::
GREAT! GET SLOUGHING! NO TIME TO LOSE!
SLIME WAITS FOR NO MAN!
DOCTOR, ARE YOU FEELING ALL RIGHT?

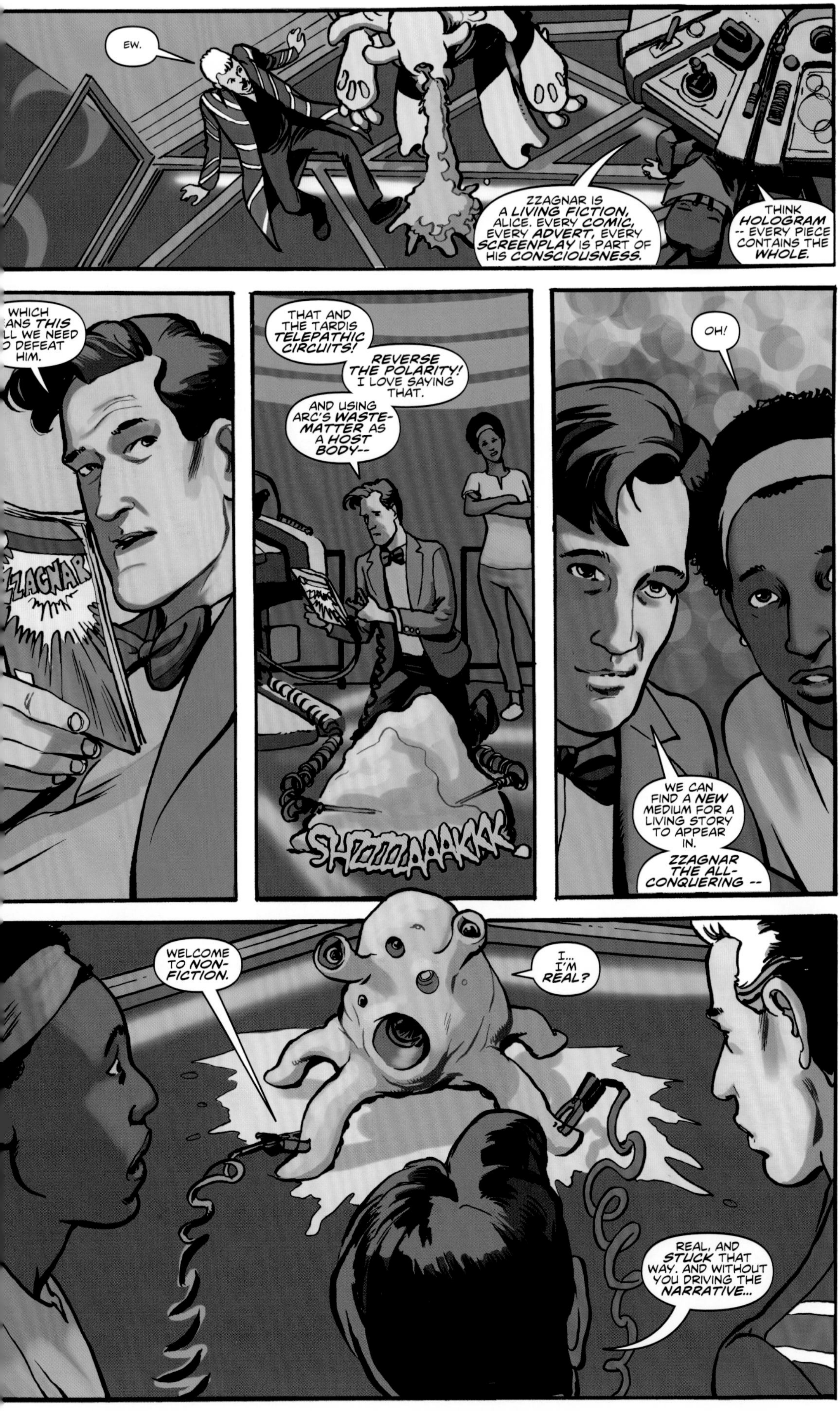
EW.
ZZAGNAR IS A LIVING FICTION, ALICE. EVERY COMIC, EVERY ADVERT, EVERY SCREENPLAY IS PART OF HIS CONSCIOUSNESS.
THINK HOLOGRAM -- EVERY PIECE CONTAINS THE WHOLE.
WHICH ANS THIS LL WE NEED O DEFEAT HIM.
ZZAGNAR
THAT AND THE TARDIS TELEPATHIC CIRCUITS!
REVERSE THE POLARITY! I LOVE SAYING THAT.
AND USING ARC'S WASTE-MATTER AS A HOST BODY--
SHZZZZLAAAKKK
OH!
WE CAN FIND A NEW MEDIUM FOR A LIVING STORY TO APPEAR IN.
ZZAGNAR THE ALL-CONQUERING --
WELCOME TO NON-FICTION.
I... I'M REAL?
REAL, AND STUCK THAT WAY. AND WITHOUT YOU DRIVING THE NARRATIVE...

YOUR STORY'S *DEAD* ON THE PAGE.

N-*NO!* THE HUMAN RACE *MUST* READ ME! THEY MUST BE *ENSLAVED* -- MADE TO READ -- OR --

-- OR HOW DO I *KNOW?*

HOW DO I KNOW IF I'M ANY *GOOD?*

DOCTOR... UNDERNEATH ALL THAT *WORLD-CONQUERING*, HE'S...

THE MOST *PATHETIC*, *PITIFUL* CREATURE IN THE UNIVERSE.

A *WRITER.*

HOW WILL YOU *KNOW?*

YOU *TRY*, AND FIND OUT -- LIKE ANYONE ELSE.

YOU... YOU THINK TH[E] PLANET *MIG[HT]* LIKE MY WOR[K] THEN? AFTE[R] EVERYTHING[...]

DUNNO. BUT HUMANS LOVE *STORIES*, ZZAGNAR. AND THEY LOVE THEM EVEN *MORE...*

"...WHEN THEY'RE *FREE.*"

ZZAGNAR
WRITER OF ZZ-MEN

1A 1B 2 2B

Bald COMICS

HYPERON

HAIL ZZ AG NAR

WHO SHOULD I MAKE IT OUT TO?

THE END

INTERLUDE

GIVE FREE OR DIE

POLICE PUBLIC CALL BOX
POLICE PUBLIC CALL BOX

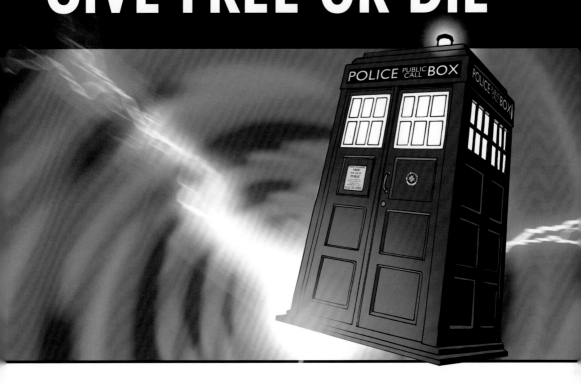

WRITERS
AL EWING & ROB WILLIAMS

ARTIST
SIMON FRASER

COLORIST
GARY CALDWELL

LETTERER
RICHARD STARKINGS AND COMICRAFT'S JIMMY BETANCOURT

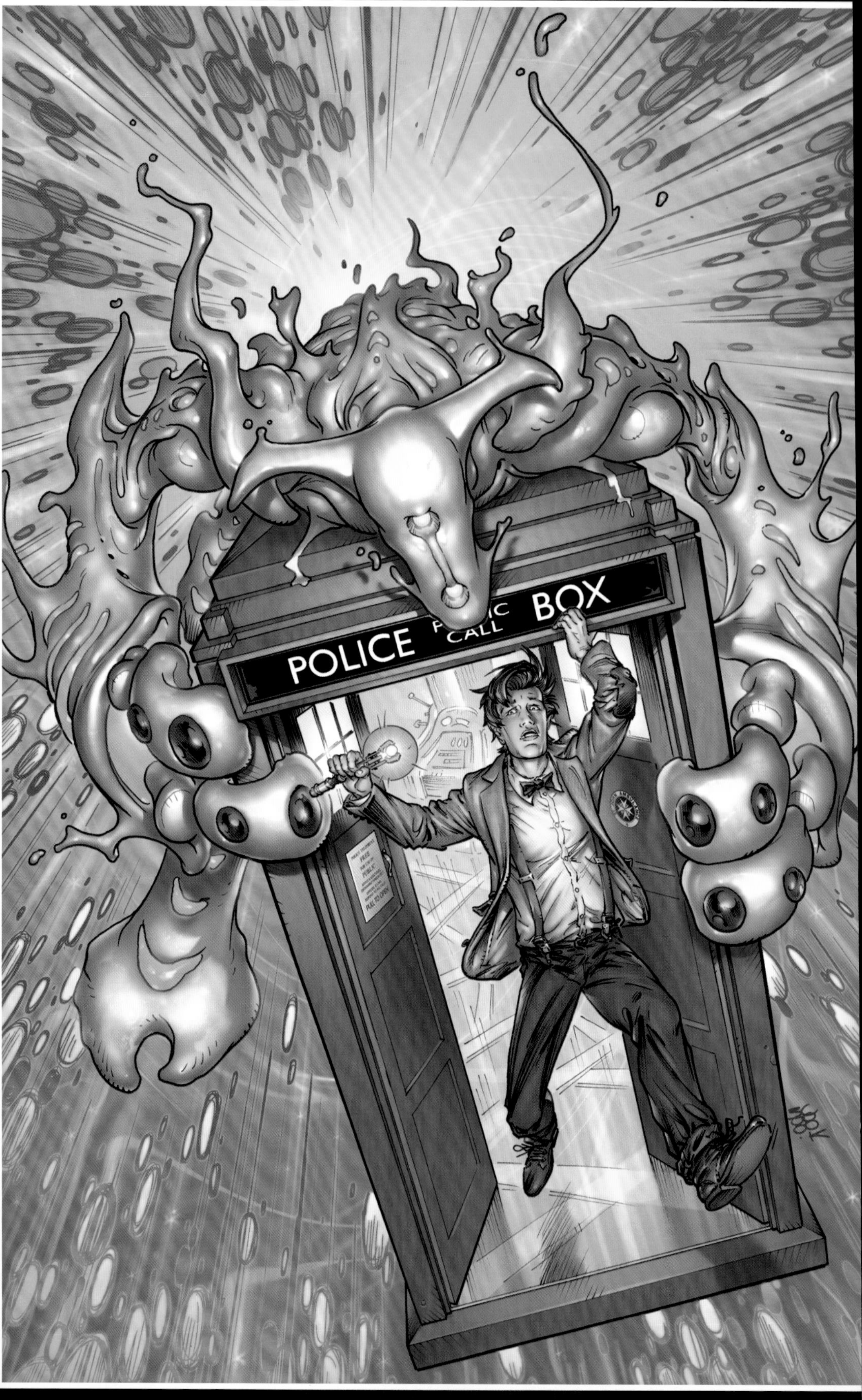
POLICE PUBLIC CALL BOX
PULL TO OPEN

CHAPTER 11 Cover A: Boo Cook

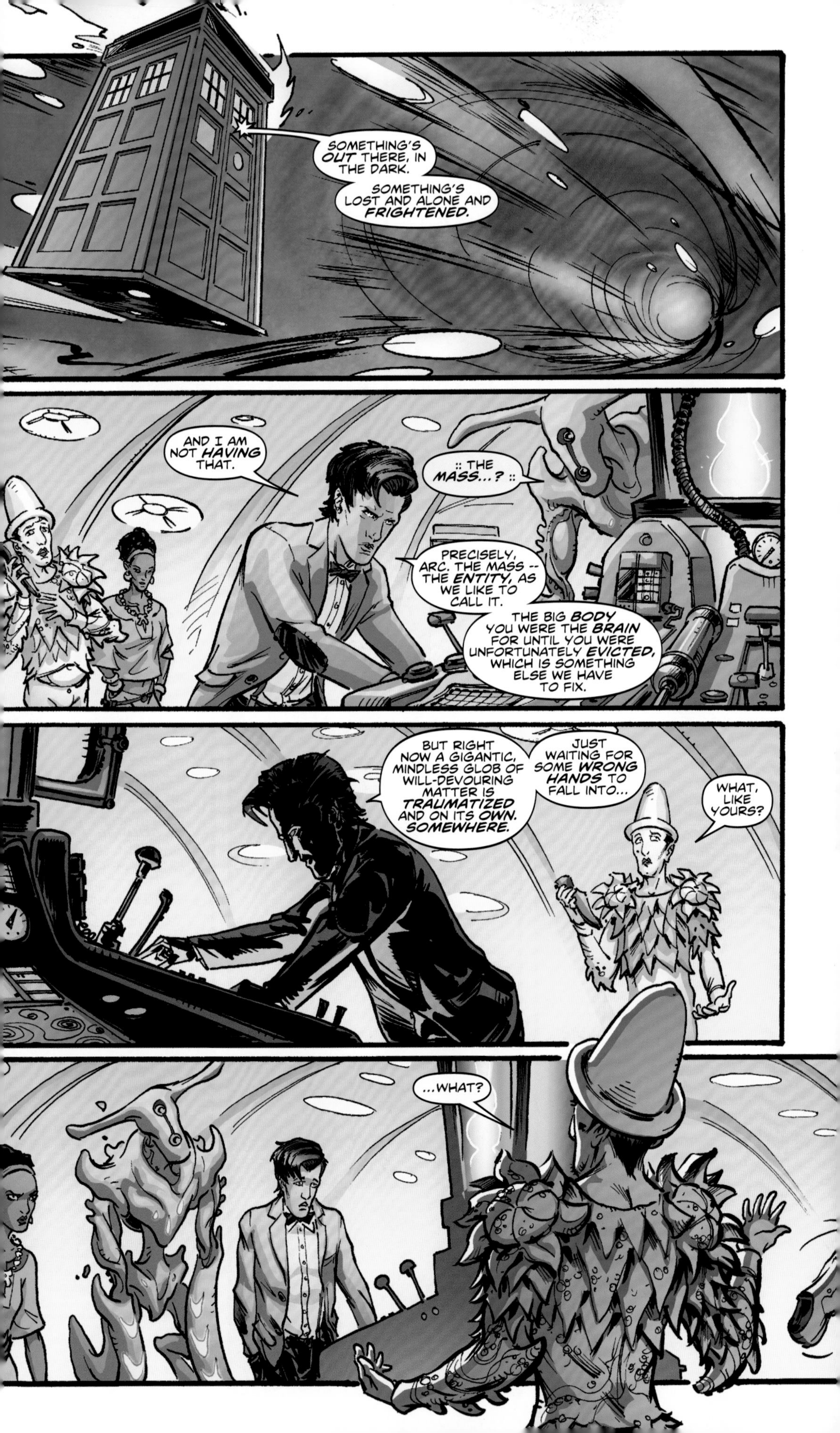
SOMETHING'S OUT THERE, IN THE DARK.
SOMETHING'S LOST AND ALONE AND FRIGHTENED.
AND I AM NOT HAVING THAT.
:: THE MASS...? ::
PRECISELY, ARC. THE MASS -- THE ENTITY, AS WE LIKE TO CALL IT.
THE BIG BODY YOU WERE THE BRAIN FOR UNTIL YOU WERE UNFORTUNATELY EVICTED, WHICH IS SOMETHING ELSE WE HAVE TO FIX.
BUT RIGHT NOW A GIGANTIC, MINDLESS GLOB OF WILL-DEVOURING MATTER IS TRAUMATIZED AND ON ITS OWN. SOMEWHERE.
JUST WAITING FOR SOME WRONG HANDS TO FALL INTO...
WHAT, LIKE YOURS?
...WHAT?

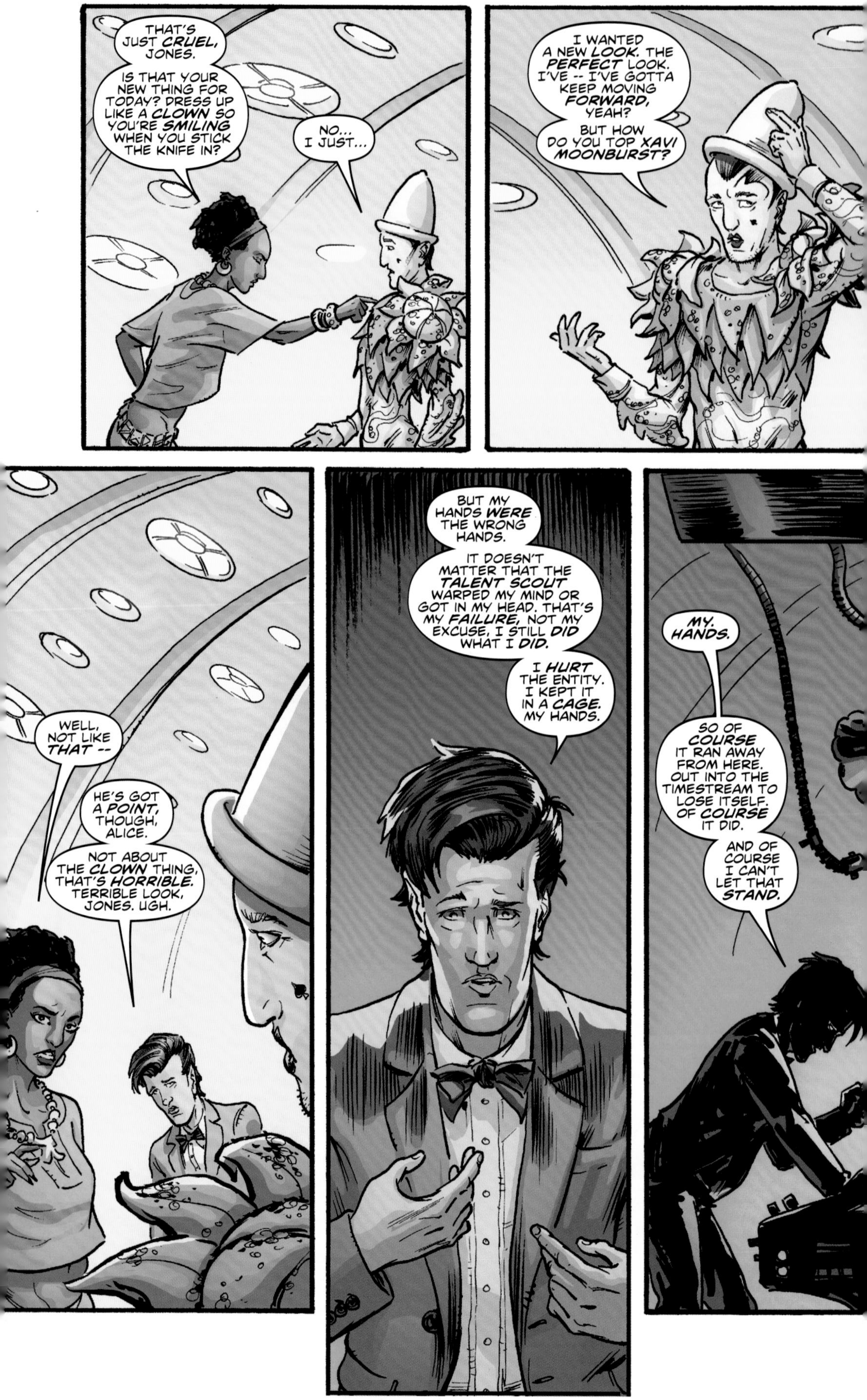
THAT'S JUST CRUEL, JONES.
IS THAT YOUR NEW THING FOR TODAY? DRESS UP LIKE A CLOWN SO YOU'RE SMILING WHEN YOU STICK THE KNIFE IN?
NO... I JUST...
I WANTED A NEW LOOK. THE PERFECT LOOK. I'VE -- I'VE GOTTA KEEP MOVING FORWARD, YEAH?
BUT HOW DO YOU TOP XAVI MOONBURST?
WELL, NOT LIKE THAT --
HE'S GOT A POINT, THOUGH, ALICE.
NOT ABOUT THE CLOWN THING, THAT'S HORRIBLE. TERRIBLE LOOK, JONES. UGH.
BUT MY HANDS WERE THE WRONG HANDS.
IT DOESN'T MATTER THAT THE TALENT SCOUT WARPED MY MIND OR GOT IN MY HEAD. THAT'S MY FAILURE, NOT MY EXCUSE, I STILL DID WHAT I DID.
I HURT THE ENTITY. I KEPT IT IN A CAGE. MY HANDS.
MY. HANDS.
SO OF COURSE IT RAN AWAY FROM HERE. OUT INTO THE TIMESTREAM TO LOSE ITSELF. OF COURSE IT DID.
AND OF COURSE I CAN'T LET THAT STAND.

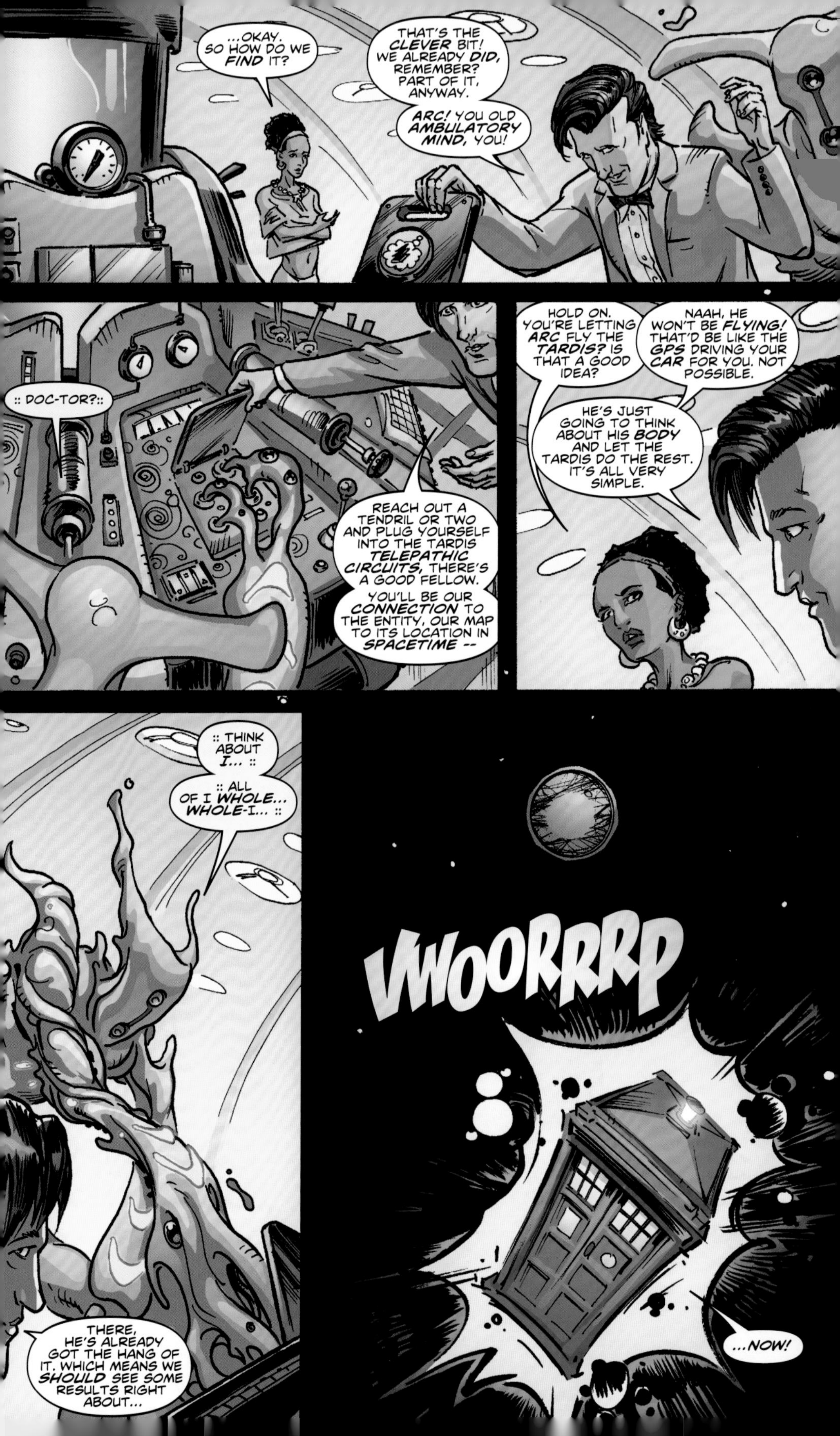

...OKAY. SO HOW DO WE FIND IT?
THAT'S THE CLEVER BIT! WE ALREADY DID, REMEMBER? PART OF IT, ANYWAY.
ARC! YOU OLD AMBULATORY MIND, YOU!
:: DOC-TOR?::
REACH OUT A TENDRIL OR TWO AND PLUG YOURSELF INTO THE TARDIS TELEPATHIC CIRCUITS, THERE'S A GOOD FELLOW.
YOU'LL BE OUR CONNECTION TO THE ENTITY, OUR MAP TO ITS LOCATION IN SPACETIME --
HOLD ON. YOU'RE LETTING ARC FLY THE TARDIS? IS THAT A GOOD IDEA?
NAAH, HE WON'T BE FLYING! THAT'D BE LIKE THE GPS DRIVING YOUR CAR FOR YOU. NOT POSSIBLE.
HE'S JUST GOING TO THINK ABOUT HIS BODY AND LET THE TARDIS DO THE REST. IT'S ALL VERY SIMPLE.
:: THINK ABOUT I... ::
:: ALL OF I WHOLE... WHOLE-I... ::
THERE, HE'S ALREADY GOT THE HANG OF IT. WHICH MEANS WE SHOULD SEE SOME RESULTS RIGHT ABOUT...
VWOORRRP
...NOW!

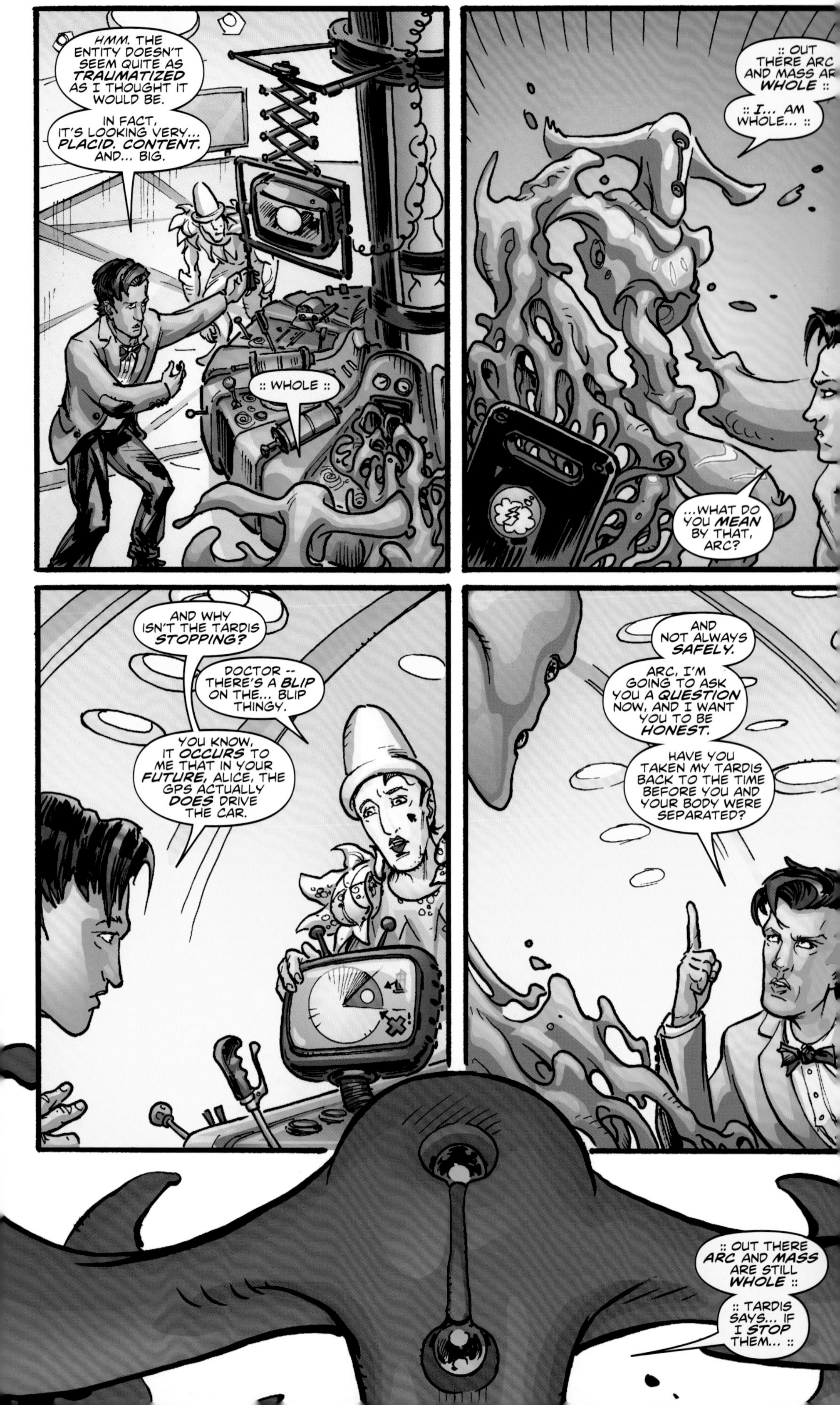
HMM. THE ENTITY DOESN'T SEEM QUITE AS TRAUMATIZED AS I THOUGHT IT WOULD BE.
IN FACT, IT'S LOOKING VERY... PLACID. CONTENT. AND... BIG.
:: WHOLE ::
:: OUT THERE ARC AND MASS AR WHOLE ::
:: I... AM WHOLE... ::
...WHAT DO YOU MEAN BY THAT, ARC?
AND WHY ISN'T THE TARDIS STOPPING?
DOCTOR -- THERE'S A BLIP ON THE... BLIP THINGY.
YOU KNOW, IT OCCURS TO ME THAT IN YOUR FUTURE, ALICE, THE GPS ACTUALLY DOES DRIVE THE CAR.
AND NOT ALWAYS SAFELY.
ARC, I'M GOING TO ASK YOU A QUESTION NOW, AND I WANT YOU TO BE HONEST.
HAVE YOU TAKEN MY TARDIS BACK TO THE TIME BEFORE YOU AND YOUR BODY WERE SEPARATED?
:: OUT THERE ARC AND MASS ARE STILL WHOLE ::
:: TARDIS SAYS... IF I STOP THEM... ::

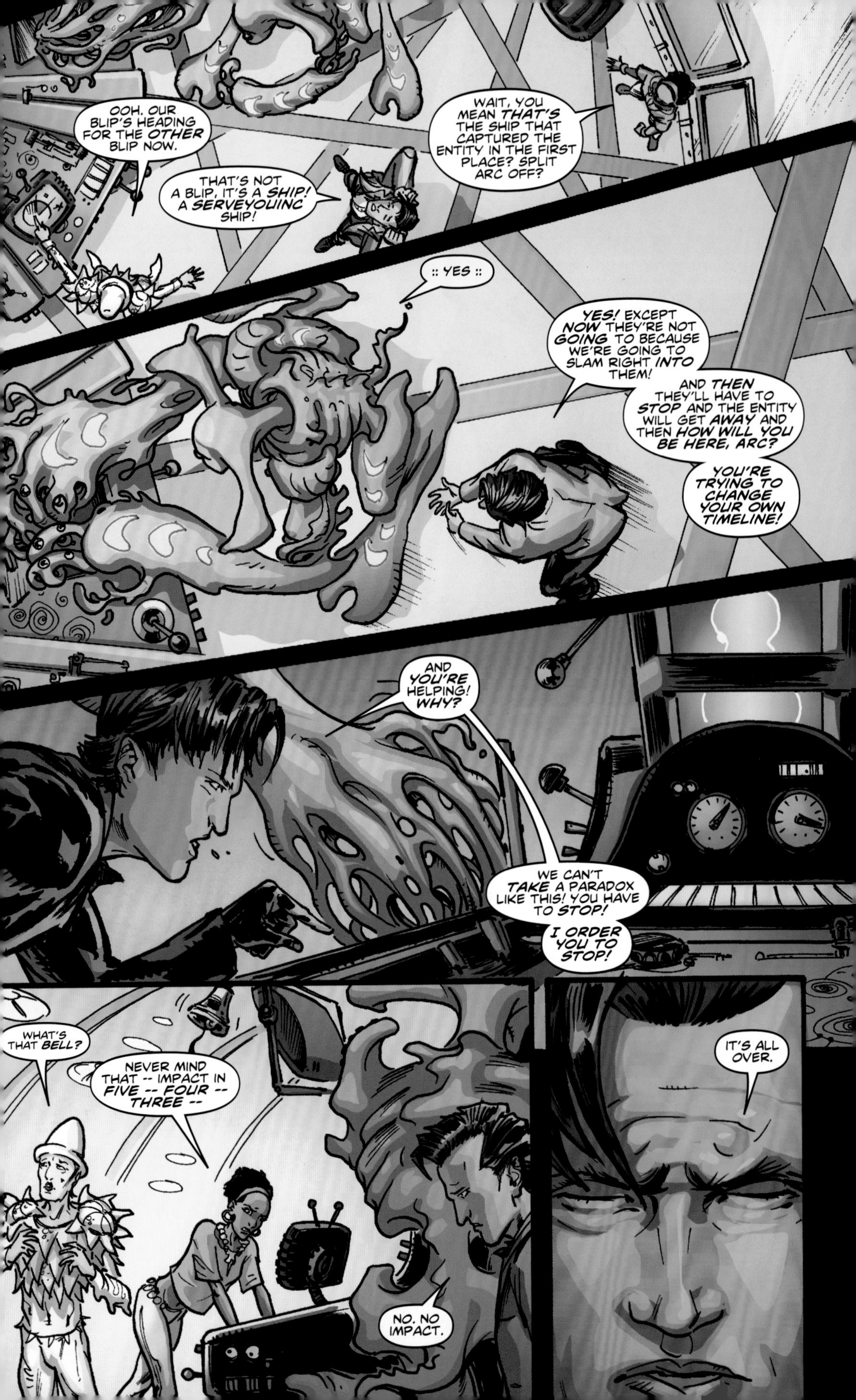
OOH. OUR BLIP'S HEADING FOR THE *OTHER* BLIP NOW.
THAT'S NOT A BLIP, IT'S A *SHIP!* A *SERVEYOUINC* SHIP!
WAIT, YOU MEAN *THAT'S* THE SHIP THAT CAPTURED THE ENTITY IN THE FIRST PLACE? SPLIT ARC OFF?
:: YES ::
YES! EXCEPT *NOW* THEY'RE NOT *GOING* TO BECAUSE WE'RE GOING TO SLAM RIGHT *INTO* THEM!
AND *THEN* THEY'LL HAVE TO *STOP* AND THE ENTITY WILL GET *AWAY* AND THEN *HOW WILL YOU BE HERE, ARC?*
YOU'RE TRYING TO CHANGE YOUR OWN TIMELINE!
AND *YOU'RE* HELPING! *WHY?*
WE CAN'T *TAKE* A PARADOX LIKE THIS! YOU HAVE TO *STOP!*
I ORDER YOU TO STOP!
WHAT'S THAT *BELL?*
NEVER MIND THAT -- IMPACT IN *FIVE -- FOUR -- THREE --*
NO. NO IMPACT.
IT'S ALL OVER.

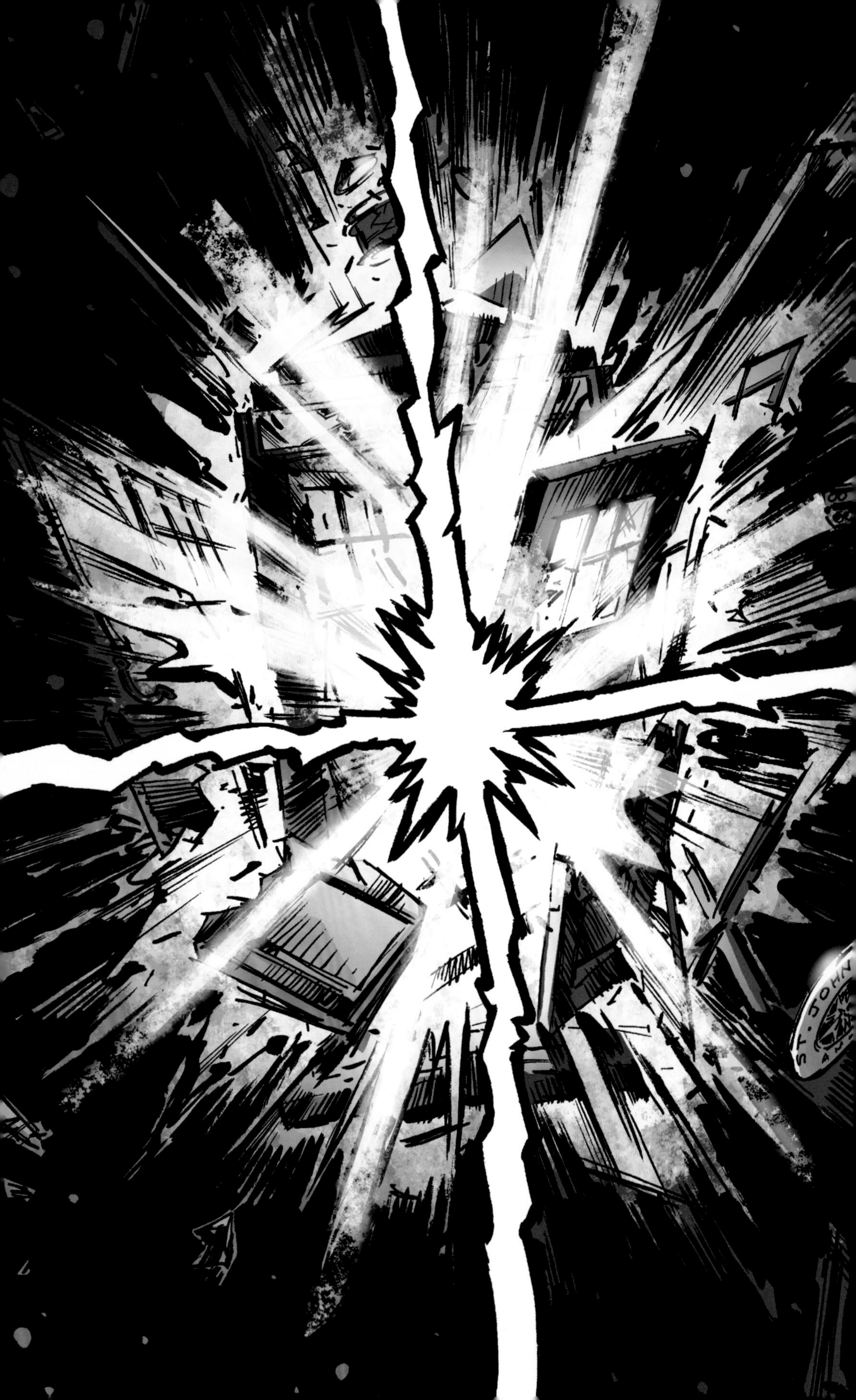

CHAPTER 11
FOUR DIMENSIONS

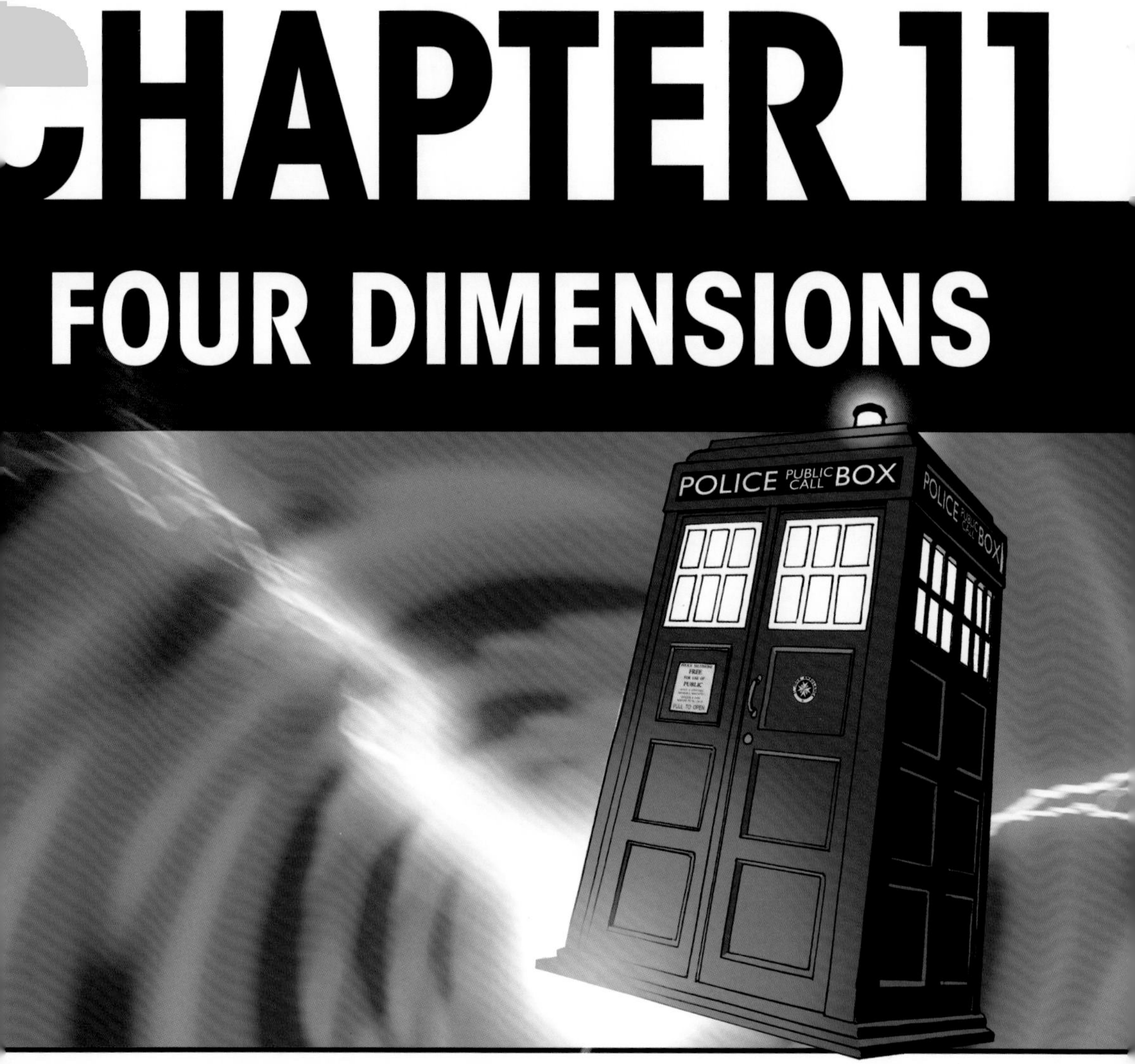
POLICE PUBLIC CALL BOX
POLICE PUBLIC CALL BOX

WRITER
AL EWING

ARTIST
BOO COOK

COLORIST
HI-FI

LETTERER
RICHARD STARKINGS AND COMICRAFT'S JIMMY BETANCOURT

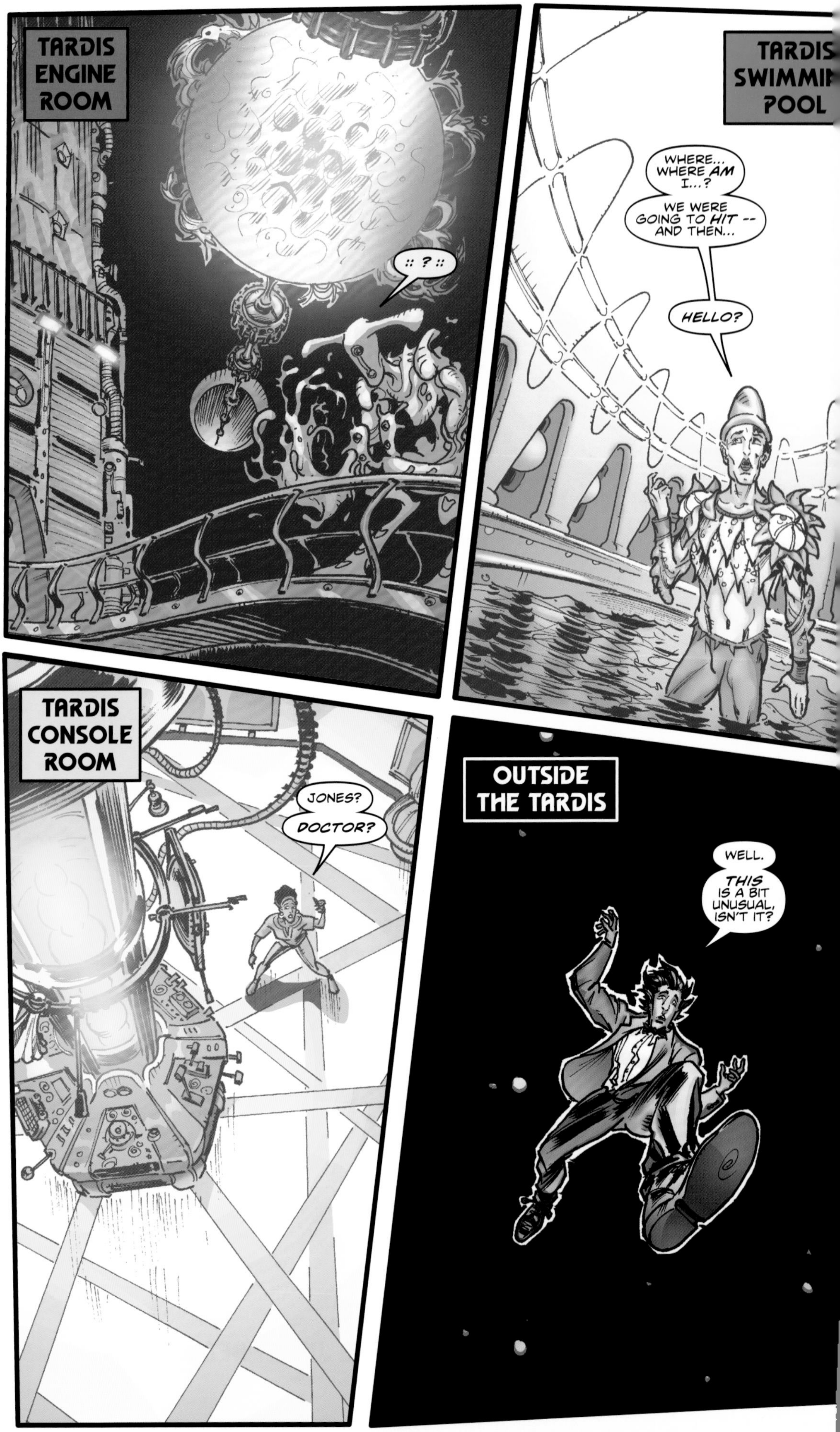
TARDIS ENGINE ROOM
:: ? ::
TARDIS SWIMMIN POOL
WHERE... WHERE AM I...?
WE WERE GOING TO HIT -- AND THEN...
HELLO?
TARDIS CONSOLE ROOM
JONES?
DOCTOR?
OUTSIDE THE TARDIS
WELL.
THIS IS A BIT UNUSUAL, ISN'T IT?

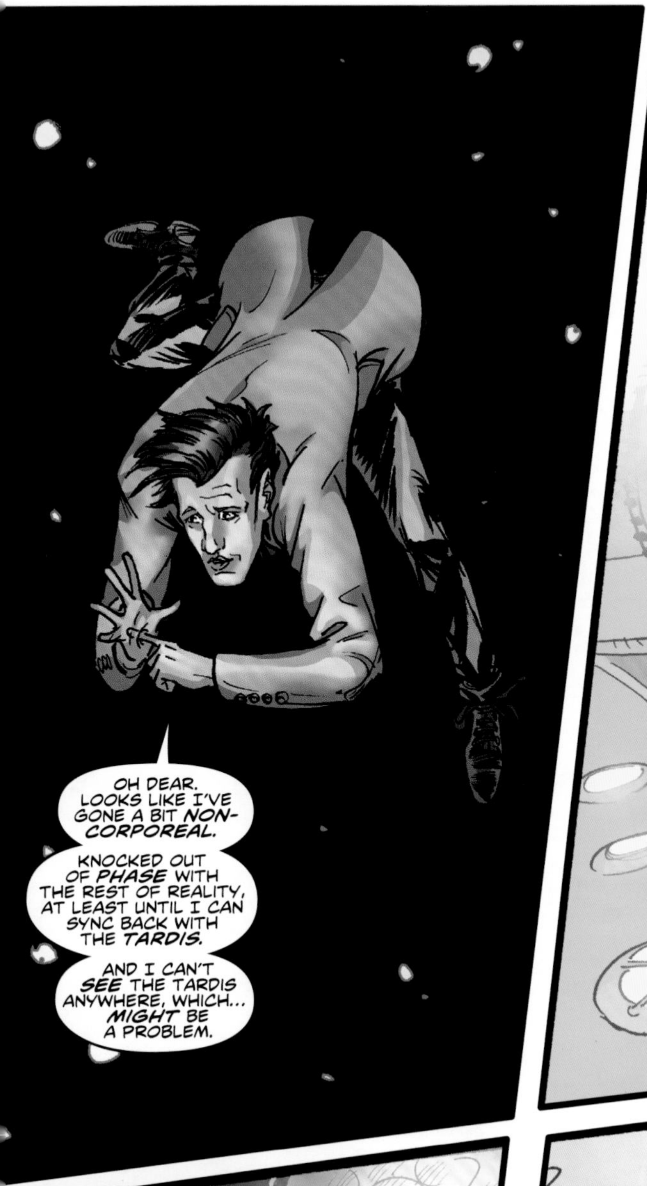
OH DEAR. LOOKS LIKE I'VE GONE A BIT NON-CORPOREAL.
KNOCKED OUT OF PHASE WITH THE REST OF REALITY, AT LEAST UNTIL I CAN SYNC BACK WITH THE TARDIS.
AND I CAN'T SEE THE TARDIS ANYWHERE, WHICH... MIGHT BE A PROBLEM.

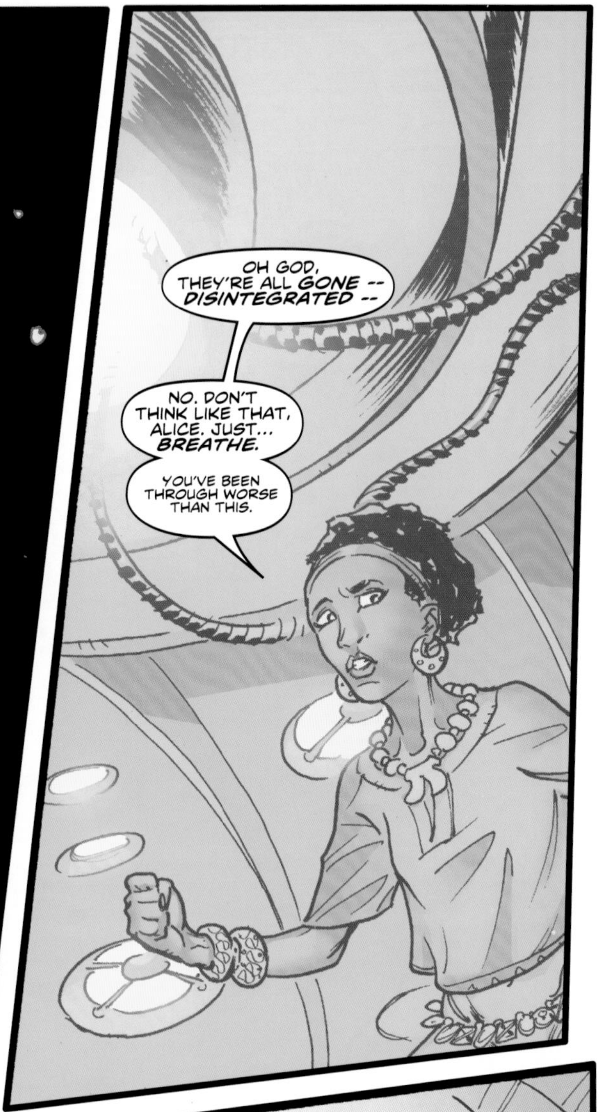
OH GOD, THEY'RE ALL GONE -- DISINTEGRATED --
NO. DON'T THINK LIKE THAT, ALICE. JUST... BREATHE.
YOU'VE BEEN THROUGH WORSE THAN THIS.

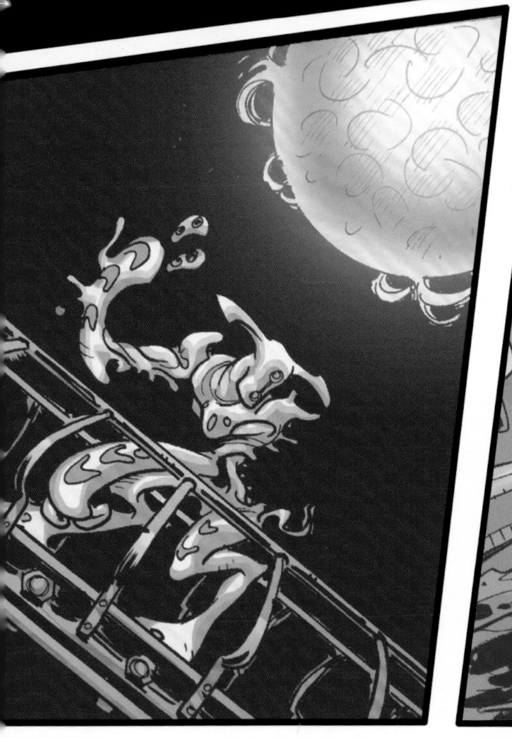

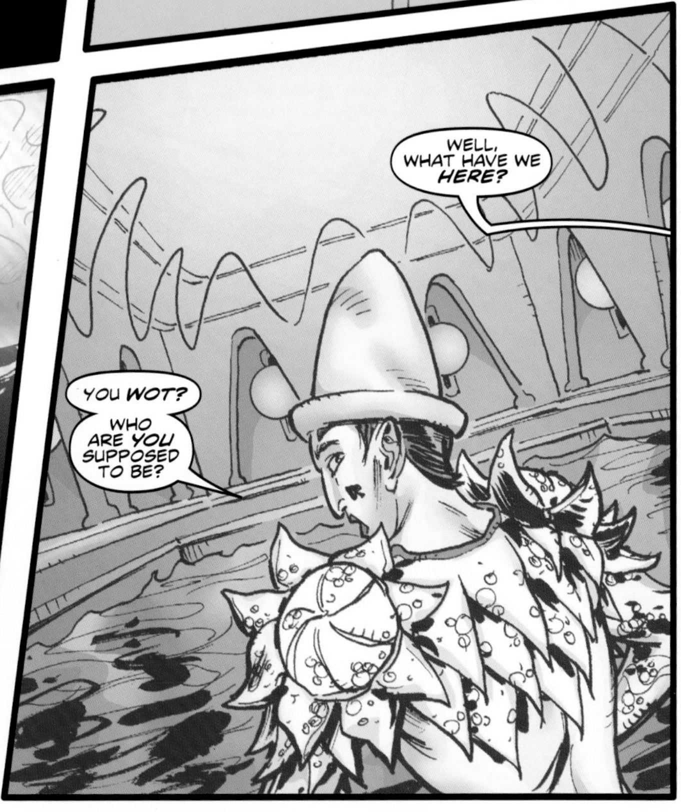
WELL, WHAT HAVE WE HERE?
YOU WOT?
WHO ARE YOU SUPPOSED TO BE?

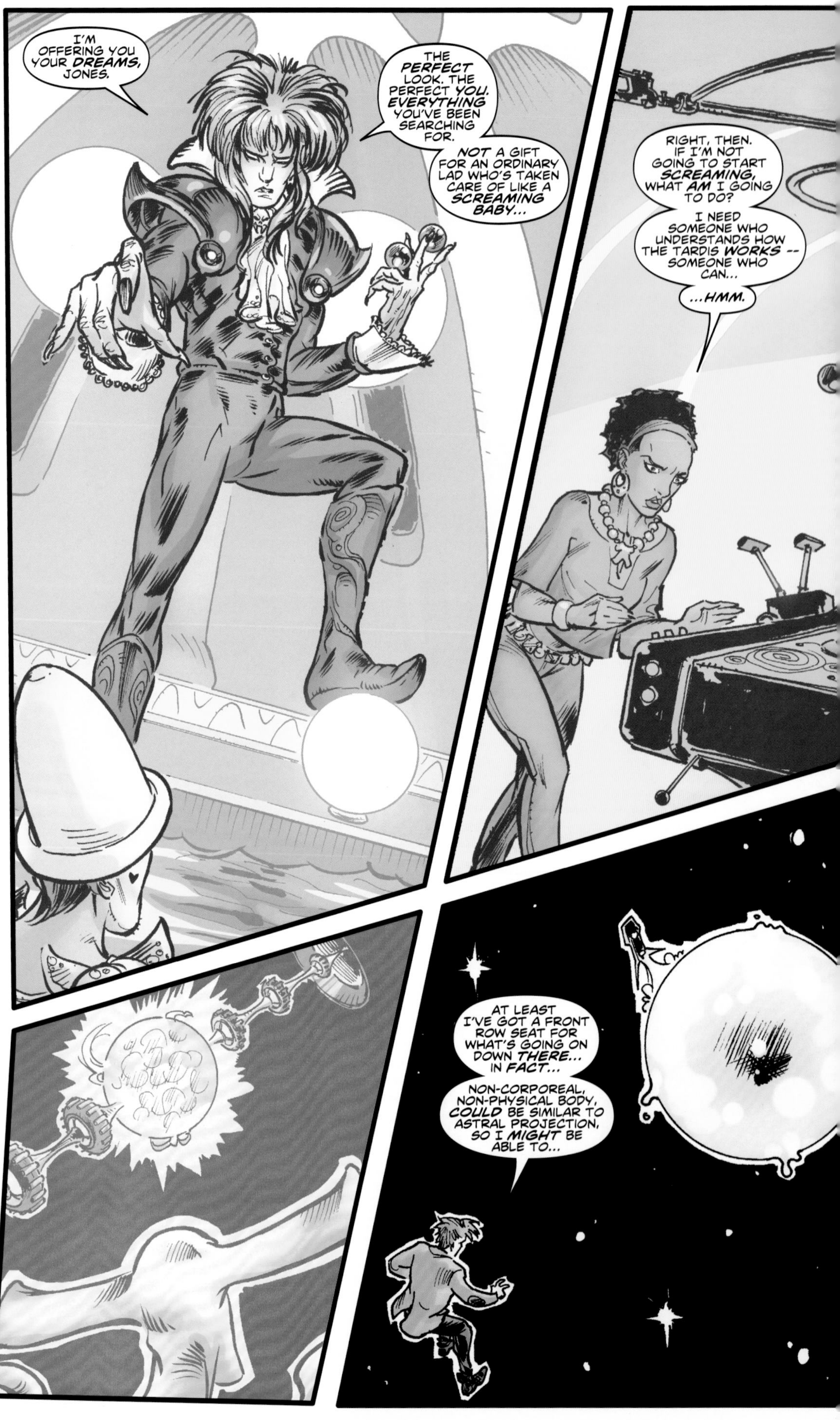
I'M OFFERING YOU YOUR DREAMS, JONES.
THE PERFECT LOOK. THE PERFECT YOU. EVERYTHING YOU'VE BEEN SEARCHING FOR.
NOT A GIFT FOR AN ORDINARY LAD WHO'S TAKEN CARE OF LIKE A SCREAMING BABY...
RIGHT, THEN. IF I'M NOT GOING TO START SCREAMING, WHAT AM I GOING TO DO?
I NEED SOMEONE WHO UNDERSTANDS HOW THE TARDIS WORKS -- SOMEONE WHO CAN...
...HMM.
AT LEAST I'VE GOT A FRONT ROW SEAT FOR WHAT'S GOING ON DOWN THERE... IN FACT...
NON-CORPOREAL, NON-PHYSICAL BODY, COULD BE SIMILAR TO ASTRAL PROJECTION, SO I MIGHT BE ABLE TO...

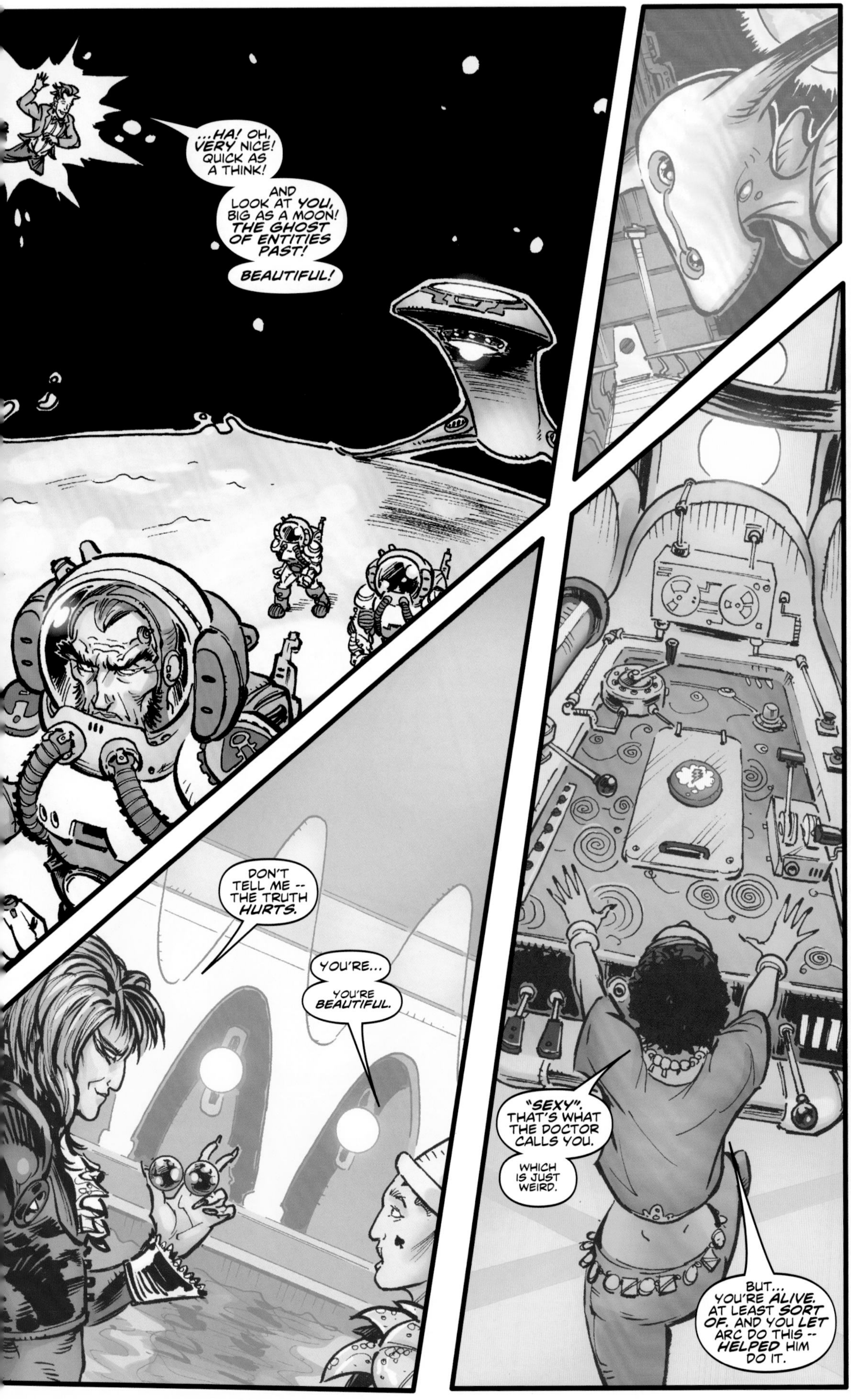
...HA! OH, VERY NICE! QUICK AS A THINK!
AND LOOK AT YOU, BIG AS A MOON! THE GHOST OF ENTITIES PAST!
BEAUTIFUL!
DON'T TELL ME -- THE TRUTH HURTS.
YOU'RE...
YOU'RE BEAUTIFUL.
"SEXY". THAT'S WHAT THE DOCTOR CALLS YOU.
WHICH IS JUST WEIRD.
BUT... YOU'RE ALIVE. AT LEAST SORT OF. AND YOU LET ARC DO THIS -- HELPED HIM DO IT.

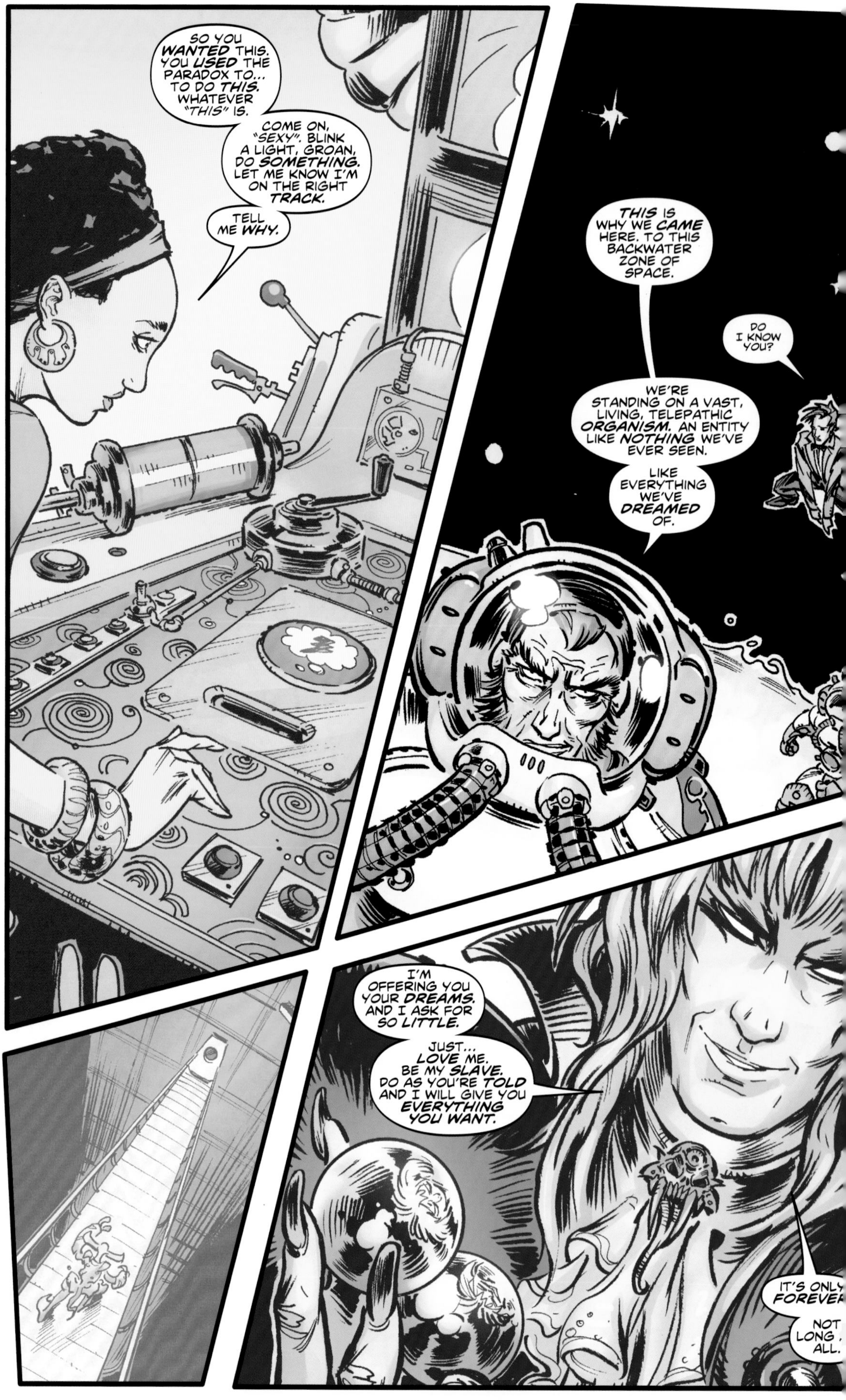
SO YOU WANTED THIS. YOU USED THE PARADOX TO... TO DO THIS. WHATEVER "THIS" IS.
COME ON, "SEXY". BLINK A LIGHT, GROAN, DO SOMETHING. LET ME KNOW I'M ON THE RIGHT TRACK.
TELL ME WHY.
THIS IS WHY WE CAME HERE. TO THIS BACKWATER ZONE OF SPACE.
WE'RE STANDING ON A VAST, LIVING, TELEPATHIC ORGANISM. AN ENTITY LIKE NOTHING WE'VE EVER SEEN.
LIKE EVERYTHING WE'VE DREAMED OF.
DO I KNOW YOU?
I'M OFFERING YOU YOUR DREAMS. AND I ASK FOR SO LITTLE.
JUST... LOVE ME. BE MY SLAVE. DO AS YOU'RE TOLD AND I WILL GIVE YOU EVERYTHING YOU WANT.
IT'S ONLY FOREVE
NOT LONG, ALL.

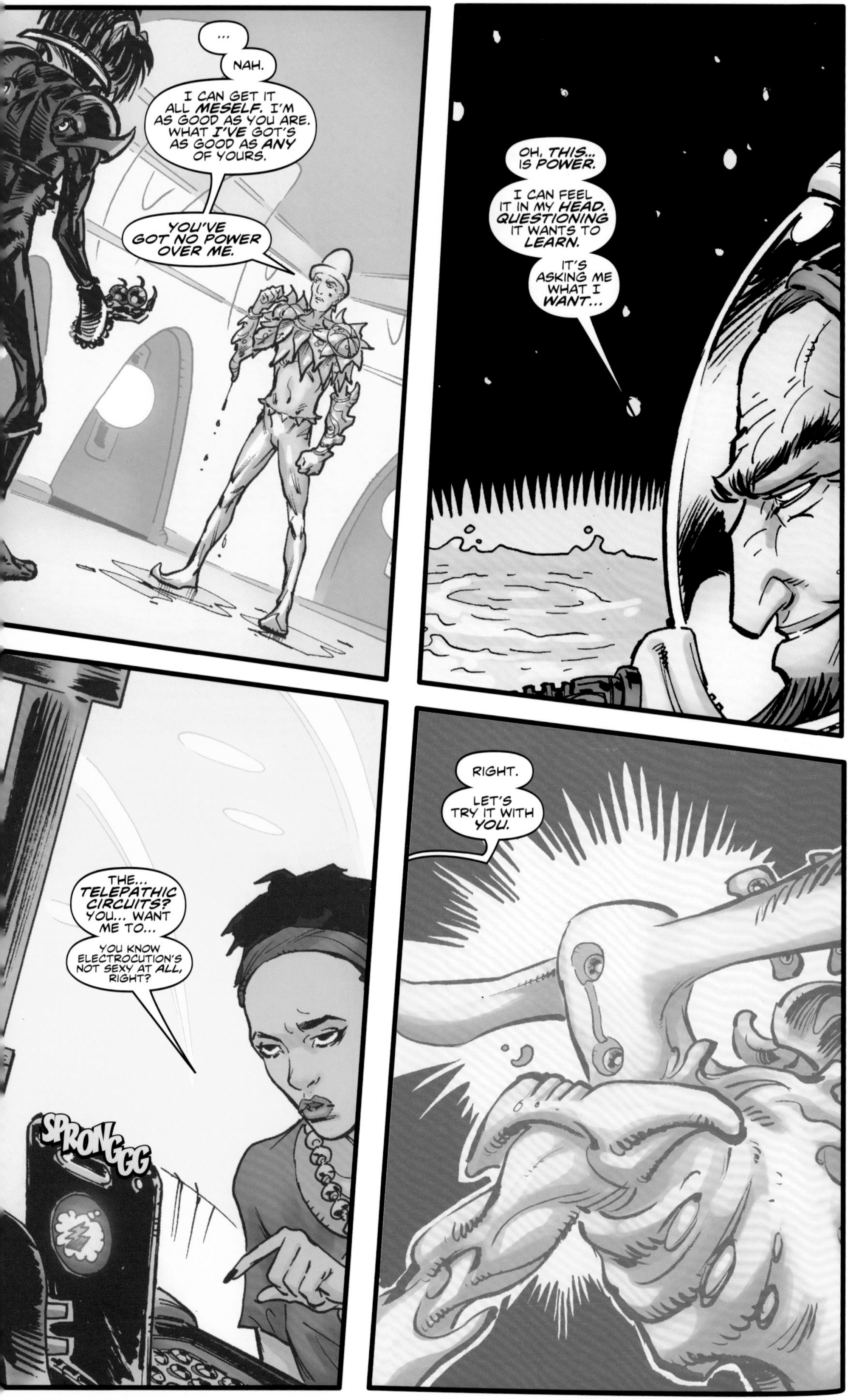
...
NAH.
I CAN GET IT ALL MESELF. I'M AS GOOD AS YOU ARE. WHAT I'VE GOT'S AS GOOD AS ANY OF YOURS.
YOU'VE GOT NO POWER OVER ME.
OH, THIS... IS POWER.
I CAN FEEL IT IN MY HEAD. QUESTIONING IT WANTS TO LEARN.
IT'S ASKING ME WHAT I WANT...
THE... TELEPATHIC CIRCUITS? YOU... WANT ME TO...
YOU KNOW ELECTROCUTION'S NOT SEXY AT ALL, RIGHT?
SPRONGGG
RIGHT.
LET'S TRY IT WITH YOU.

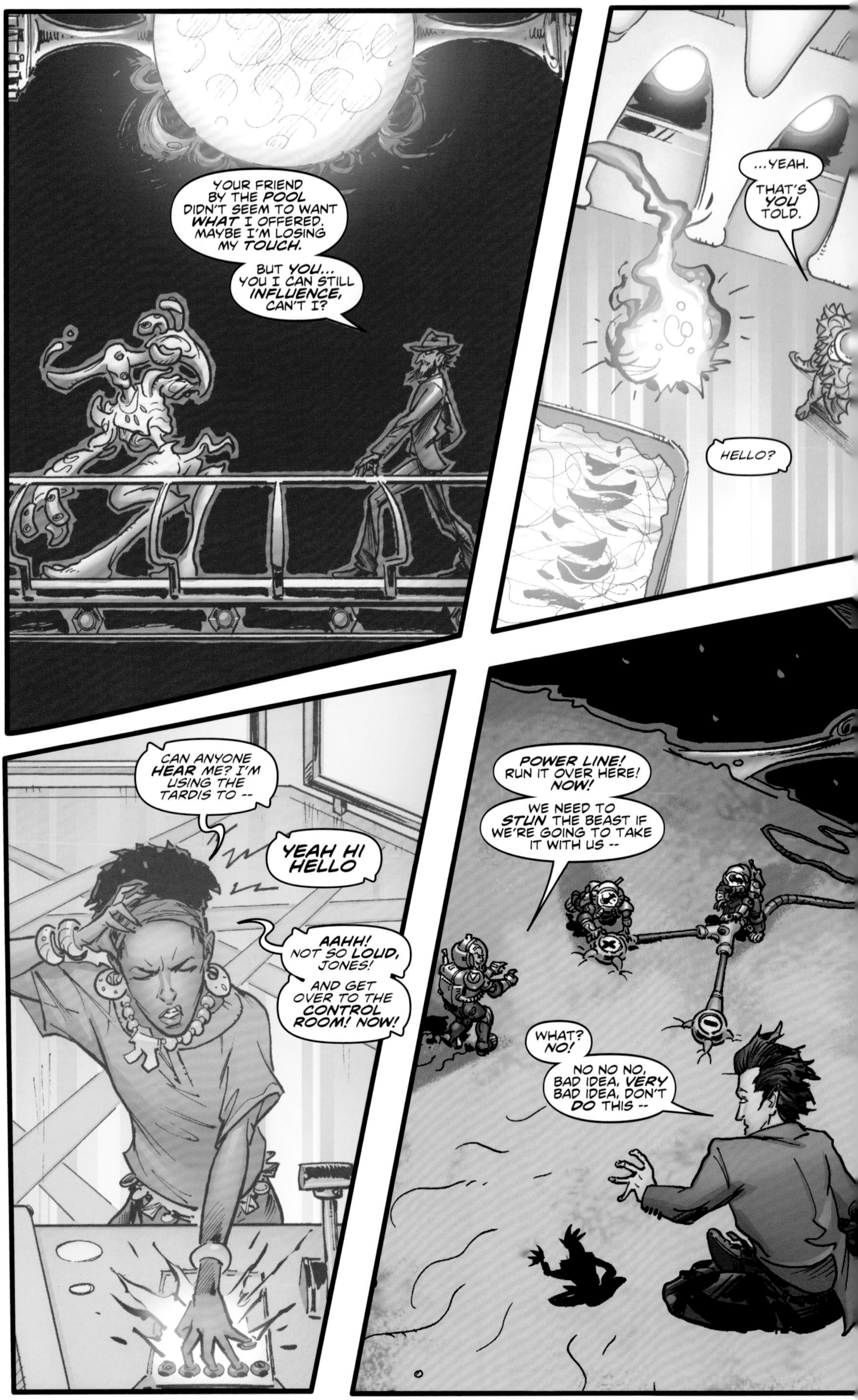
YOUR FRIEND BY THE POOL DIDN'T SEEM TO WANT WHAT I OFFERED. MAYBE I'M LOSING MY TOUCH.
BUT YOU... YOU I CAN STILL INFLUENCE, CAN'T I?
...YEAH.
THAT'S YOU TOLD.
HELLO?
CAN ANYONE HEAR ME? I'M USING THE TARDIS TO --
YEAH HI HELLO
AAHH! NOT SO LOUD, JONES!
AND GET OVER TO THE CONTROL ROOM! NOW!
POWER LINE! RUN IT OVER HERE! NOW!
WE NEED TO STUN THE BEAST IF WE'RE GOING TO TAKE IT WITH US --
WHAT? NO!
NO NO NO, BAD IDEA, VERY BAD IDEA, DON'T DO THIS --

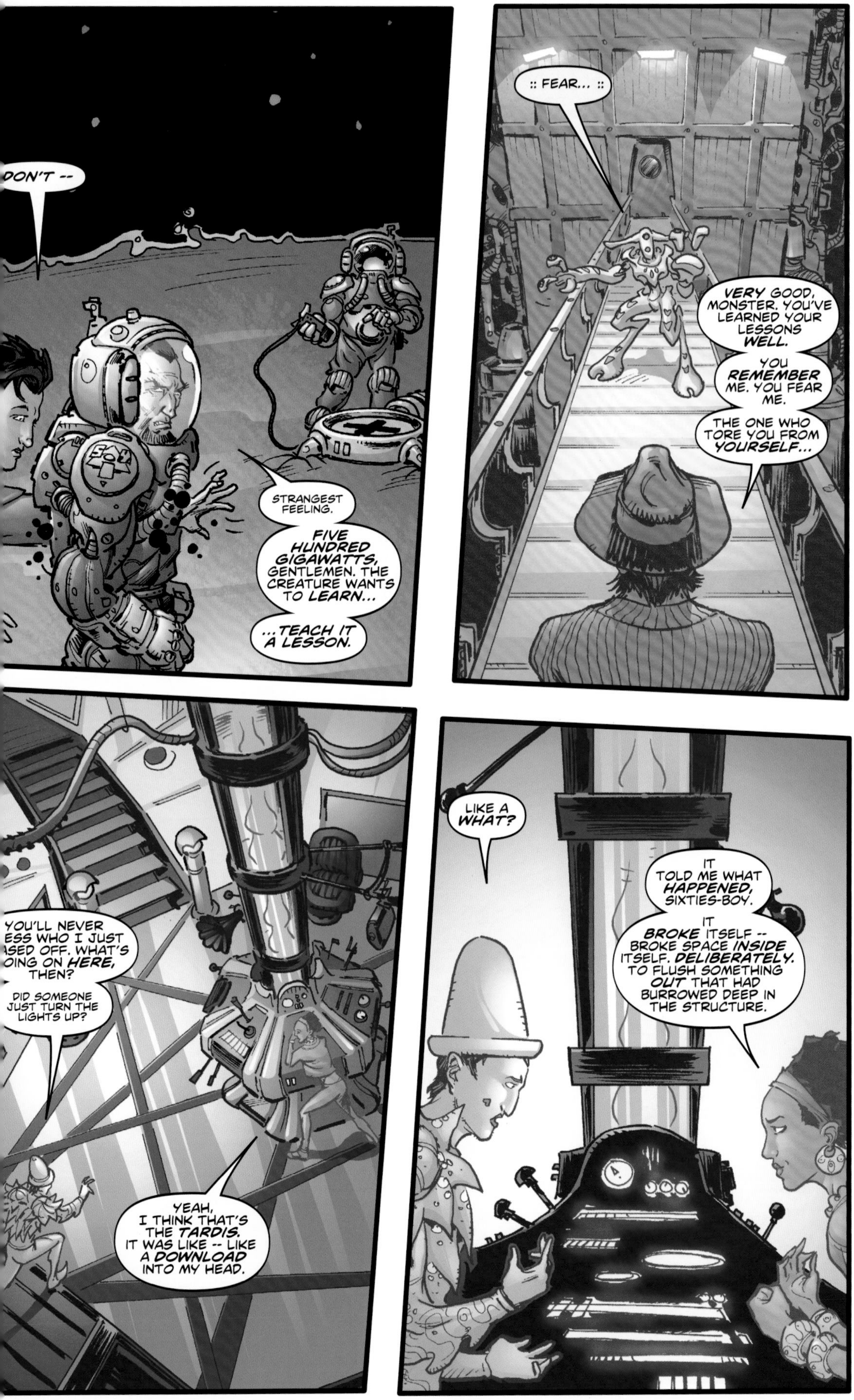
DON'T --
STRANGEST FEELING.
FIVE HUNDRED GIGAWATTS, GENTLEMEN. THE CREATURE WANTS TO LEARN...
...TEACH IT A LESSON.
:: FEAR... ::
VERY GOOD, MONSTER. YOU'VE LEARNED YOUR LESSONS WELL.
YOU REMEMBER ME. YOU FEAR ME.
THE ONE WHO TORE YOU FROM YOURSELF...
YOU'LL NEVER ESS WHO I JUST ASED OFF. WHAT'S OING ON HERE, THEN?
DID SOMEONE JUST TURN THE LIGHTS UP?
YEAH, I THINK THAT'S THE TARDIS. IT WAS LIKE -- LIKE A DOWNLOAD INTO MY HEAD.
LIKE A WHAT?
IT TOLD ME WHAT HAPPENED, SIXTIES-BOY.
IT BROKE ITSELF -- BROKE SPACE INSIDE ITSELF. DELIBERATELY. TO FLUSH SOMETHING OUT THAT HAD BURROWED DEEP IN THE STRUCTURE.

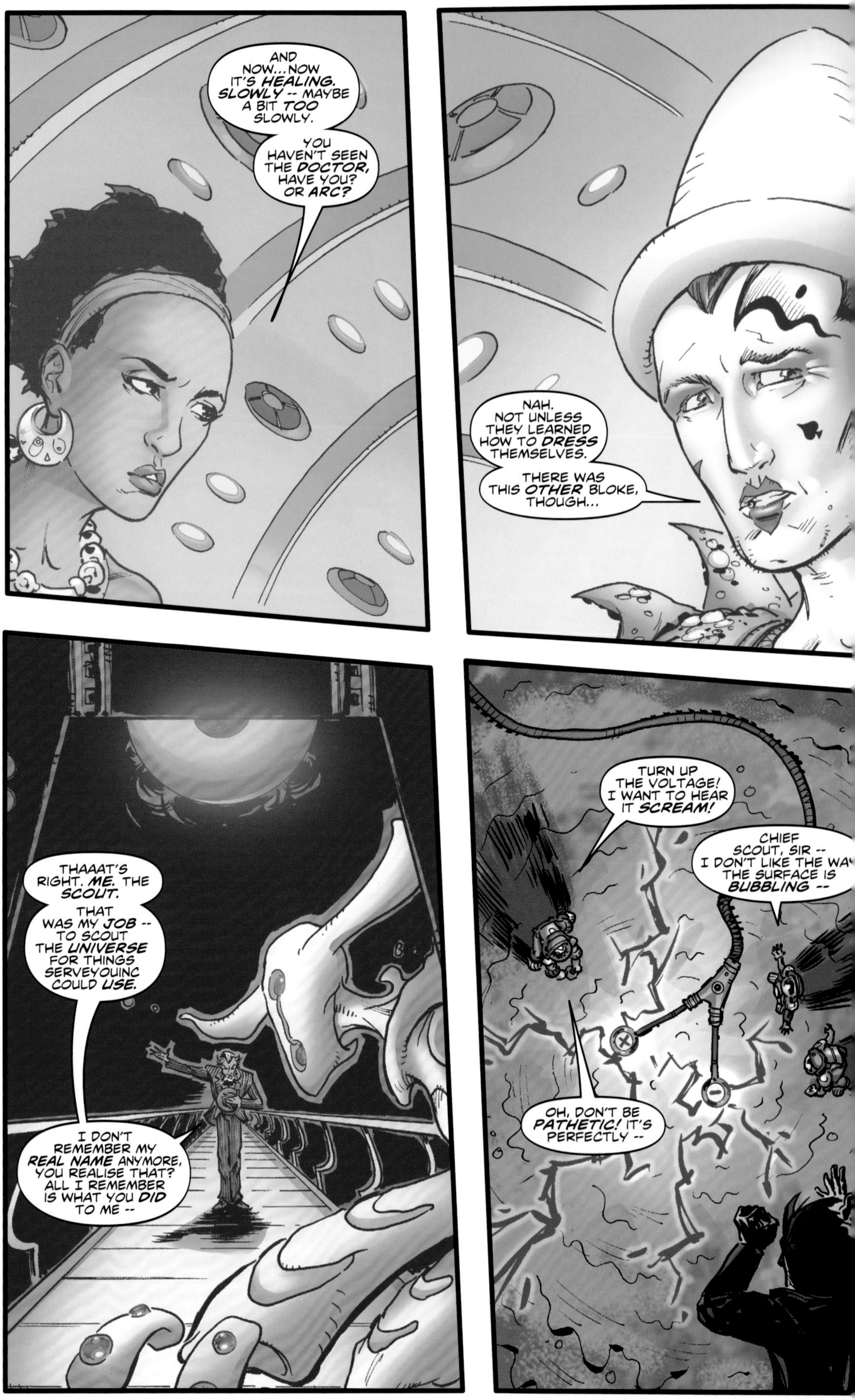

AND NOW... NOW IT'S HEALING. SLOWLY -- MAYBE A BIT TOO SLOWLY.
YOU HAVEN'T SEEN THE DOCTOR, HAVE YOU? OR ARC?
NAH. NOT UNLESS THEY LEARNED HOW TO DRESS THEMSELVES.
THERE WAS THIS OTHER BLOKE, THOUGH...
THAAAT'S RIGHT. ME. THE SCOUT.
THAT WAS MY JOB -- TO SCOUT THE UNIVERSE FOR THINGS SERVEYOUINC COULD USE.
I DON'T REMEMBER MY REAL NAME ANYMORE, YOU REALISE THAT? ALL I REMEMBER IS WHAT YOU DID TO ME --
TURN UP THE VOLTAGE! I WANT TO HEAR IT SCREAM!
CHIEF SCOUT, SIR -- I DON'T LIKE THE WA THE SURFACE IS BUBBLING --
OH, DON'T BE PATHETIC! IT'S PERFECTLY --

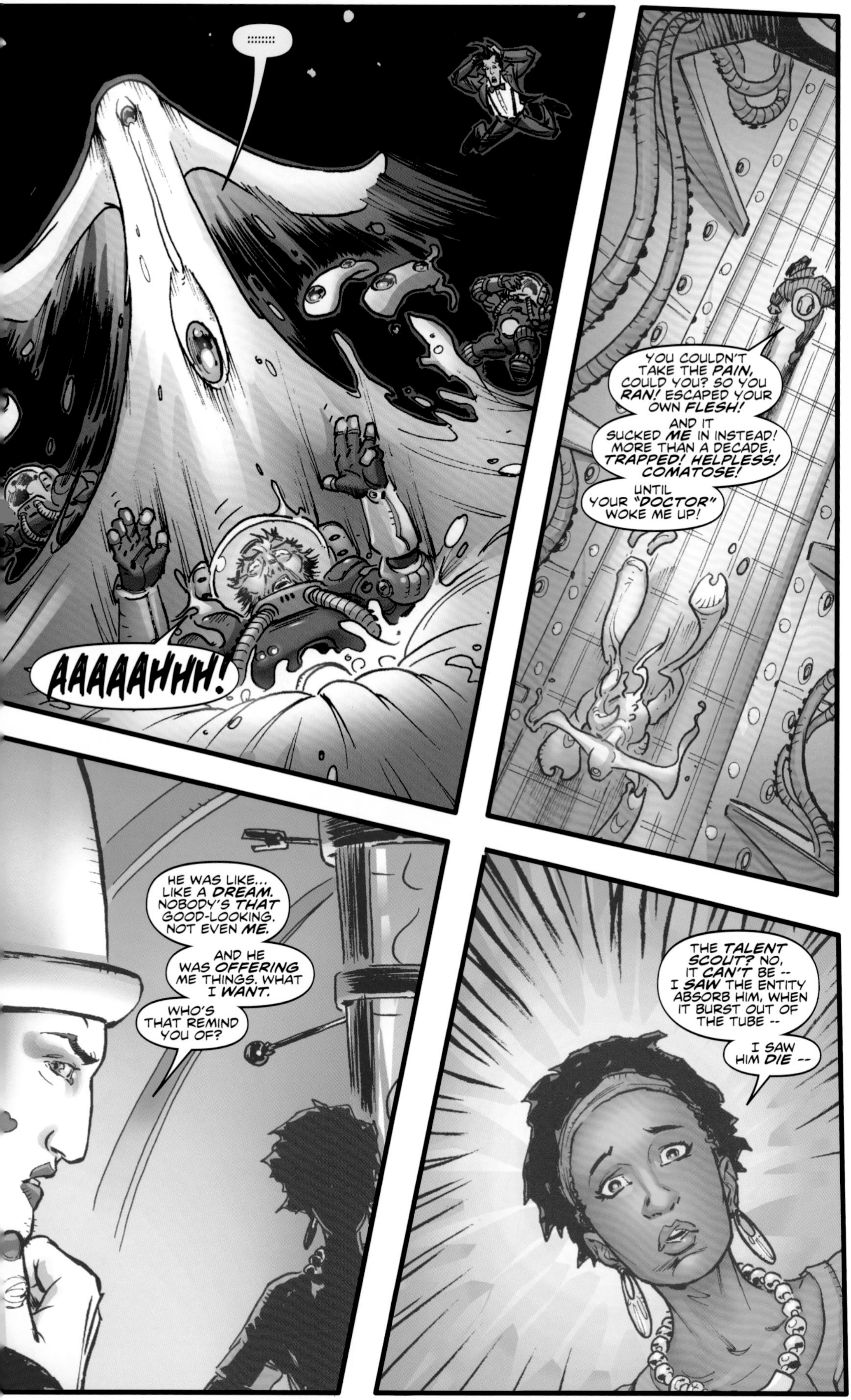

AAAAAHHH!
YOU COULDN'T TAKE THE PAIN, COULD YOU? SO YOU RAN! ESCAPED YOUR OWN FLESH!
AND IT SUCKED ME IN INSTEAD! MORE THAN A DECADE, TRAPPED! HELPLESS! COMATOSE!
UNTIL YOUR "DOCTOR" WOKE ME UP!
HE WAS LIKE... LIKE A DREAM. NOBODY'S THAT GOOD-LOOKING. NOT EVEN ME.
AND HE WAS OFFERING ME THINGS. WHAT I WANT.
WHO'S THAT REMIND YOU OF?
THE TALENT SCOUT? NO, IT CAN'T BE -- I SAW THE ENTITY ABSORB HIM, WHEN IT BURST OUT OF THE TUBE --
I SAW HIM DIE --

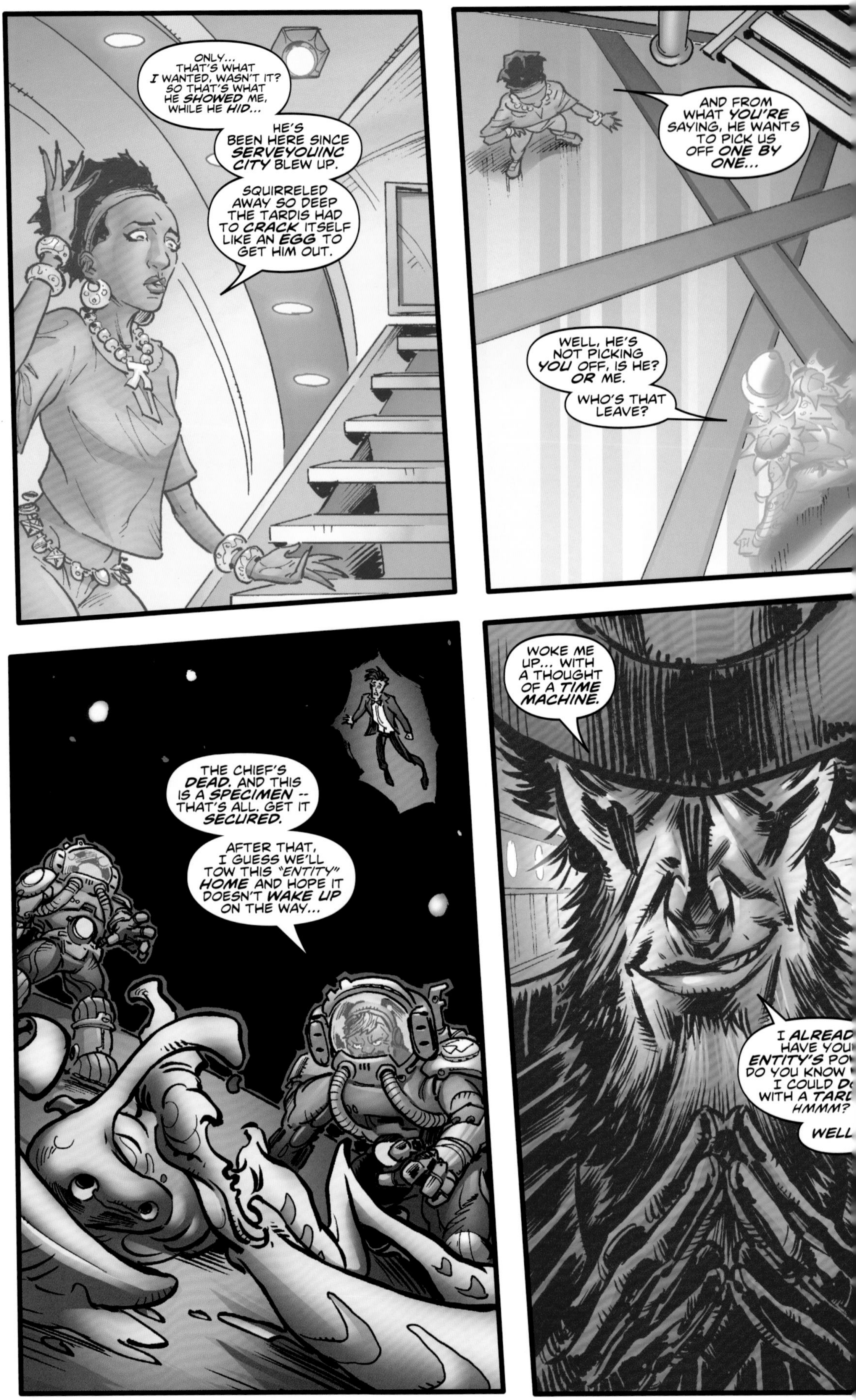
ONLY... THAT'S WHAT I WANTED, WASN'T IT? SO THAT'S WHAT HE SHOWED ME, WHILE HE HID...
HE'S BEEN HERE SINCE SERVEYOUINC CITY BLEW UP.
SQUIRRELED AWAY SO DEEP THE TARDIS HAD TO CRACK ITSELF LIKE AN EGG TO GET HIM OUT.
AND FROM WHAT YOU'RE SAYING, HE WANTS TO PICK US OFF ONE BY ONE...
WELL, HE'S NOT PICKING YOU OFF, IS HE? OR ME.
WHO'S THAT LEAVE?
THE CHIEF'S DEAD. AND THIS IS A SPECIMEN -- THAT'S ALL. GET IT SECURED.
AFTER THAT, I GUESS WE'LL TOW THIS "ENTITY" HOME AND HOPE IT DOESN'T WAKE UP ON THE WAY...
WOKE ME UP... WITH A THOUGHT OF A TIME MACHINE.
I ALREAD HAVE YOU ENTITY'S PO DO YOU KNOW I COULD D WITH A TARD HMMM?
WELL

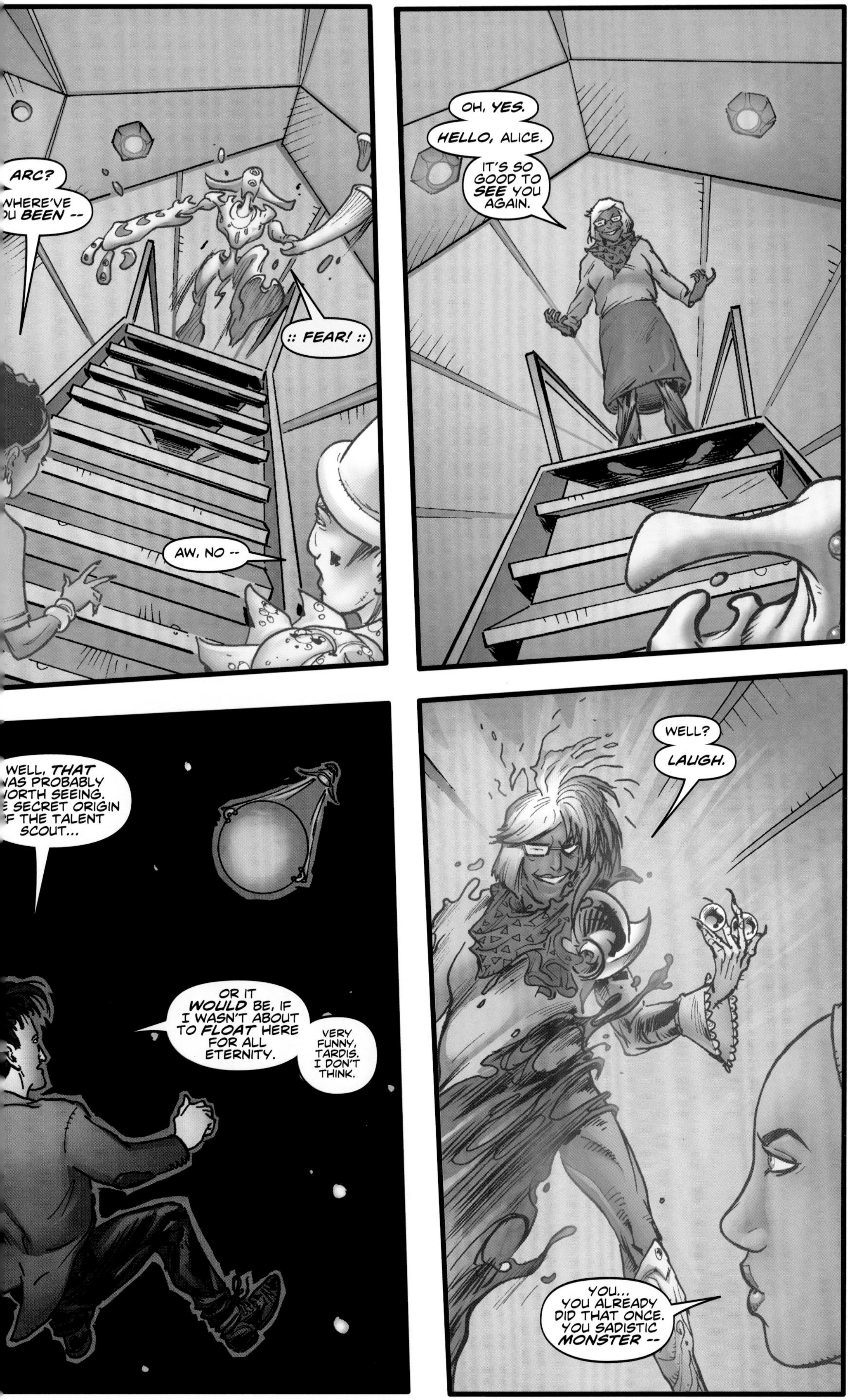
ARC?
WHERE'VE YOU BEEN --
:: FEAR! ::
AW, NO --
OH, YES.
HELLO, ALICE.
IT'S SO GOOD TO SEE YOU AGAIN.
WELL, THAT WAS PROBABLY WORTH SEEING. THE SECRET ORIGIN OF THE TALENT SCOUT...
OR IT WOULD BE, IF I WASN'T ABOUT TO FLOAT HERE FOR ALL ETERNITY.
VERY FUNNY, TARDIS. I DON'T THINK.
WELL?
LAUGH.
YOU... YOU ALREADY DID THAT ONCE. YOU SADISTIC MONSTER --

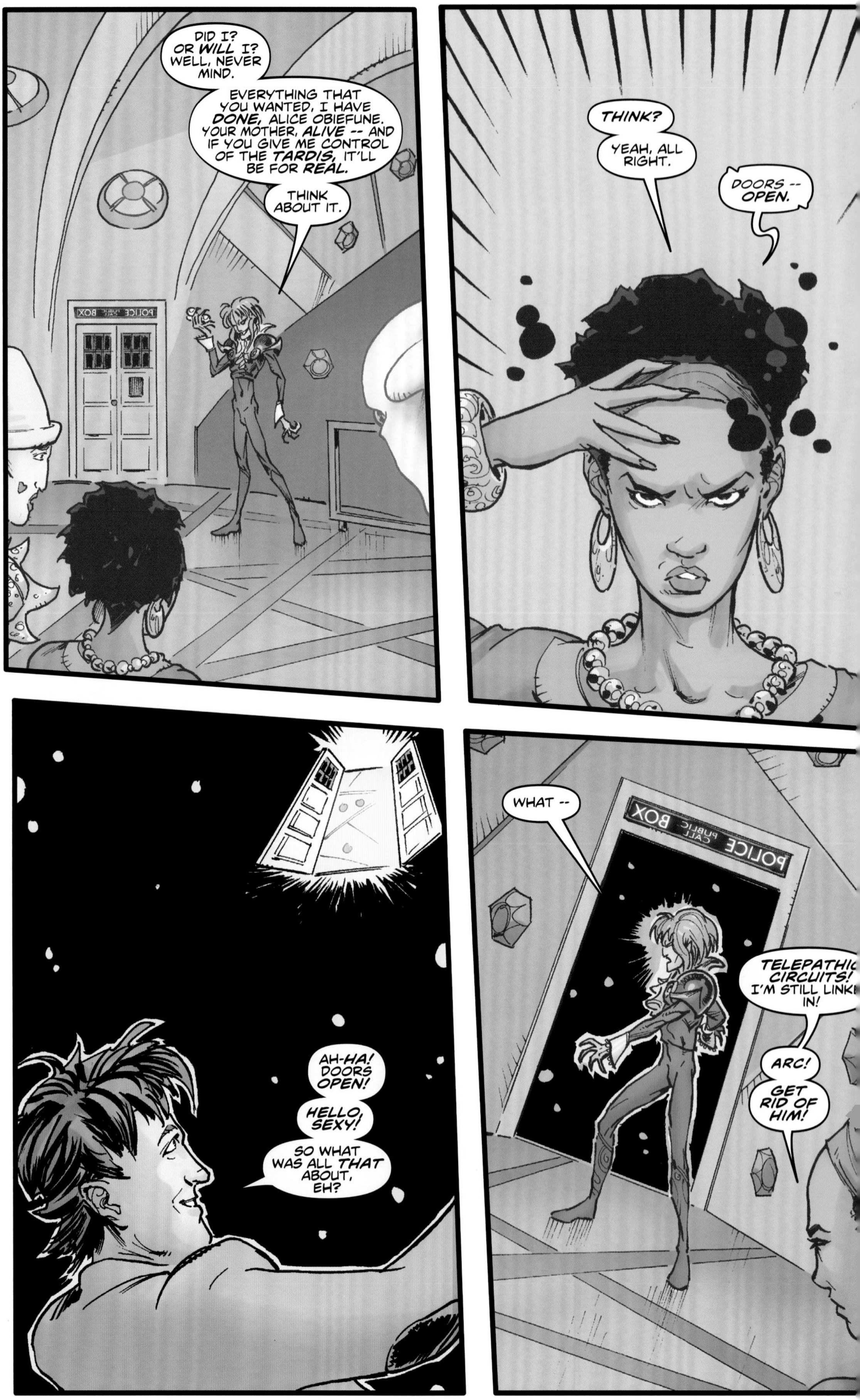
DID I? OR WILL I? WELL, NEVER MIND.
EVERYTHING THAT YOU WANTED, I HAVE DONE, ALICE OBIEFUNE. YOUR MOTHER, ALIVE -- AND IF YOU GIVE ME CONTROL OF THE TARDIS, IT'LL BE FOR REAL.
THINK ABOUT IT.
POLICE PUBLIC CALL BOX
THINK?
YEAH, ALL RIGHT.
DOORS -- OPEN.
AH-HA! DOORS OPEN!
HELLO, SEXY!
SO WHAT WAS ALL THAT ABOUT, EH?
WHAT --
POLICE PUBLIC CALL BOX
TELEPATHIC CIRCUITS! I'M STILL LINK IN!
ARC!
GET RID OF HIM!

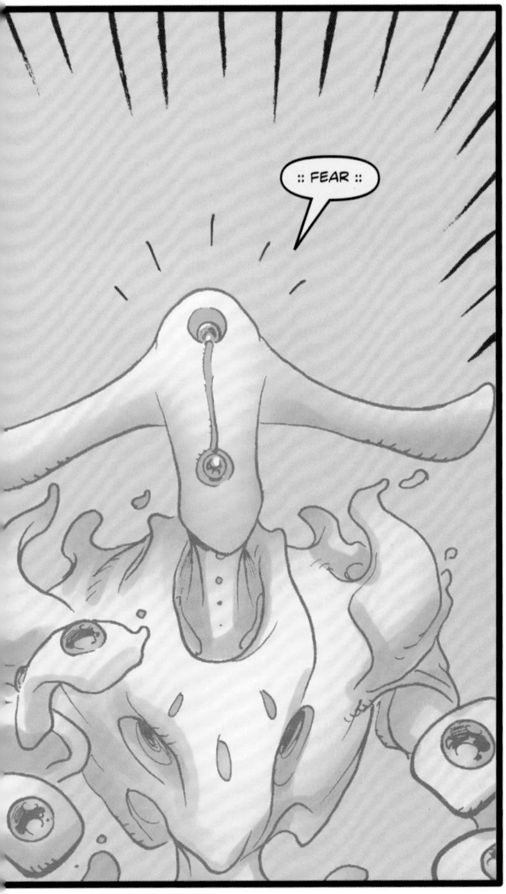
:: FEAR ::

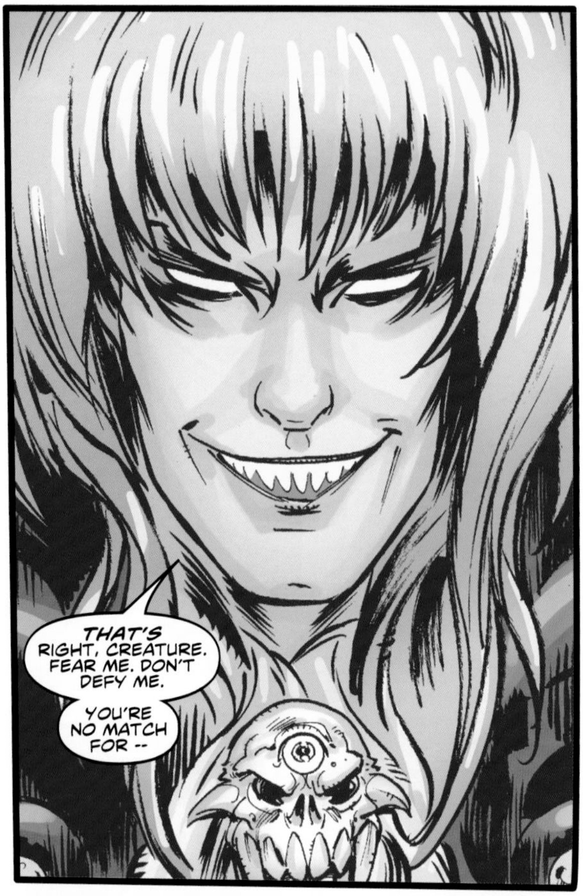
THAT'S RIGHT, CREATURE. FEAR ME. DON'T DEFY ME.
YOU'RE NO MATCH FOR --

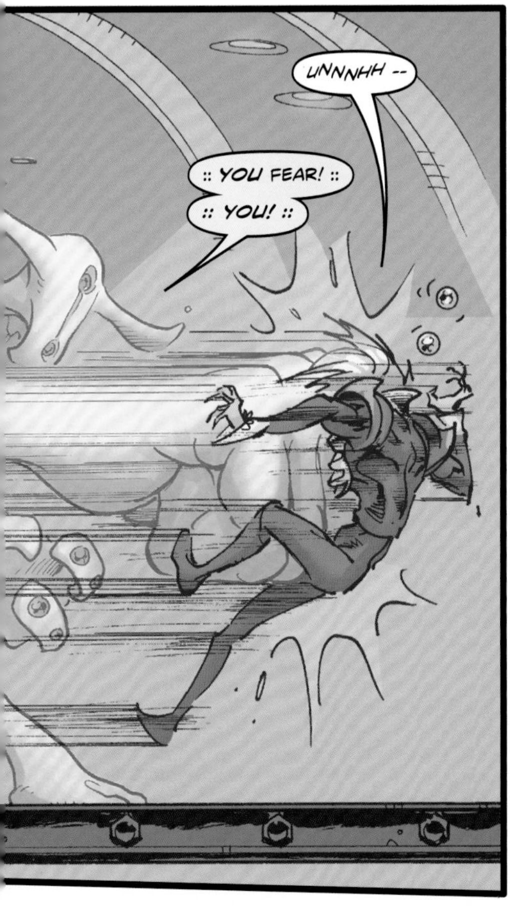
UNNNHH --
:: YOU FEAR! ::
:: YOU! ::

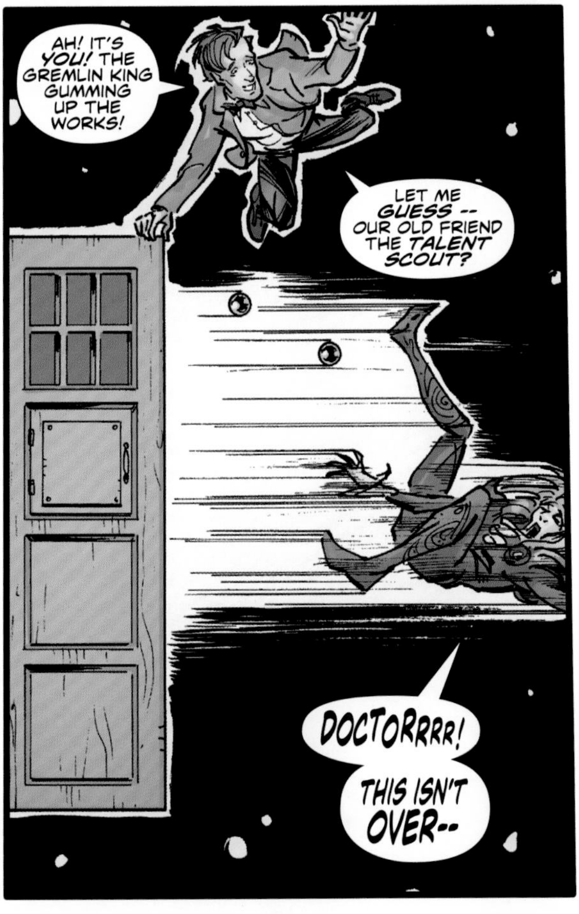
AH! IT'S YOU! THE GREMLIN KING GUMMING UP THE WORKS!
LET ME GUESS -- OUR OLD FRIEND THE TALENT SCOUT?
DOCTORRRR!
THIS ISN'T OVER--

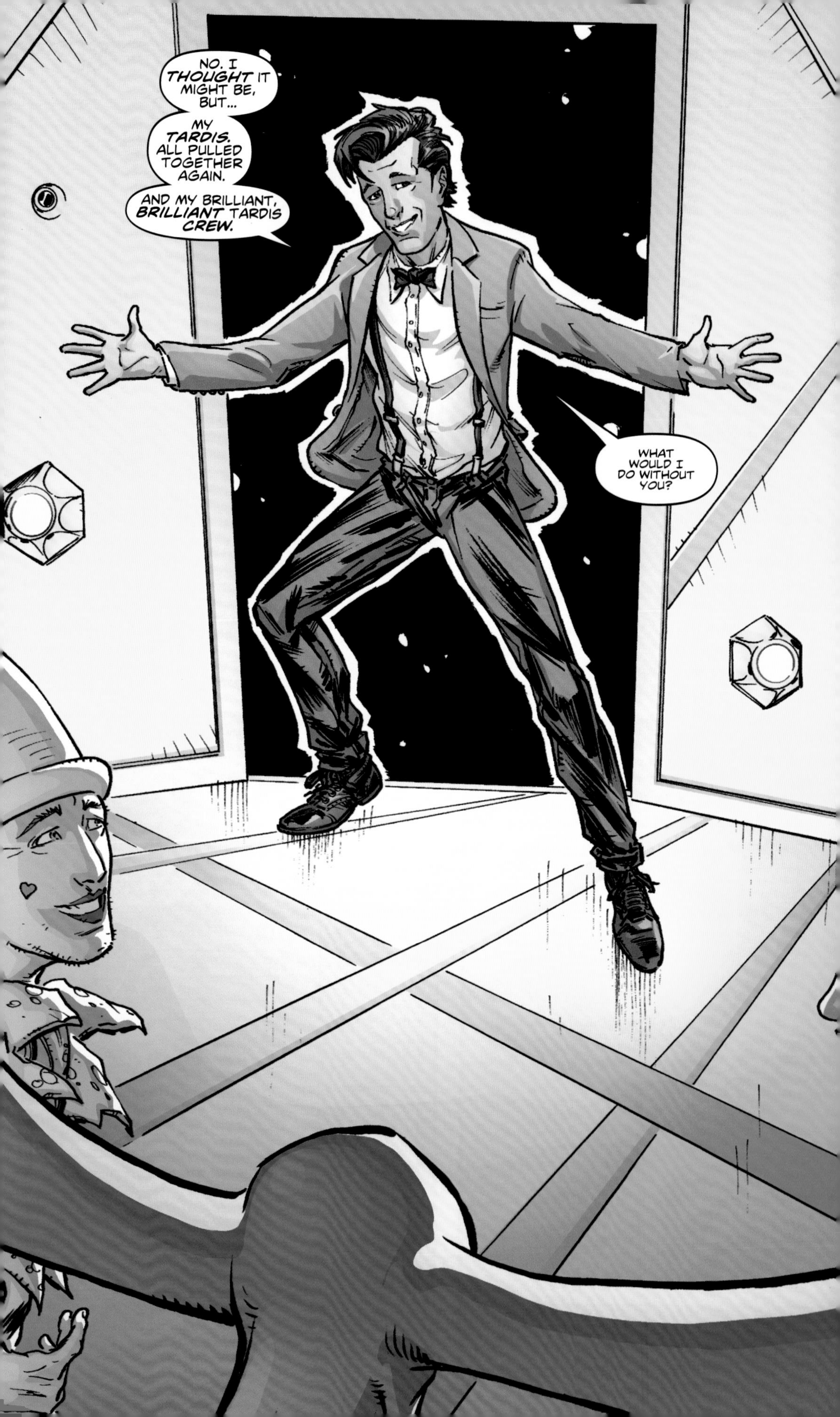
NO. I *THOUGHT* IT MIGHT BE, BUT...
MY *TARDIS.* ALL PULLED TOGETHER AGAIN.
AND MY BRILLIANT, *BRILLIANT* TARDIS *CREW.*
WHAT WOULD I DO WITHOUT YOU?

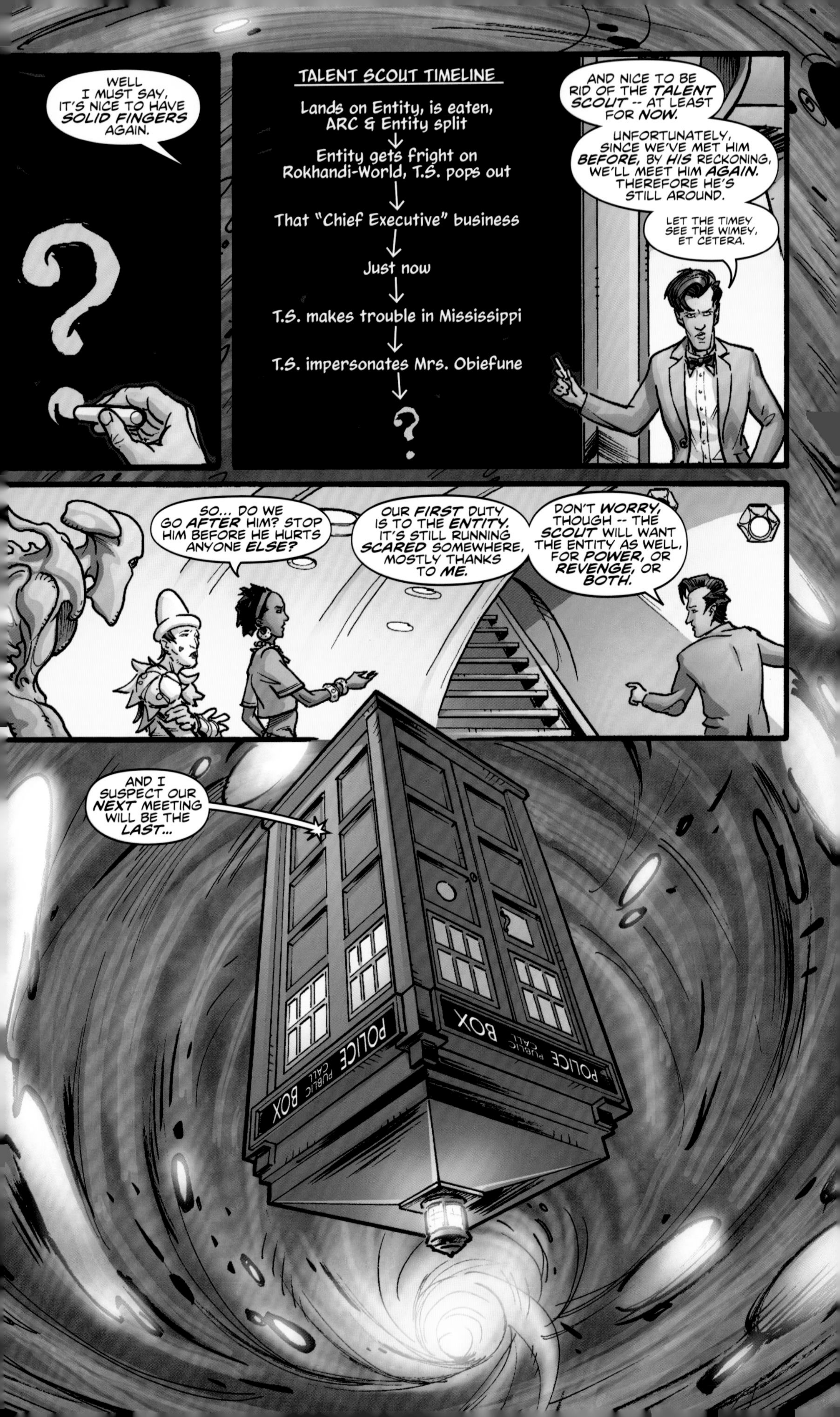

WELL I MUST SAY, IT'S NICE TO HAVE SOLID FINGERS AGAIN.
TALENT SCOUT TIMELINE
Lands on Entity, is eaten, ARC & Entity split
Entity gets fright on Rokhandi-World, T.S. pops out
That "Chief Executive" business
Just now
T.S. makes trouble in Mississippi
T.S. impersonates Mrs. Obiefune
?
AND NICE TO BE RID OF THE TALENT SCOUT -- AT LEAST FOR NOW.
UNFORTUNATELY, SINCE WE'VE MET HIM BEFORE, BY HIS RECKONING, WE'LL MEET HIM AGAIN. THEREFORE HE'S STILL AROUND.
LET THE TIMEY SEE THE WIMEY, ET CETERA.
SO... DO WE GO AFTER HIM? STOP HIM BEFORE HE HURTS ANYONE ELSE?
OUR FIRST DUTY IS TO THE ENTITY. IT'S STILL RUNNING SCARED SOMEWHERE, MOSTLY THANKS TO ME.
DON'T WORRY, THOUGH -- THE SCOUT WILL WANT THE ENTITY AS WELL, FOR POWER, OR REVENGE, OR BOTH.
AND I SUSPECT OUR NEXT MEETING WILL BE THE LAST...
POLICE PUBLIC CALL BOX
POLICE PUBLIC CALL BOX

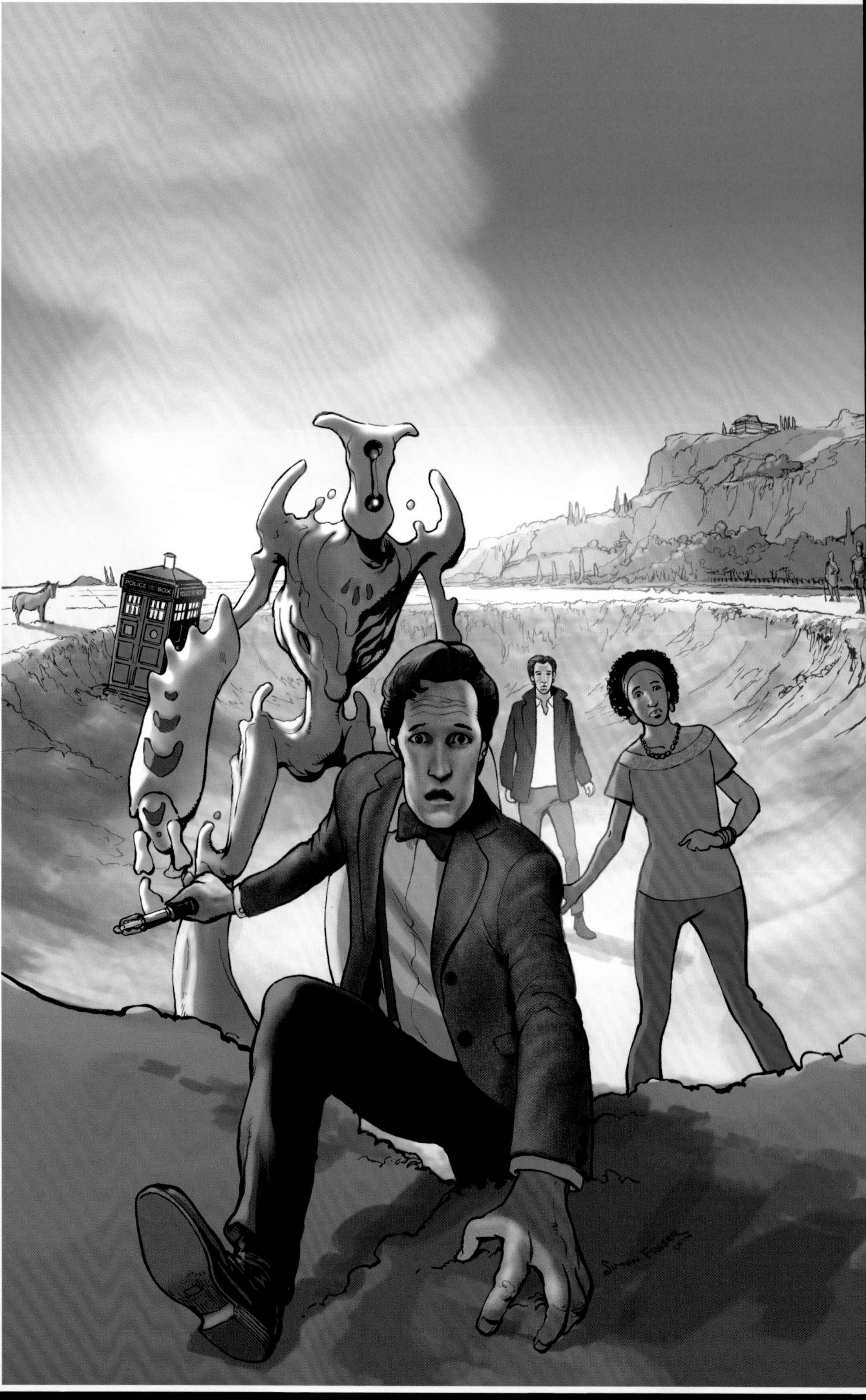
POLICE BOX
SIMON FRASER

CHAPTER 12 Cover A: Simon Fraser

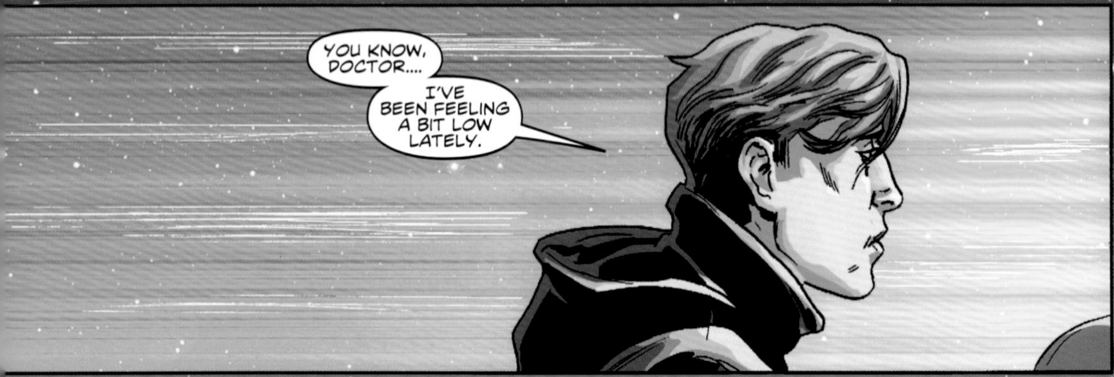
YOU KNOW, DOCTOR....
I'VE BEEN FEELING A BIT LOW LATELY.

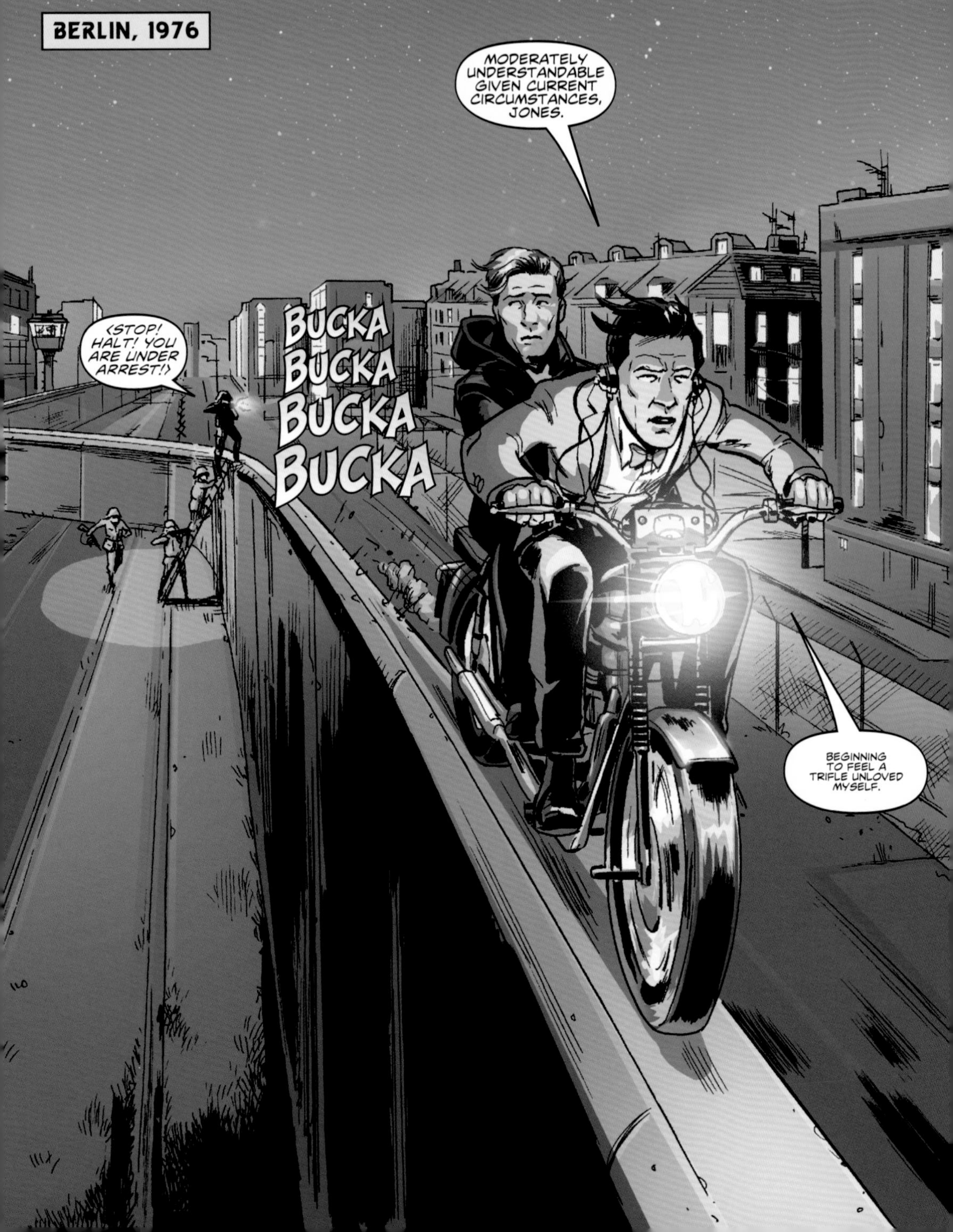
BERLIN, 1976
MODERATELY UNDERSTANDABLE GIVEN CURRENT CIRCUMSTANCES, JONES.
<STOP! HALT! YOU ARE UNDER ARREST!>
BUCKA BUCKA BUCKA BUCKA
BEGINNING TO FEEL A TRIFLE UNLOVED MYSELF.

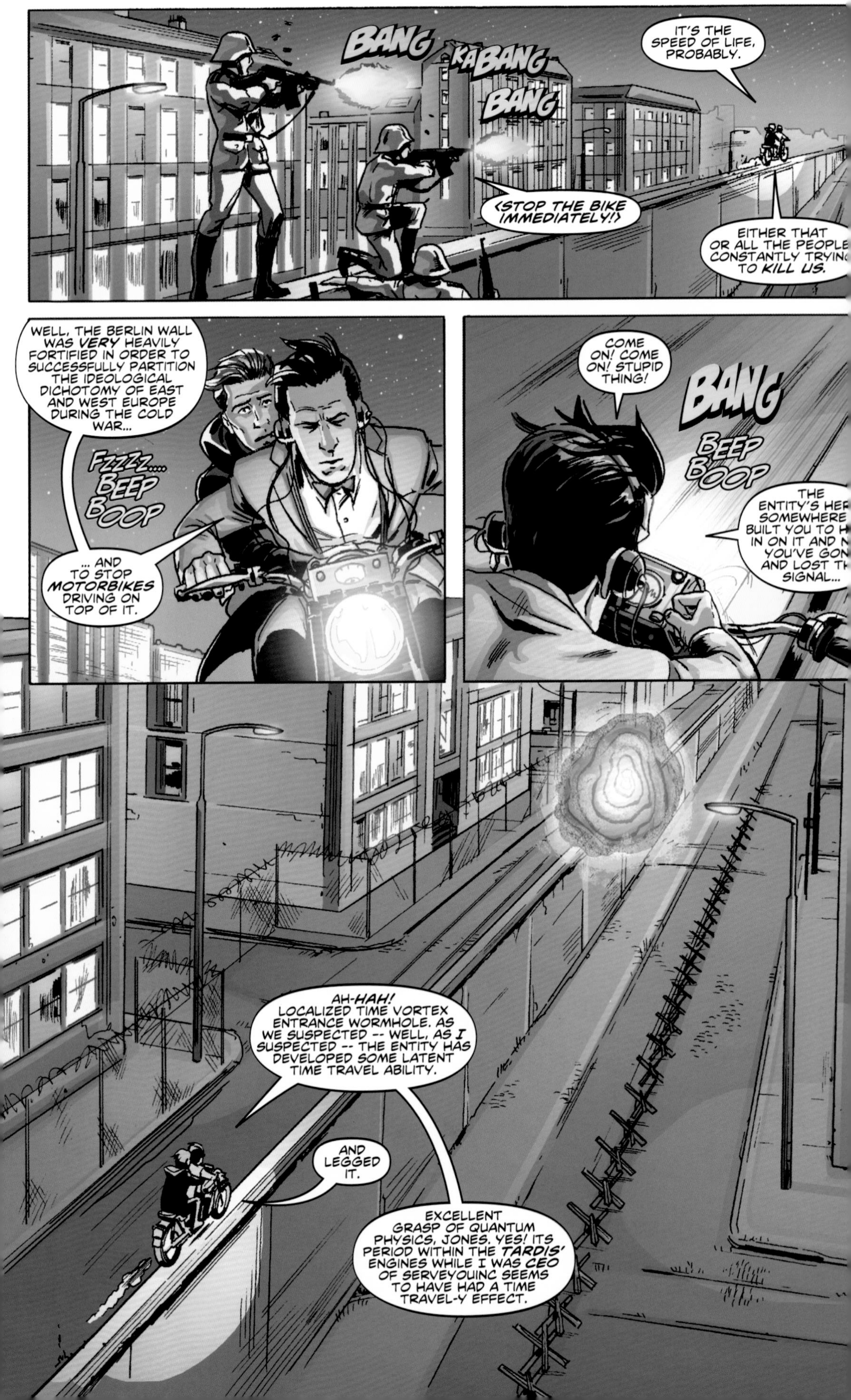
BANG
KABANG
BANG
IT'S THE SPEED OF LIFE, PROBABLY.
‹STOP THE BIKE IMMEDIATELY!›
EITHER THAT OR ALL THE PEOPLE CONSTANTLY TRYING TO KILL US.
WELL, THE BERLIN WALL WAS VERY HEAVILY FORTIFIED IN ORDER TO SUCCESSFULLY PARTITION THE IDEOLOGICAL DICHOTOMY OF EAST AND WEST EUROPE DURING THE COLD WAR...
FZZZZ.... BEEP BOOP
... AND TO STOP MOTORBIKES DRIVING ON TOP OF IT.
COME ON! COME ON! STUPID THING!
BANG
BEEP BOOP
AH-HAH! LOCALIZED TIME VORTEX ENTRANCE WORMHOLE. AS WE SUSPECTED -- WELL, AS I SUSPECTED -- THE ENTITY HAS DEVELOPED SOME LATENT TIME TRAVEL ABILITY.
AND LEGGED IT.
EXCELLENT GRASP OF QUANTUM PHYSICS, JONES. YES! ITS PERIOD WITHIN THE TARDIS' ENGINES WHILE I WAS CEO OF SERVEYOUINC SEEMS TO HAVE HAD A TIME TRAVEL-Y EFFECT.

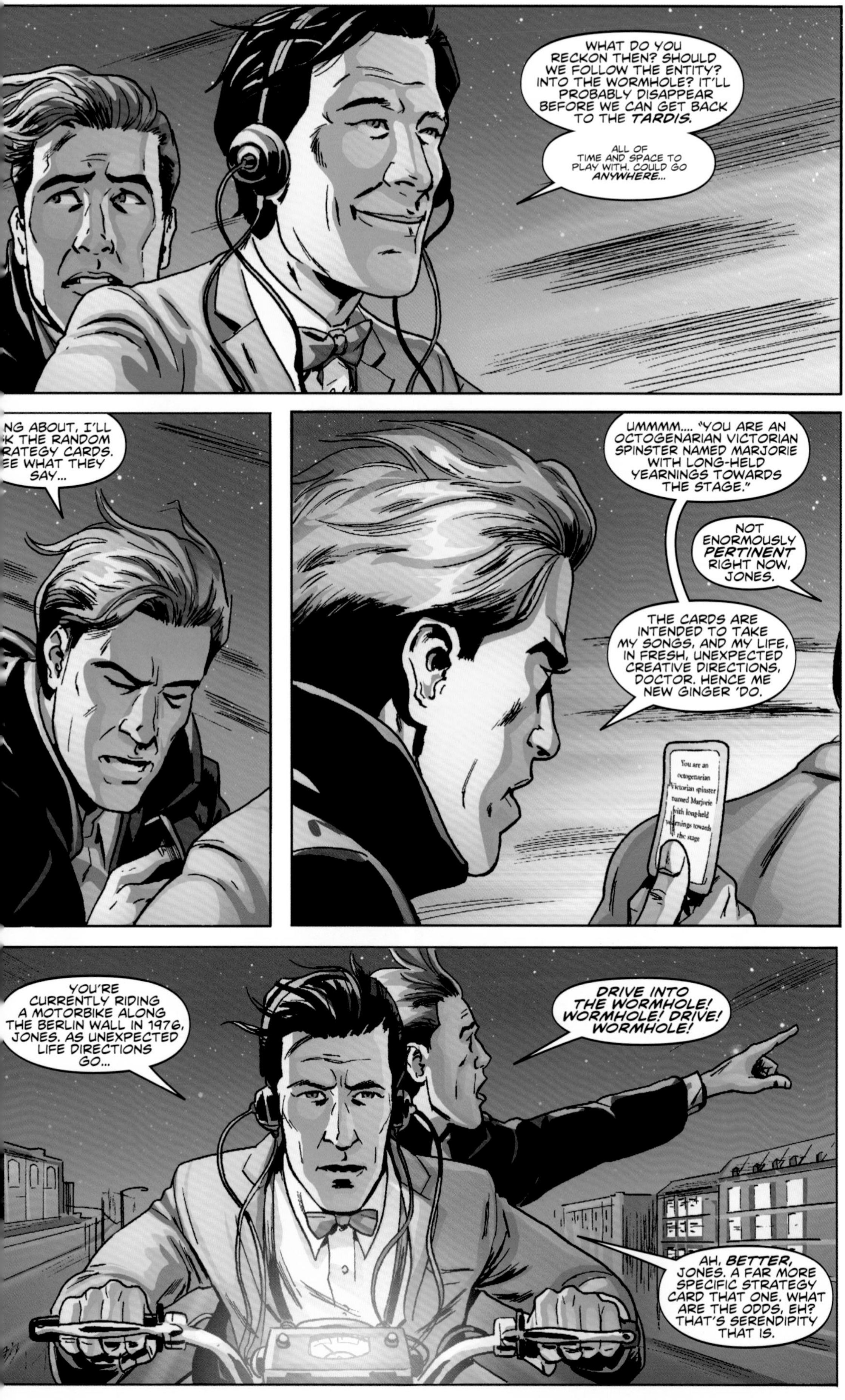

WHAT DO YOU RECKON THEN? SHOULD WE FOLLOW THE ENTITY? INTO THE WORMHOLE? IT'LL PROBABLY DISAPPEAR BEFORE WE CAN GET BACK TO THE *TARDIS.*
ALL OF TIME AND SPACE TO PLAY WITH. COULD GO *ANYWHERE...*
NG ABOUT, I'LL K THE RANDOM RATEGY CARDS. EE WHAT THEY SAY...
UMMMM.... "YOU ARE AN OCTOGENARIAN VICTORIAN SPINSTER NAMED MARJORIE WITH LONG-HELD YEARNINGS TOWARDS THE STAGE."
NOT ENORMOUSLY *PERTINENT* RIGHT NOW, JONES.
THE CARDS ARE INTENDED TO TAKE MY SONGS, AND MY LIFE, IN FRESH, UNEXPECTED CREATIVE DIRECTIONS, DOCTOR. HENCE ME NEW GINGER 'DO.
You are an octogenarian Victorian spinster named Marjorie with long-held yearnings towards the stage
YOU'RE CURRENTLY RIDING A MOTORBIKE ALONG THE BERLIN WALL IN 1976, JONES. AS UNEXPECTED LIFE DIRECTIONS GO...
DRIVE INTO THE WORMHOLE! WORMHOLE! DRIVE! WORMHOLE!
AH, *BETTER,* JONES. A FAR MORE SPECIFIC STRATEGY CARD THAT ONE. WHAT ARE THE ODDS, EH? THAT'S SERENDIPITY THAT IS.

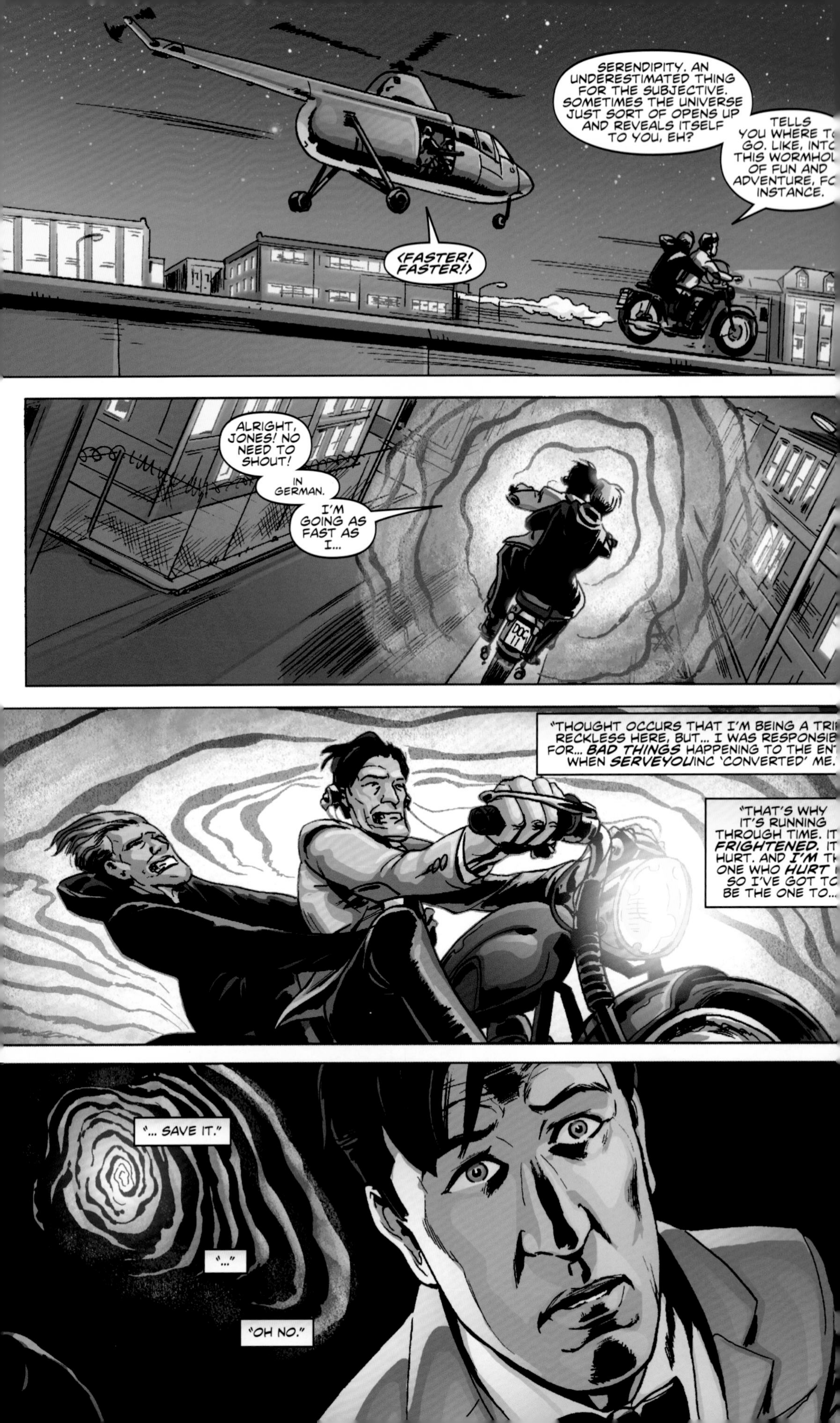
SERENDIPITY. AN UNDERESTIMATED THING FOR THE SUBJECTIVE. SOMETIMES THE UNIVERSE JUST SORT OF OPENS UP AND REVEALS ITSELF TO YOU, EH?
TELLS YOU WHERE T GO. LIKE, INT THIS WORMHOL OF FUN AND ADVENTURE, F INSTANCE.
‹FASTER! FASTER!›
ALRIGHT, JONES! NO NEED TO SHOUT!
IN GERMAN.
I'M GOING AS FAST AS I...
"THOUGHT OCCURS THAT I'M BEING A TRI RECKLESS HERE, BUT... I WAS RESPONSIB FOR... *BAD THINGS* HAPPENING TO THE EN WHEN *SERVEYOU*INC 'CONVERTED' ME.
"THAT'S WHY IT'S RUNNING THROUGH TIME. IT *FRIGHTENED.* IT HURT. AND *I'M* TH ONE WHO *HURT* SO I'VE GOT T BE THE ONE TO...
"... SAVE IT."
"..."
"OH NO."

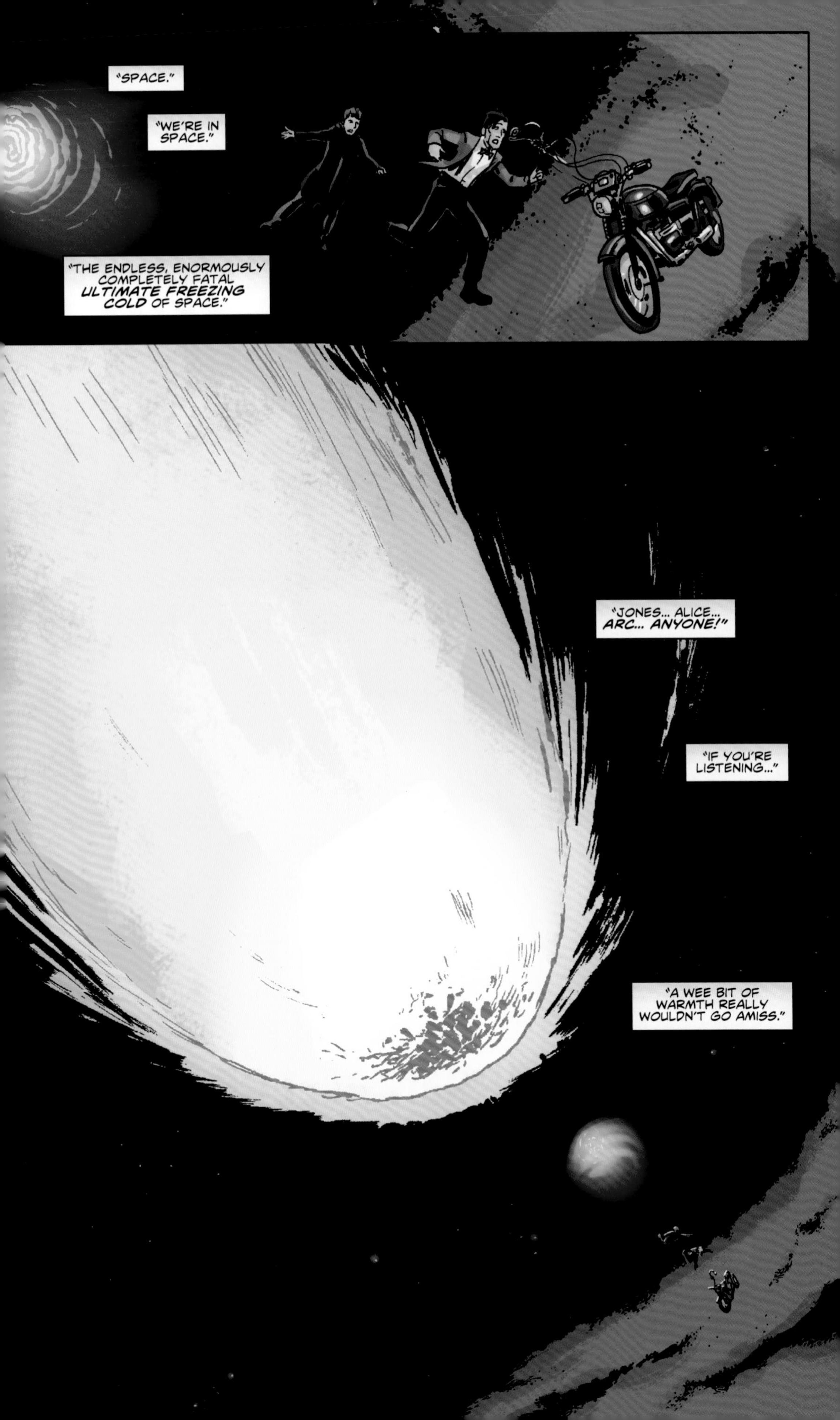
"SPACE."
"WE'RE IN SPACE."
"THE ENDLESS, ENORMOUSLY COMPLETELY FATAL ULTIMATE FREEZING COLD OF SPACE."
"JONES... ALICE... ARC... ANYONE!"
"IF YOU'RE LISTENING..."
"A WEE BIT OF WARMTH REALLY WOULDN'T GO AMISS."

CHAPTER 12

CONVERSION PART 1

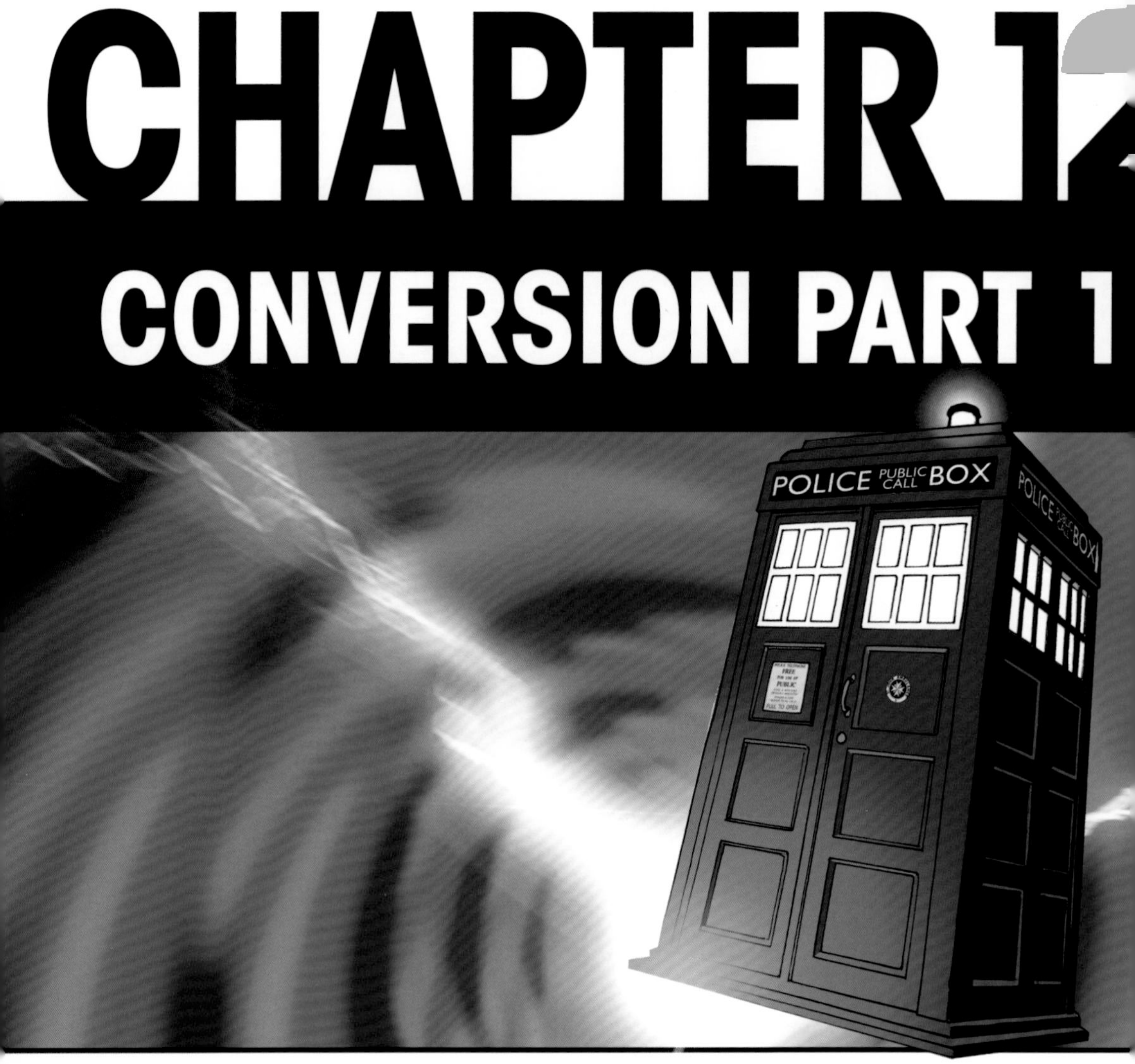
POLICE PUBLIC CALL BOX
PULL TO OPEN

WRITER
ROB WILLIAMS

ARTIST
WARREN PLEECE

COLORIST
HI-FI

LETTERER
RICHARD STARKINGS AND COMICRAFT'S JIMMY BETANCOURT

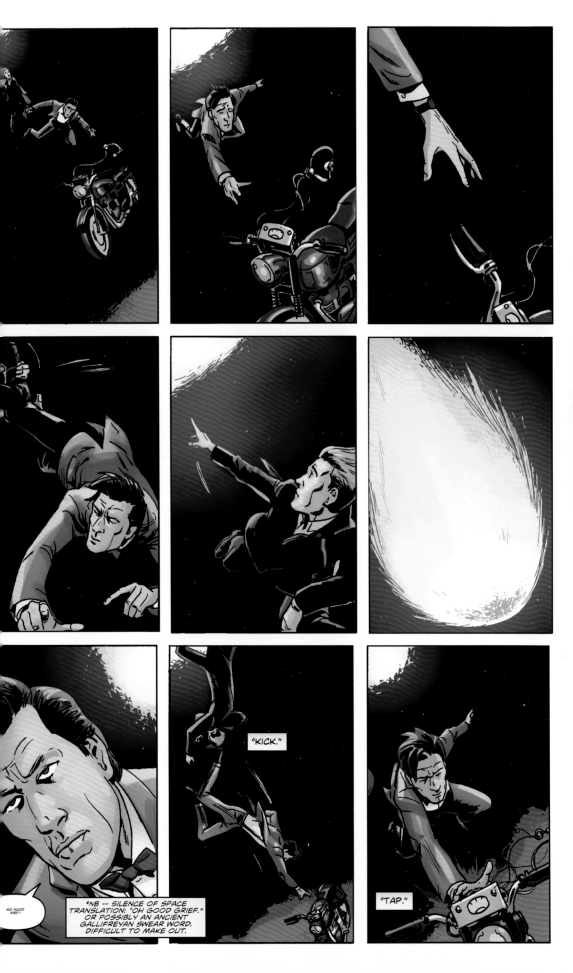

"KICK."

"NB -- SILENCE OF SPACE
TRANSLATION: "OH GOOD GRIEF."
OR POSSIBLY AN ANCIENT
GALLIFREYAN SWEAR WORD.
DIFFICULT TO MAKE OUT.

"NO MOOD
MIEF."

"TAP."

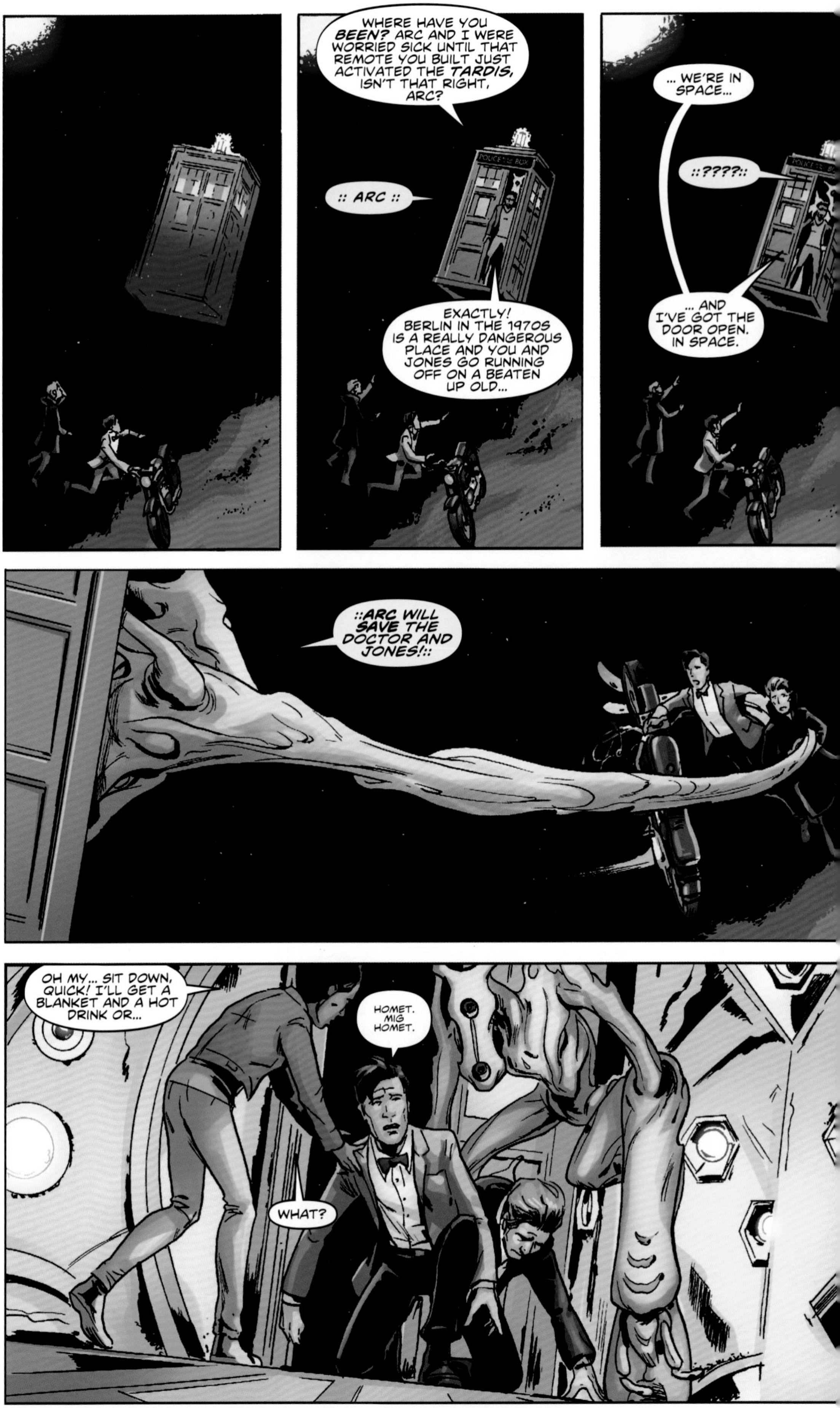
WHERE HAVE YOU BEEN? ARC AND I WERE WORRIED SICK UNTIL THAT REMOTE YOU BUILT JUST ACTIVATED THE TARDIS, ISN'T THAT RIGHT, ARC?
:: ARC ::
EXACTLY! BERLIN IN THE 1970S IS A REALLY DANGEROUS PLACE AND YOU AND JONES GO RUNNING OFF ON A BEATEN UP OLD...
... WE'RE IN SPACE...
::????::
... AND I'VE GOT THE DOOR OPEN. IN SPACE.
::ARC WILL SAVE THE DOCTOR AND JONES!::
OH MY... SIT DOWN, QUICK! I'LL GET A BLANKET AND A HOT DRINK OR...
HOMET. MIG HOMET.
WHAT?

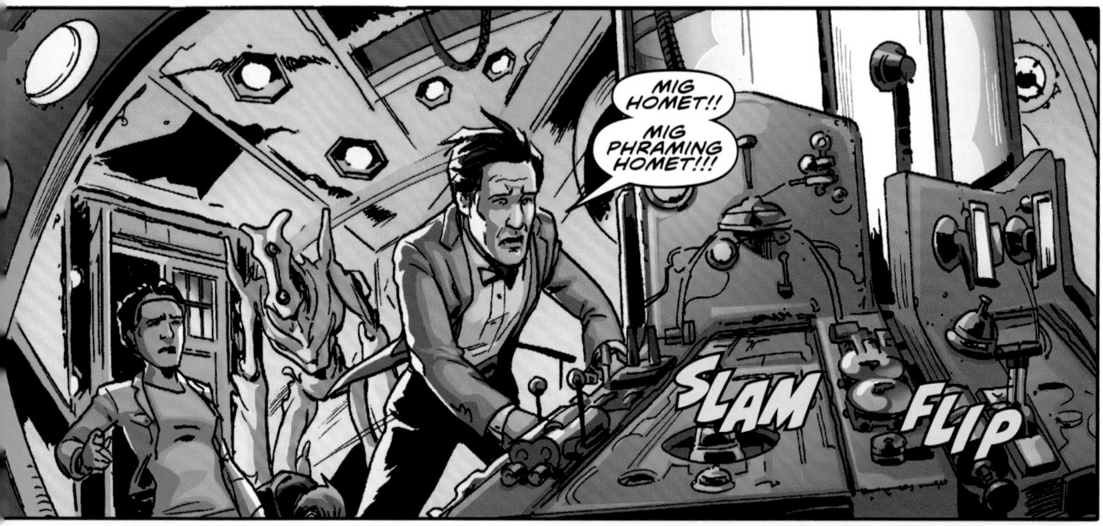
MIG HOMET!!
MIG PHRAMING HOMET!!!
SLAM
FLIP

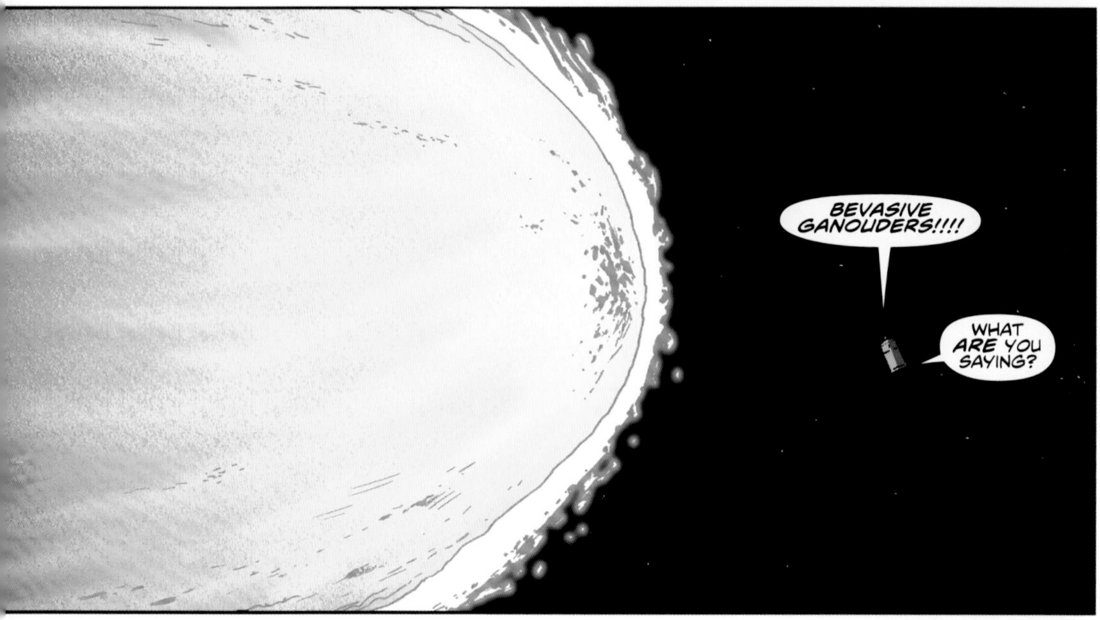
BEVASIVE GANOUDERS!!!!
WHAT ARE YOU SAYING?

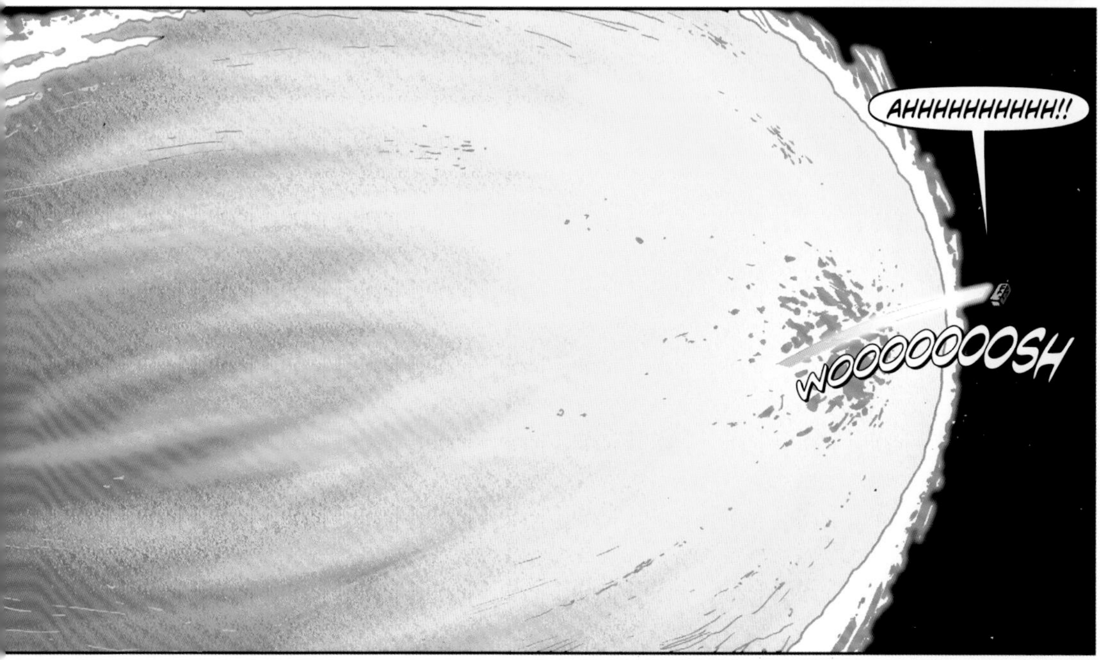
AHHHHHHHHHH!!
WOOOOOOOOSH

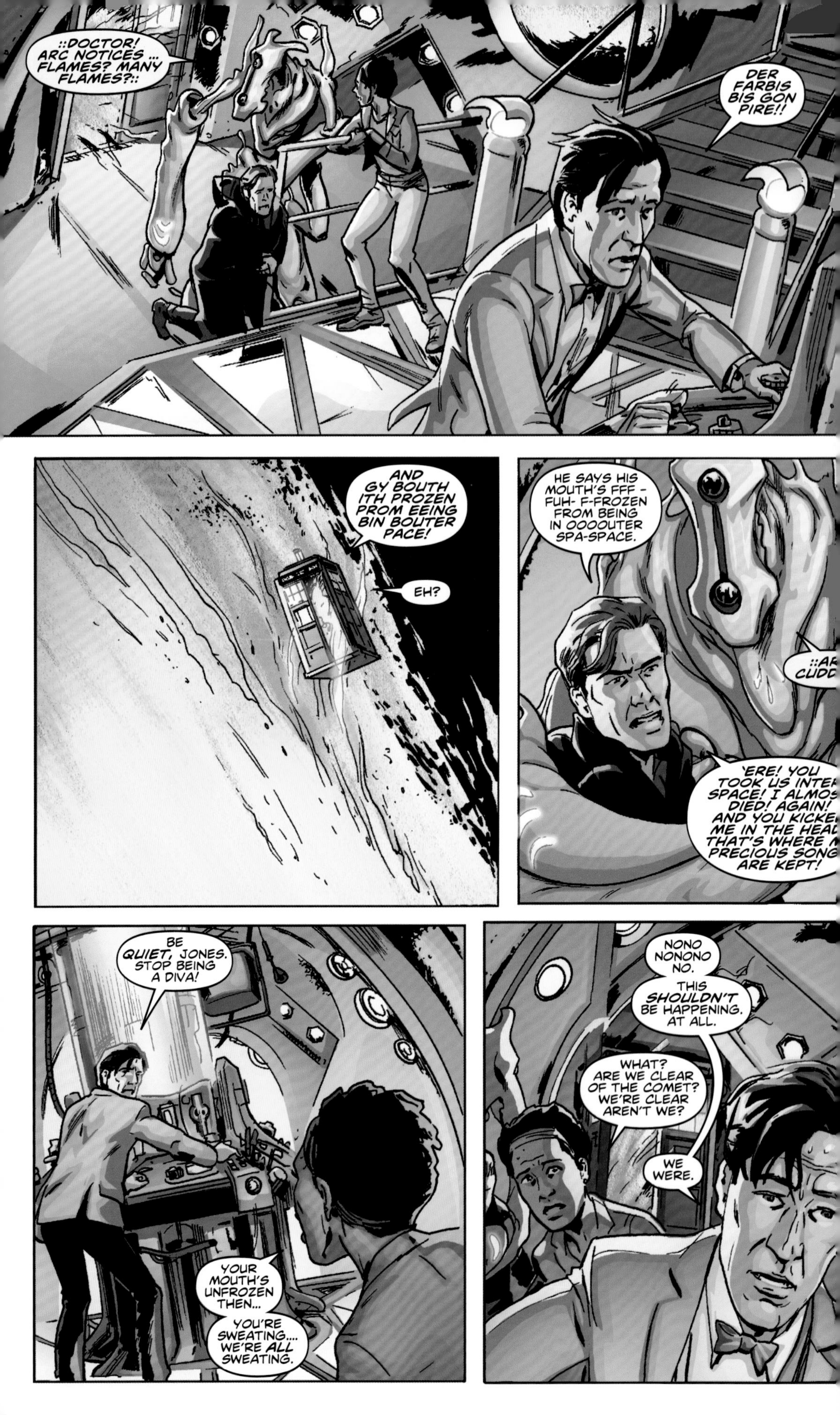
::DOCTOR! ARC NOTICES ... FLAMES? MANY FLAMES?::
DER FARBIS BIS GON PIRE!!
AND GY BOUTH ITH PROZEN PROM EEING BIN BOUTER PACE!
EH?
HE SAYS HIS MOUTH'S FFF - FUH- F-FROZEN FROM BEING IN OOOOUTER SPA-SPACE.
::AR CUDD
'ERE! YOU TOOK US INTER SPACE! I ALMOS DIED! AGAIN! AND YOU KICKE ME IN THE HEAD THAT'S WHERE M PRECIOUS SONG ARE KEPT!
BE QUIET, JONES. STOP BEING A DIVA!
YOUR MOUTH'S UNFROZEN THEN...
YOU'RE SWEATING.... WE'RE ALL SWEATING.
NONO NONONO NO.
THIS SHOULDN'T BE HAPPENING. AT ALL.
WHAT? ARE WE CLEAR OF THE COMET? WE'RE CLEAR AREN'T WE?
WE WERE.

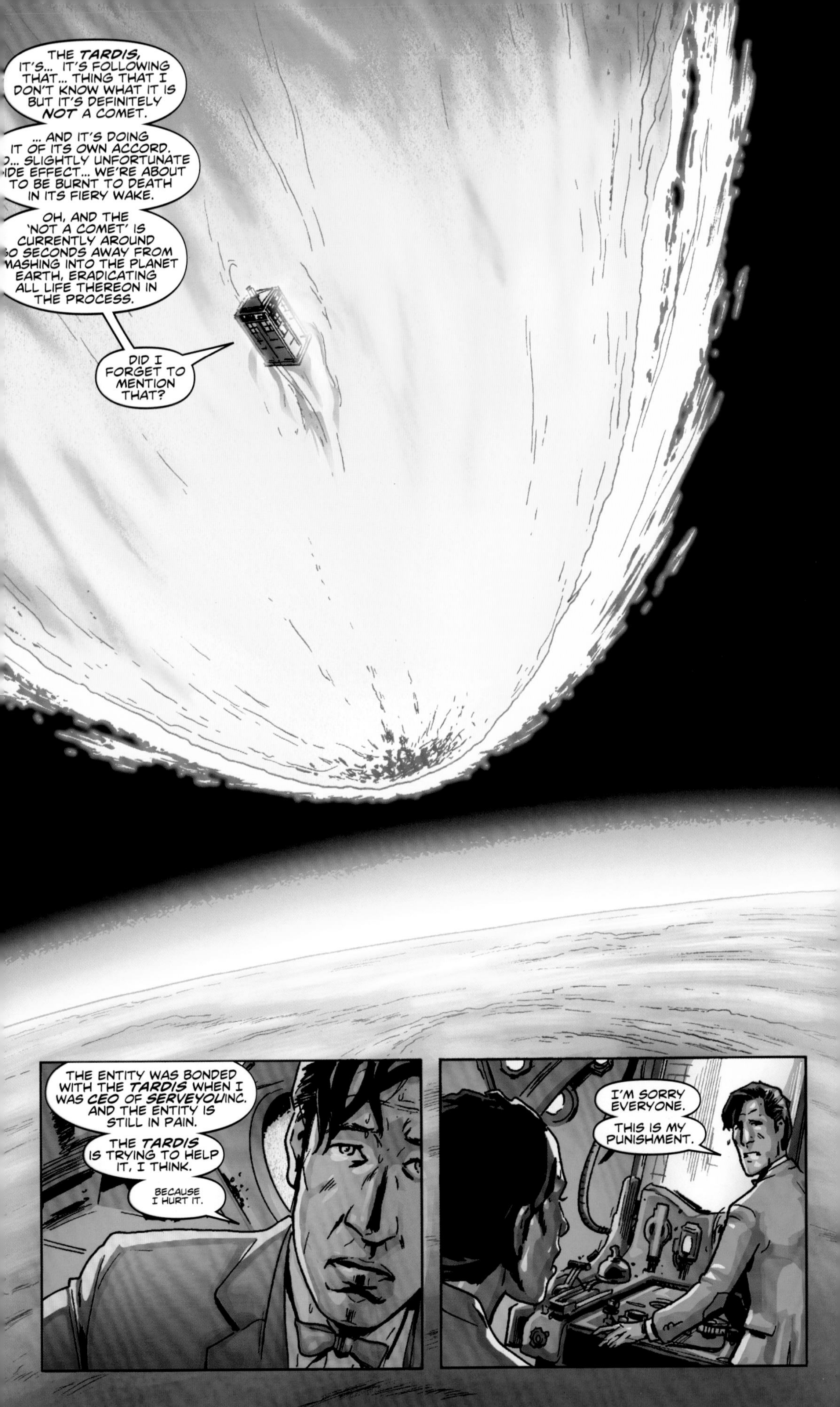
THE TARDIS, IT'S... IT'S FOLLOWING THAT... THING THAT I DON'T KNOW WHAT IT IS BUT IT'S DEFINITELY NOT A COMET.
... AND IT'S DOING IT OF ITS OWN ACCORD. ... SLIGHTLY UNFORTUNATE IDE EFFECT... WE'RE ABOUT TO BE BURNT TO DEATH IN ITS FIERY WAKE.
OH, AND THE 'NOT A COMET' IS CURRENTLY AROUND O SECONDS AWAY FROM MASHING INTO THE PLANET EARTH, ERADICATING ALL LIFE THEREON IN THE PROCESS.
DID I FORGET TO MENTION THAT?
THE ENTITY WAS BONDED WITH THE TARDIS WHEN I WAS CEO OF SERVEYOU INC. AND THE ENTITY IS STILL IN PAIN.
THE TARDIS IS TRYING TO HELP IT, I THINK.
BECAUSE I HURT IT.
I'M SORRY EVERYONE.
THIS IS MY PUNISHMENT.

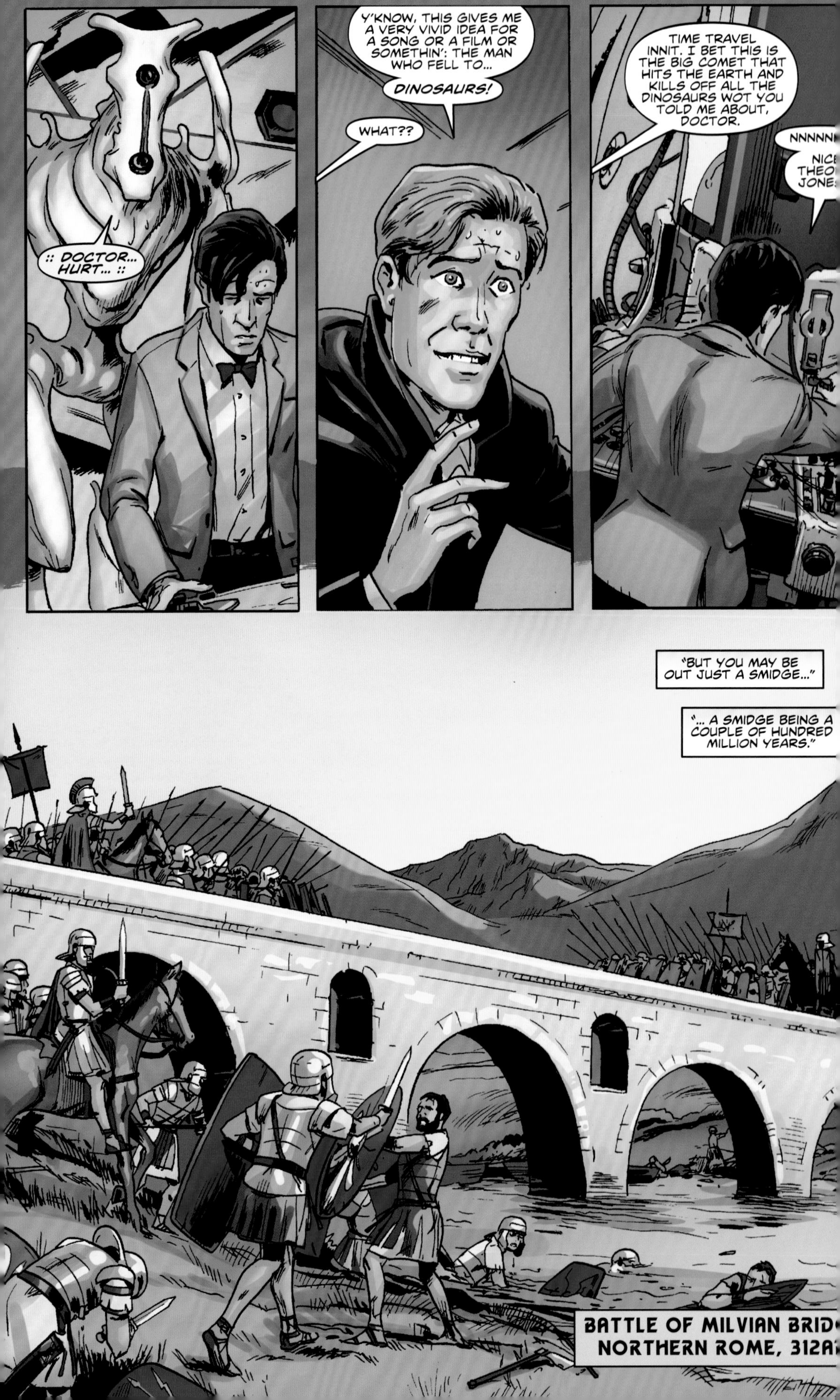
:: DOCTOR... HURT... ::
Y'KNOW, THIS GIVES ME A VERY VIVID IDEA FOR A SONG OR A FILM OR SOMETHIN': THE MAN WHO FELL TO...
DINOSAURS!
WHAT??
TIME TRAVEL INNIT. I BET THIS IS THE BIG COMET THAT HITS THE EARTH AND KILLS OFF ALL THE DINOSAURS WOT YOU TOLD ME ABOUT, DOCTOR.
NNNNN
NICE THEO JONES
"BUT YOU MAY BE OUT JUST A SMIDGE..."
"... A SMIDGE BEING A COUPLE OF HUNDRED MILLION YEARS."
BATTLE OF MILVIAN BRID
NORTHERN ROME, 312A

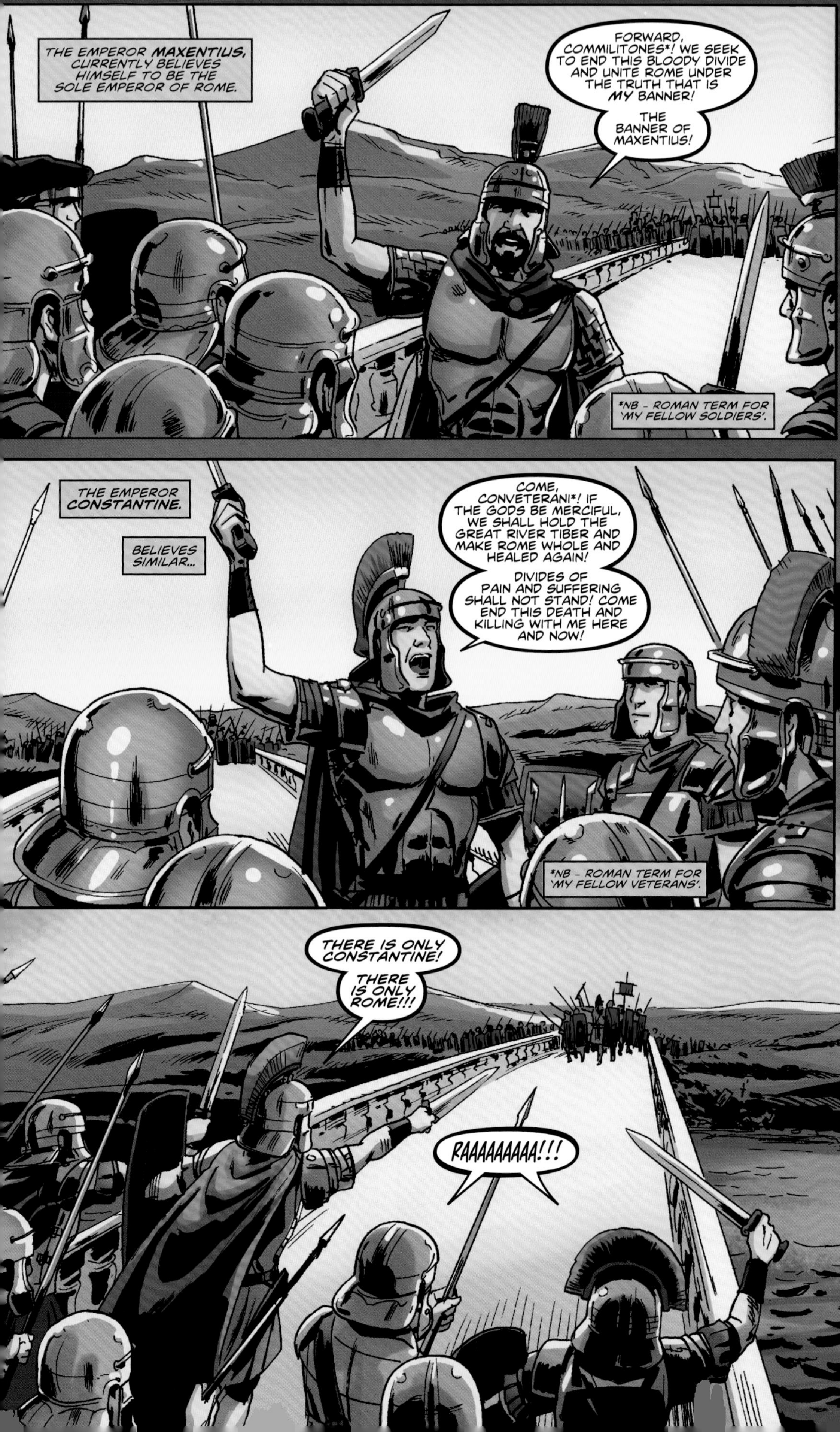
THE EMPEROR MAXENTIUS, CURRENTLY BELIEVES HIMSELF TO BE THE SOLE EMPEROR OF ROME.
FORWARD, COMMILITONES*! WE SEEK TO END THIS BLOODY DIVIDE AND UNITE ROME UNDER THE TRUTH THAT IS MY BANNER!
THE BANNER OF MAXENTIUS!
*NB - ROMAN TERM FOR 'MY FELLOW SOLDIERS'.
THE EMPEROR CONSTANTINE.
BELIEVES SIMILAR...
COME, CONVETERANI*! IF THE GODS BE MERCIFUL, WE SHALL HOLD THE GREAT RIVER TIBER AND MAKE ROME WHOLE AND HEALED AGAIN!
DIVIDES OF PAIN AND SUFFERING SHALL NOT STAND! COME END THIS DEATH AND KILLING WITH ME HERE AND NOW!
*NB - ROMAN TERM FOR 'MY FELLOW VETERANS'.
THERE IS ONLY CONSTANTINE!
THERE IS ONLY ROME!!!
RAAAAAAAAA!!!

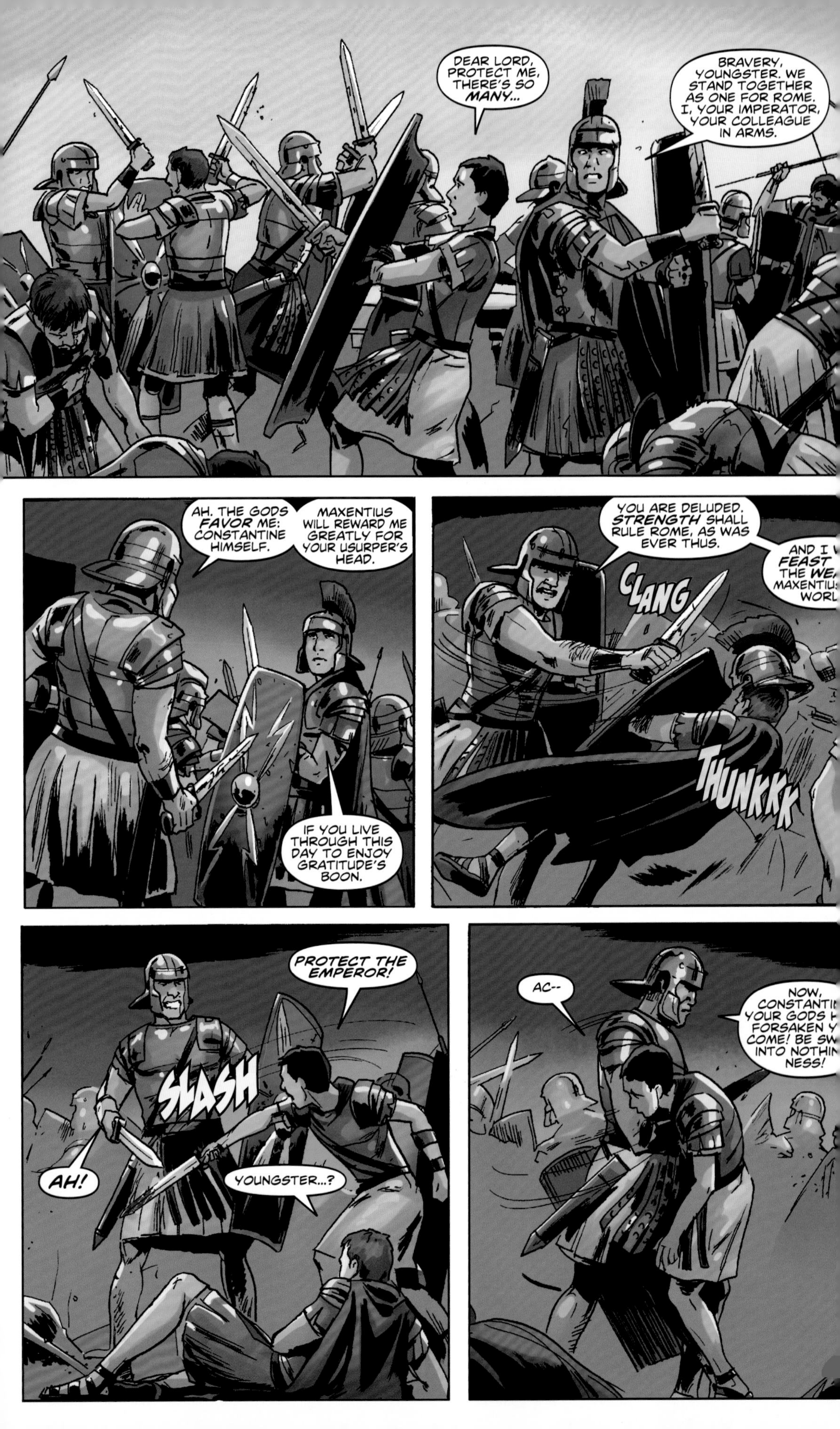
DEAR LORD, PROTECT ME, THERE'S SO MANY...
BRAVERY, YOUNGSTER. WE STAND TOGETHER AS ONE FOR ROME. I, YOUR IMPERATOR, YOUR COLLEAGUE IN ARMS.
AH. THE GODS FAVOR ME: CONSTANTINE HIMSELF.
MAXENTIUS WILL REWARD ME GREATLY FOR YOUR USURPER'S HEAD.
IF YOU LIVE THROUGH THIS DAY TO ENJOY GRATITUDE'S BOON.
YOU ARE DELUDED. STRENGTH SHALL RULE ROME, AS WAS EVER THUS.
CLANG
AND I FEAST THE MAXENTIUS WORL
THUNKKK
PROTECT THE EMPEROR!
SLASH
AH!
YOUNGSTER...?
AC--
NOW, CONSTANTI YOUR GODS FORSAKEN COME! BE SW INTO NOTHIN NESS!

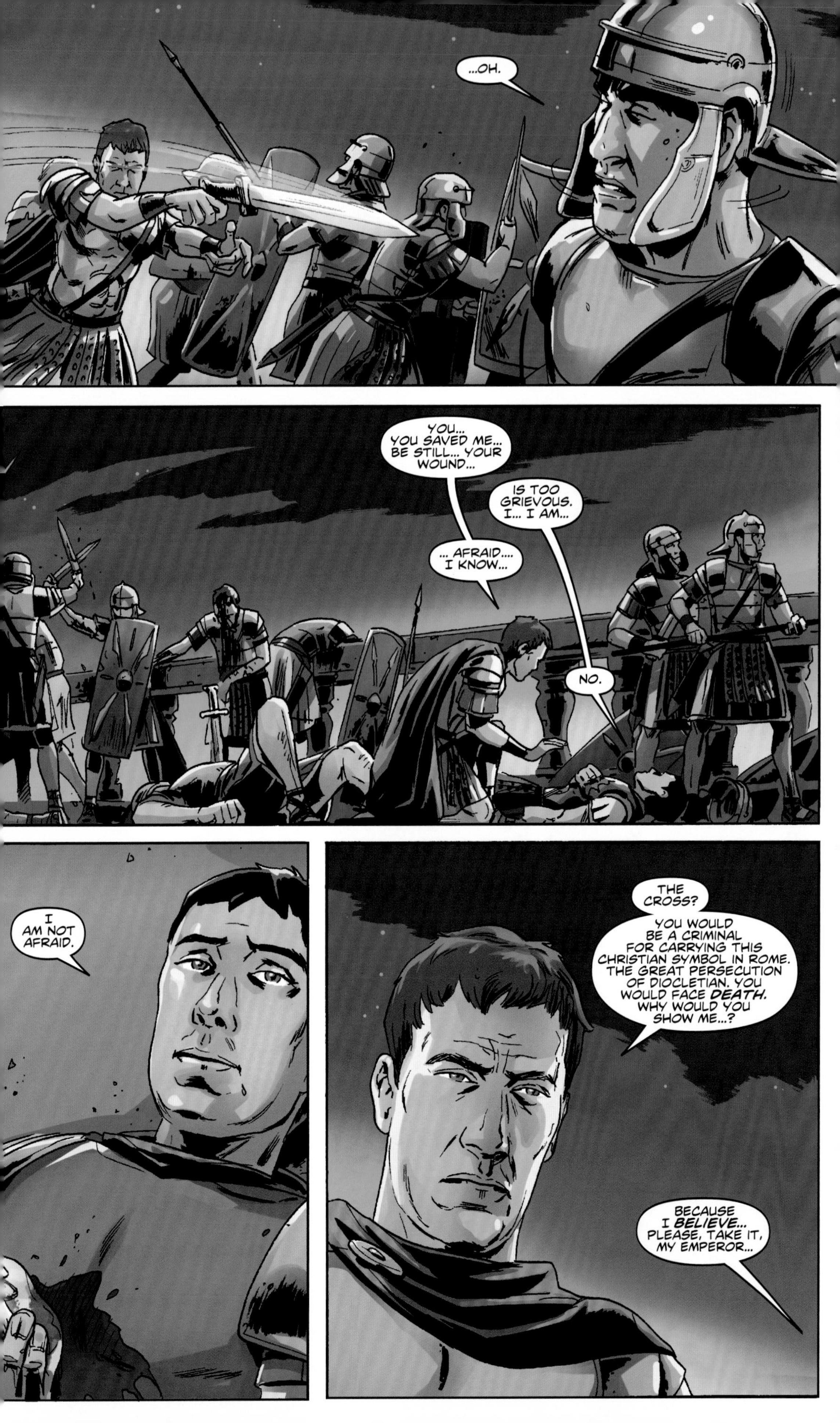
...OH.
YOU... YOU SAVED ME... BE STILL... YOUR WOUND...
IS TOO GRIEVOUS. I... I AM...
... AFRAID.... I KNOW...
NO.
I AM NOT AFRAID.
THE CROSS?
YOU WOULD BE A CRIMINAL FOR CARRYING THIS CHRISTIAN SYMBOL IN ROME. THE GREAT PERSECUTION OF DIOCLETIAN. YOU WOULD FACE *DEATH.* WHY WOULD YOU SHOW ME...?
BECAUSE I *BELIEVE*... PLEASE, TAKE IT, MY EMPEROR...

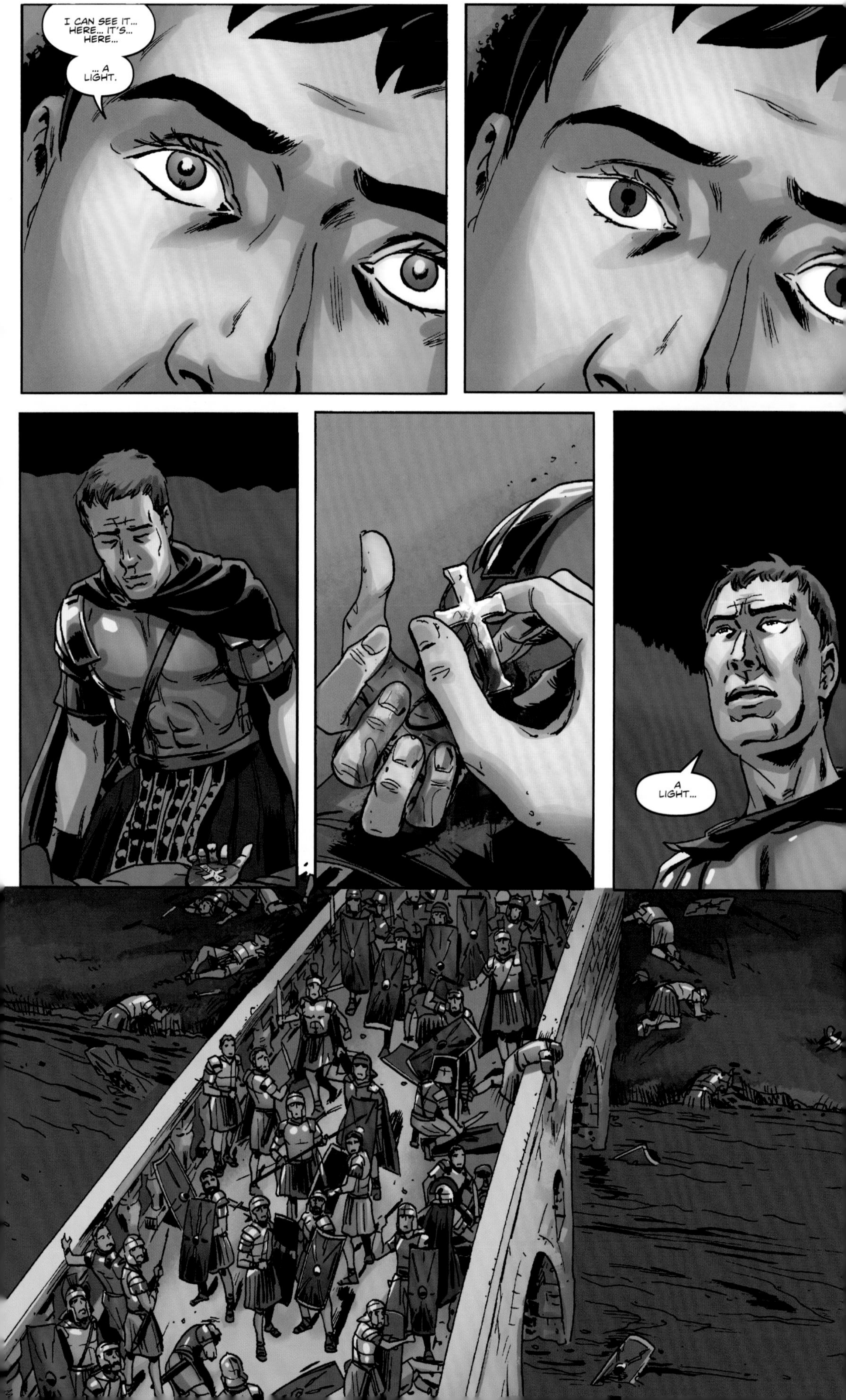
I CAN SEE IT... HERE... IT'S... HERE...
... A LIGHT.
A LIGHT...

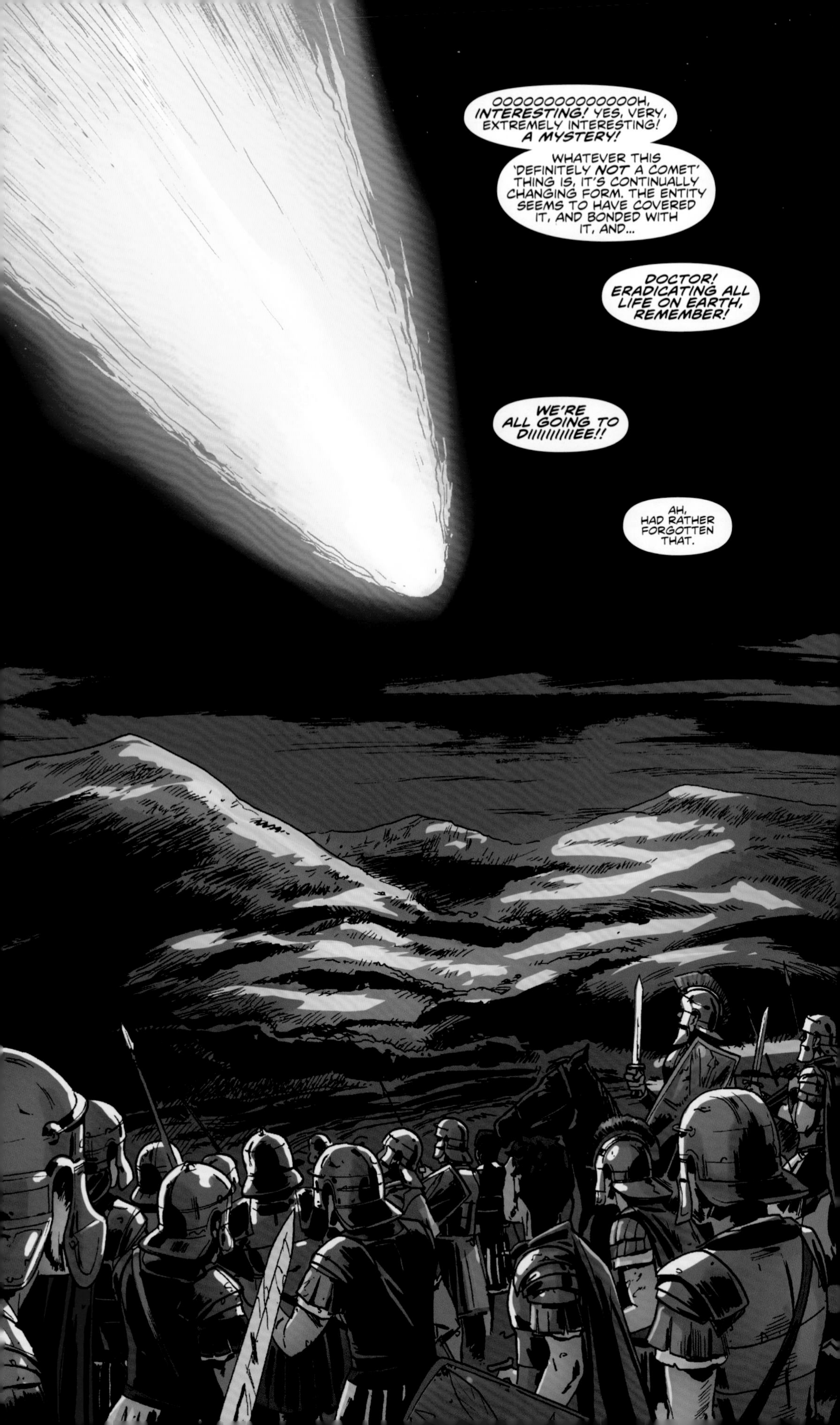
OOOOOOOOOOOOOOOH, INTERESTING! YES, VERY, EXTREMELY INTERESTING! A MYSTERY!
WHATEVER THIS 'DEFINITELY NOT A COMET' THING IS, IT'S CONTINUALLY CHANGING FORM. THE ENTITY SEEMS TO HAVE COVERED IT, AND BONDED WITH IT, AND...
DOCTOR! ERADICATING ALL LIFE ON EARTH, REMEMBER!
WE'RE ALL GOING TO DIIIIIIIIIEE!!
AH, HAD RATHER FORGOTTEN THAT.

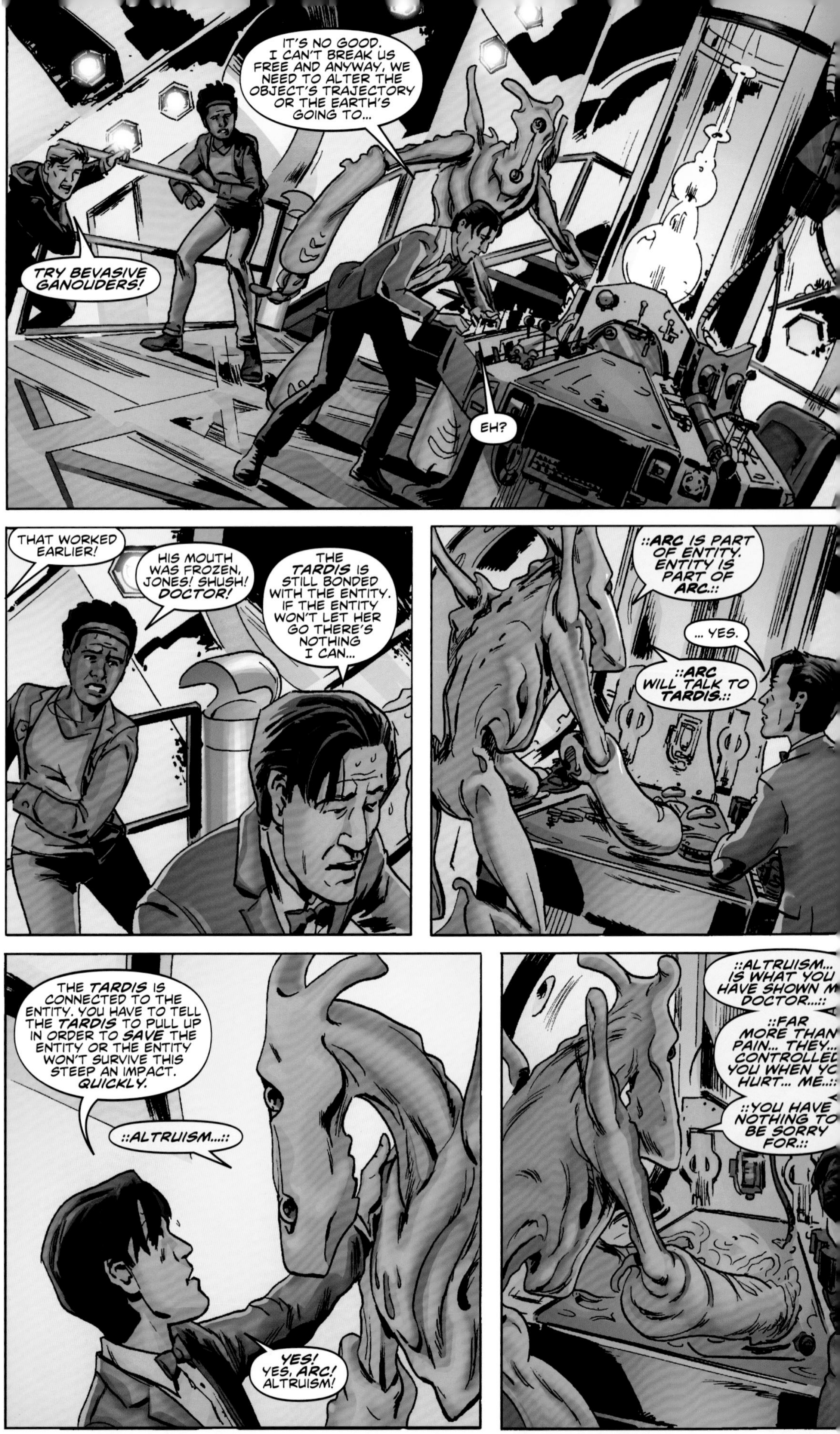
IT'S NO GOOD. I CAN'T BREAK US FREE AND ANYWAY, WE NEED TO ALTER THE OBJECT'S TRAJECTORY OR THE EARTH'S GOING TO...
TRY BEVASIVE GANOUDERS!
EH?
THAT WORKED EARLIER!
HIS MOUTH WAS FROZEN, JONES! SHUSH! DOCTOR!
THE TARDIS IS STILL BONDED WITH THE ENTITY. IF THE ENTITY WON'T LET HER GO THERE'S NOTHING I CAN...
::ARC IS PART OF ENTITY. ENTITY IS PART OF ARC.::
... YES.
::ARC WILL TALK TO TARDIS.::
THE TARDIS IS CONNECTED TO THE ENTITY. YOU HAVE TO TELL THE TARDIS TO PULL UP IN ORDER TO SAVE THE ENTITY OR THE ENTITY WON'T SURVIVE THIS STEEP AN IMPACT. QUICKLY.
::ALTRUISM...::
YES! YES, ARC! ALTRUISM!
::ALTRUISM... IS WHAT YOU HAVE SHOWN M DOCTOR...::
::FAR MORE THAN PAIN... THEY... CONTROLLE YOU WHEN YO HURT... ME...::
::YOU HAVE NOTHING TO BE SORRY FOR.::

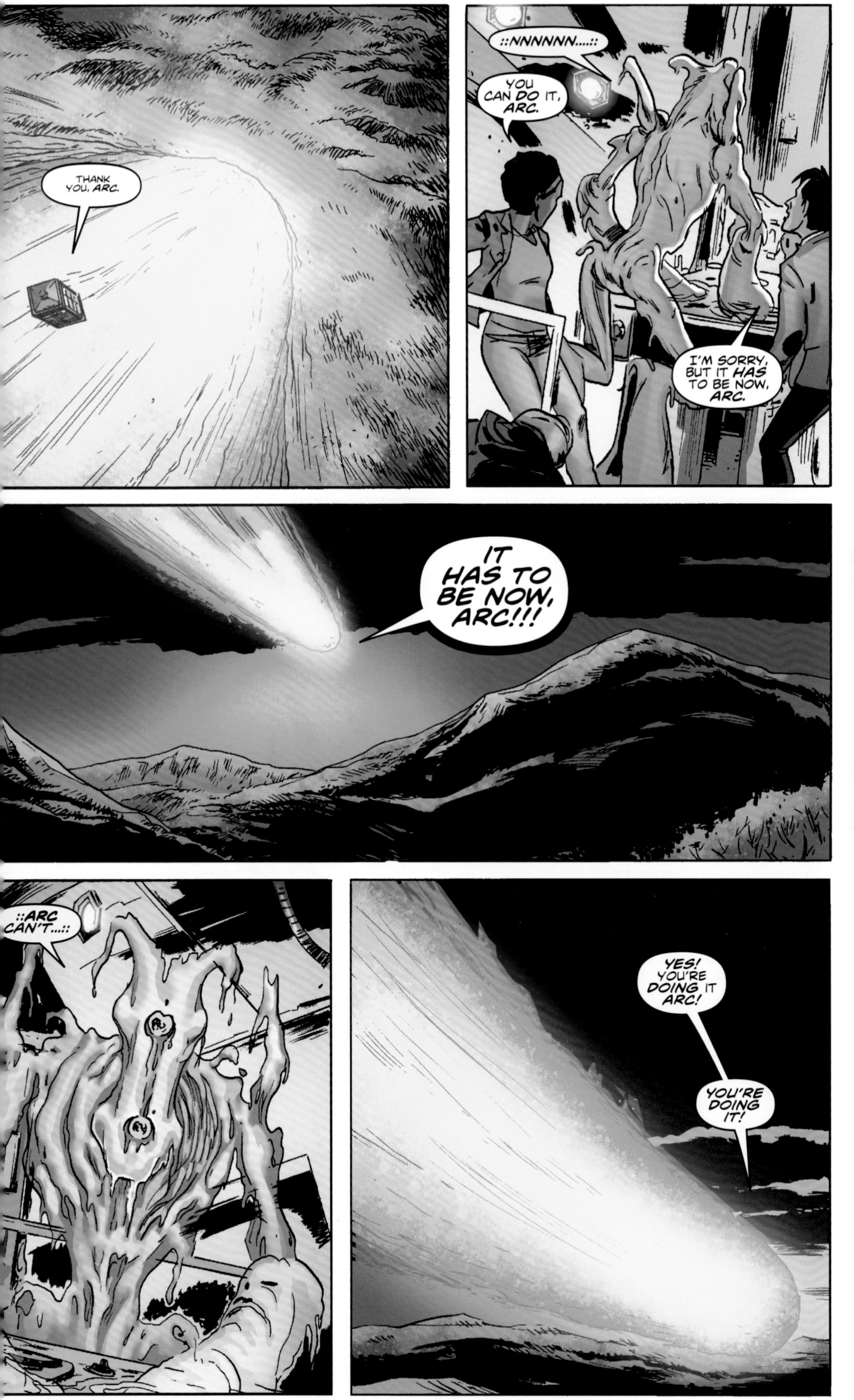
THANK YOU, ARC.
::NNNNNN....::
YOU CAN DO IT, ARC.
I'M SORRY, BUT IT HAS TO BE NOW, ARC.
IT HAS TO BE NOW, ARC!!!
::ARC CAN'T....::
YES! YOU'RE DOING IT ARC!
YOU'RE DOING IT!

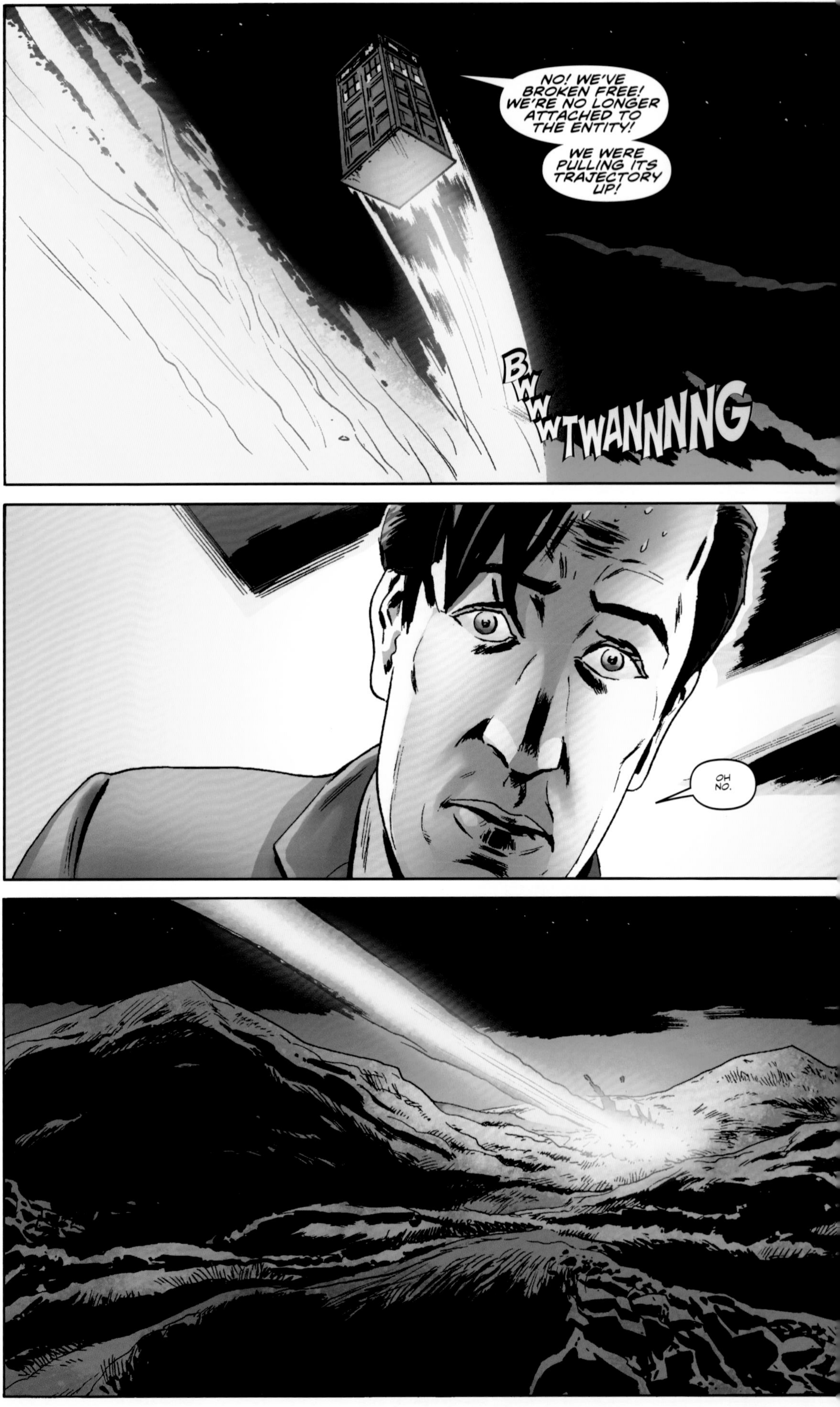
NO! WE'VE BROKEN FREE! WE'RE NO LONGER ATTACHED TO THE ENTITY!
WE WERE PULLING ITS TRAJECTORY UP!
BWWWTWANNNNG
OH NO.

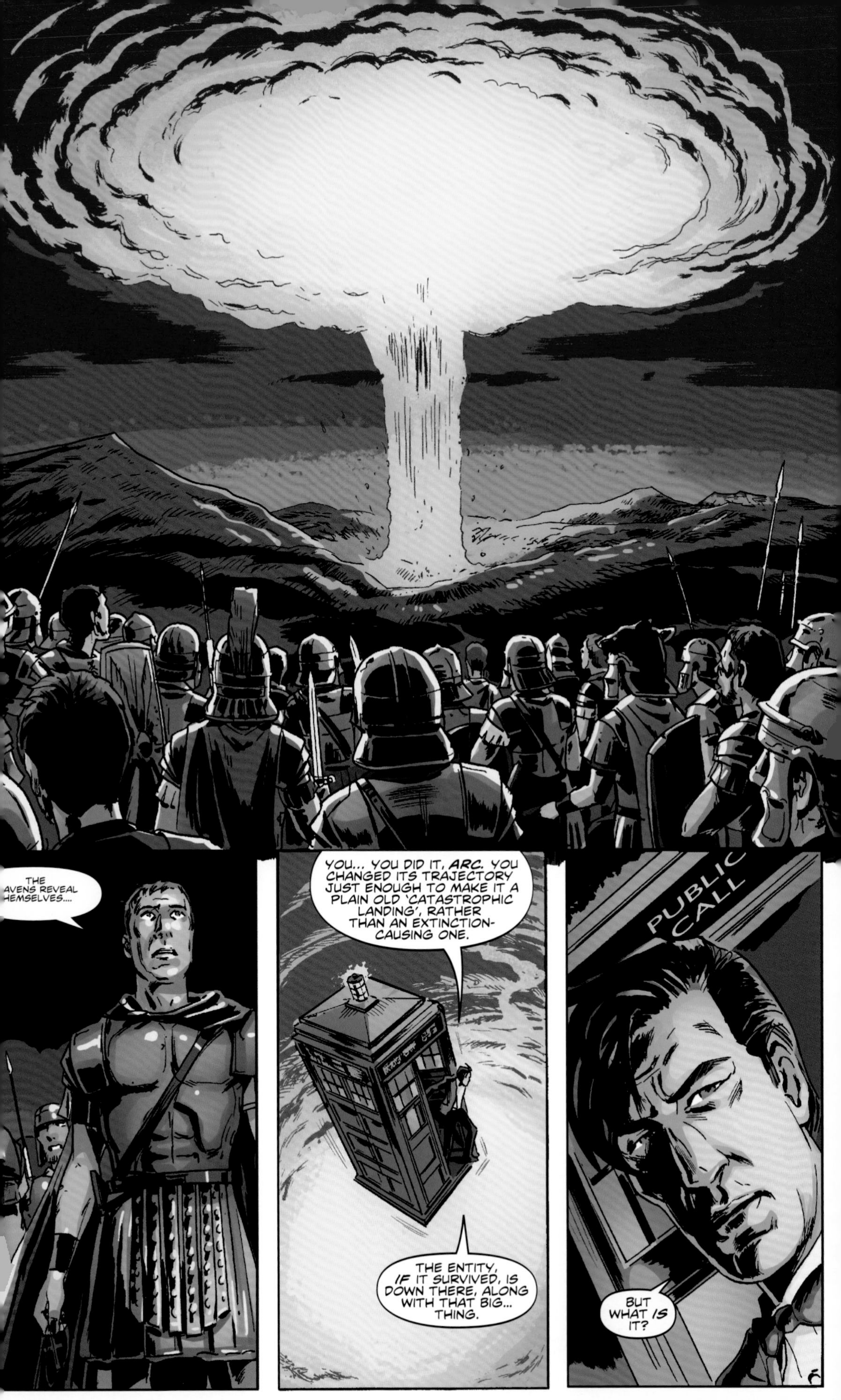
THE
AVENS REVEAL
HEMSELVES....
YOU... YOU DID IT, ARC. YOU CHANGED ITS TRAJECTORY JUST ENOUGH TO MAKE IT A PLAIN OLD 'CATASTROPHIC LANDING', RATHER THAN AN EXTINCTION-CAUSING ONE.
PUBLIC CALL
THE ENTITY, IF IT SURVIVED, IS DOWN THERE, ALONG WITH THAT BIG... THING.
BUT WHAT IS IT?

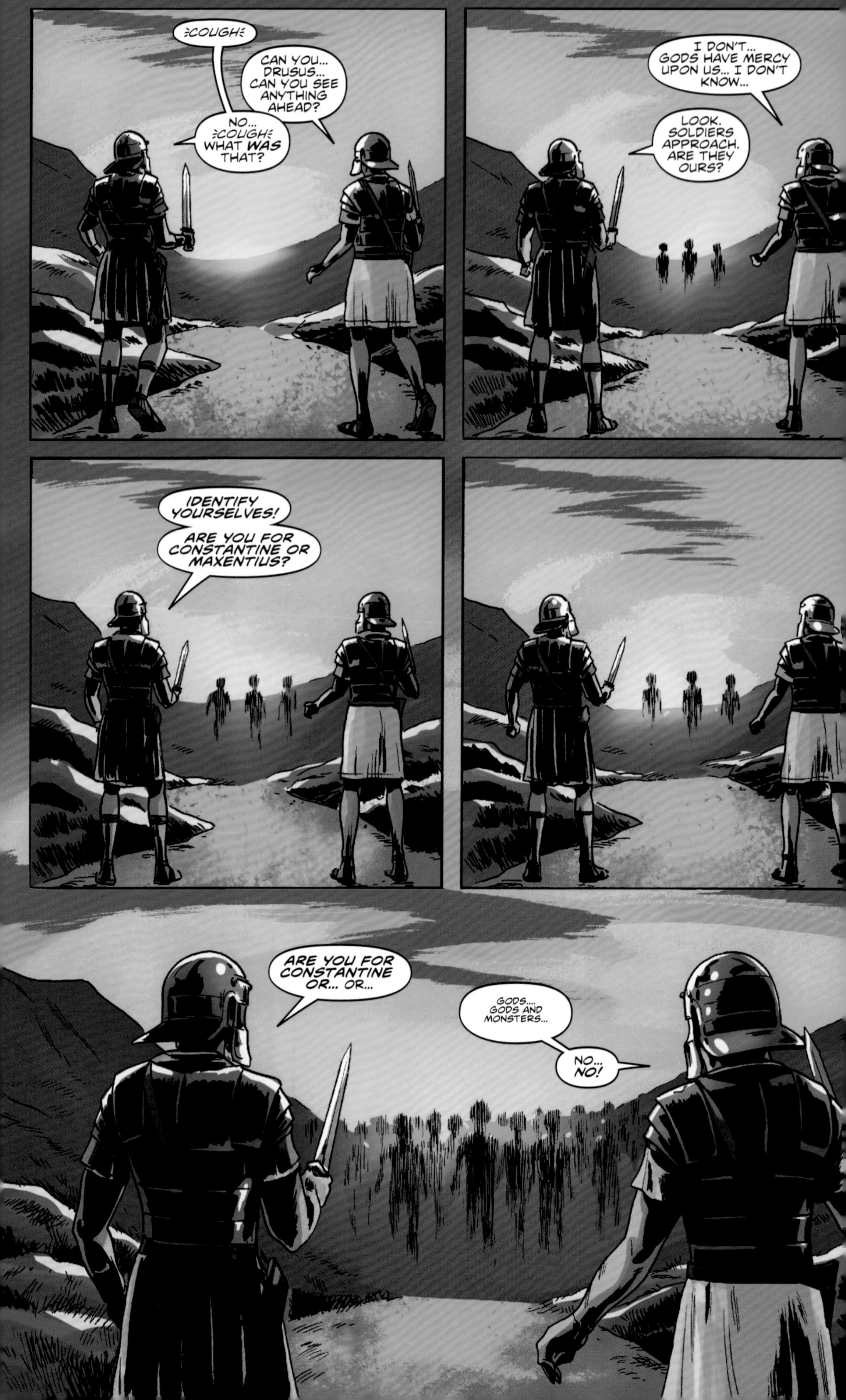
⁞COUGH⁞
CAN YOU... DRUSUS... CAN YOU SEE ANYTHING AHEAD?
NO... ⁞COUGH⁞ WHAT WAS THAT?
I DON'T... GODS HAVE MERCY UPON US... I DON'T KNOW...
LOOK. SOLDIERS APPROACH. ARE THEY OURS?
IDENTIFY YOURSELVES!
ARE YOU FOR CONSTANTINE OR MAXENTIUS?
ARE YOU FOR CONSTANTINE OR... OR...
GODS.... GODS AND MONSTERS...
NO... NO!

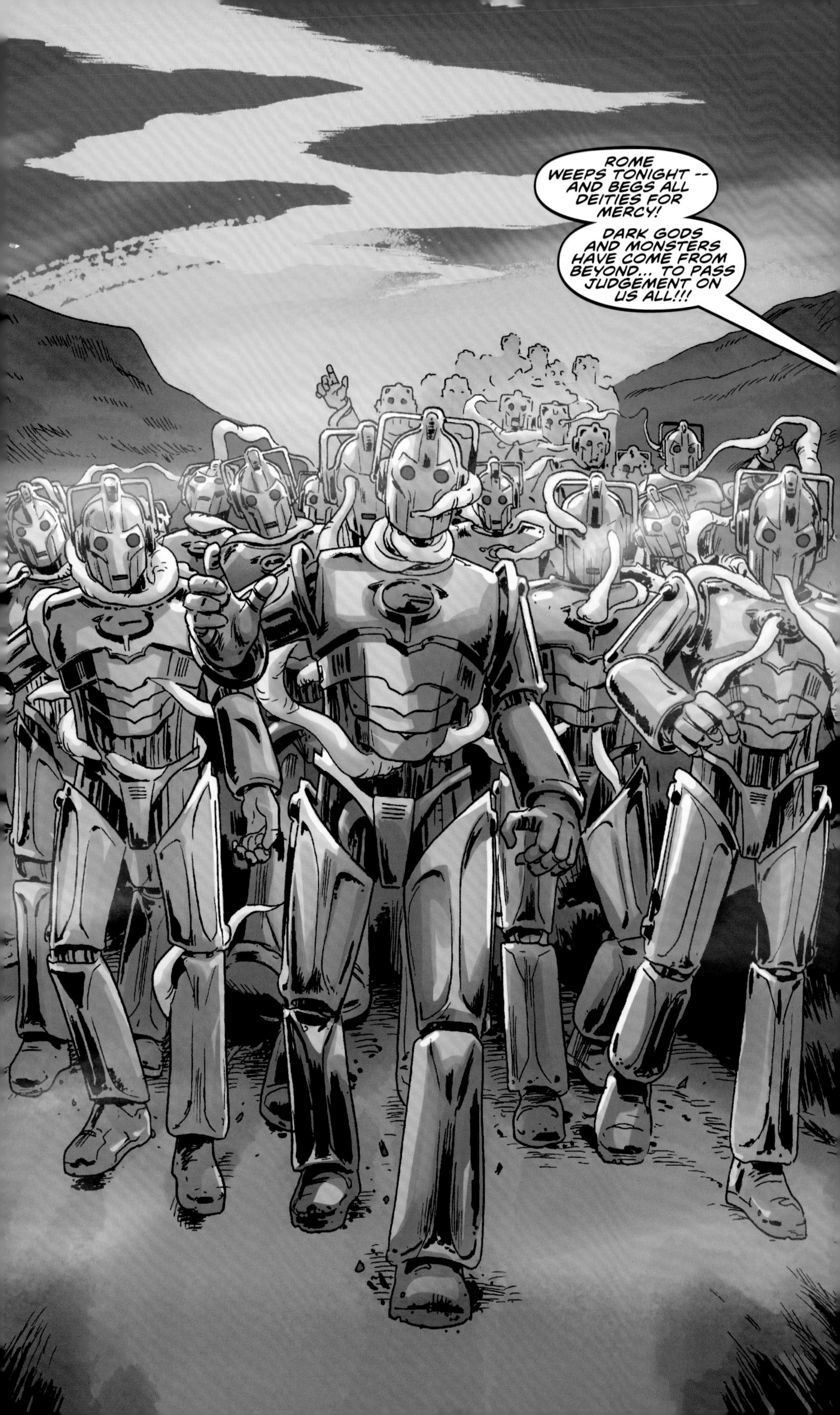
ROME WEEPS TONIGHT -- AND BEGS ALL DEITIES FOR MERCY!
DARK GODS AND MONSTERS HAVE COME FROM BEYOND... TO PASS JUDGEMENT ON US ALL!!!

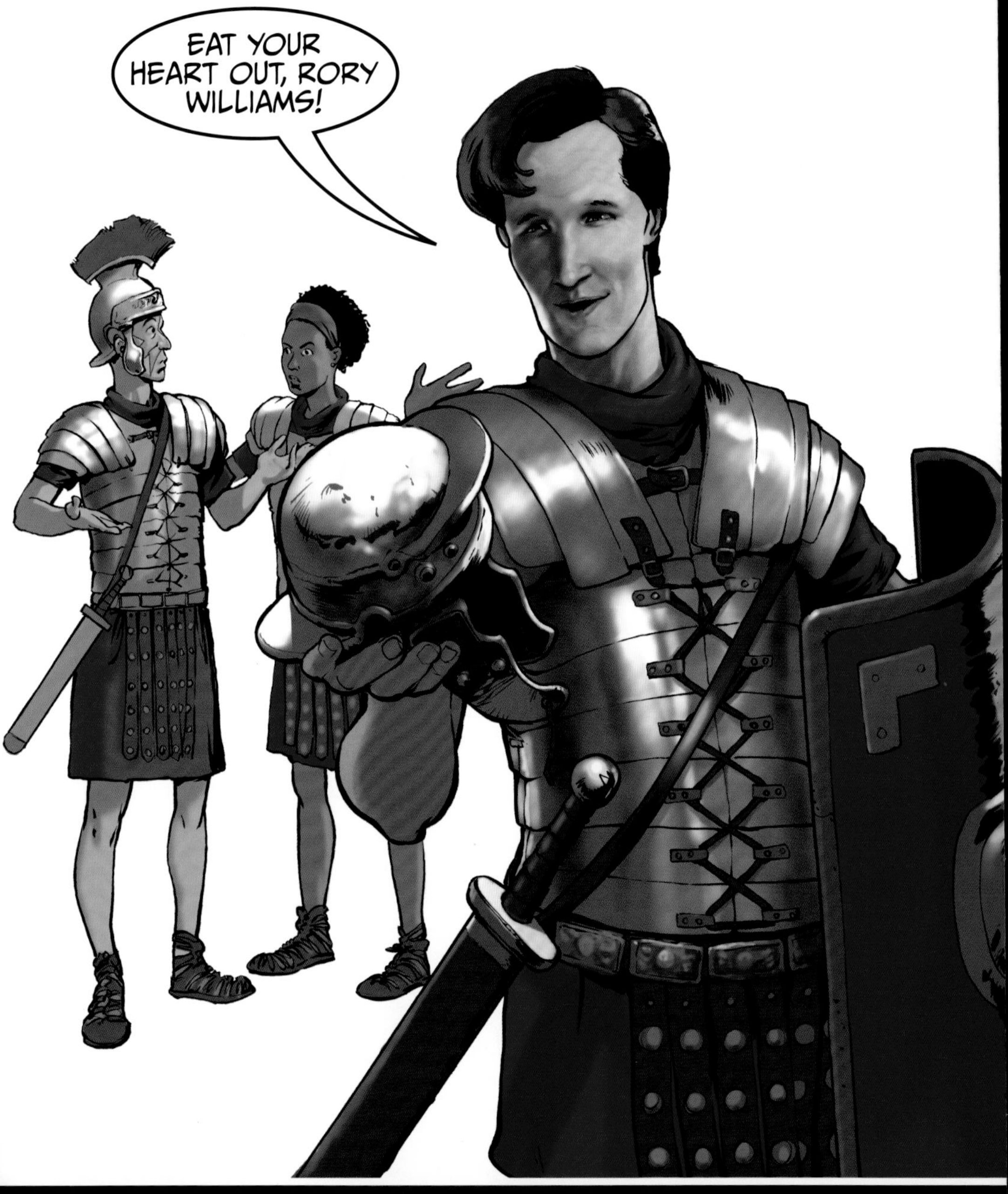
EAT YOUR HEART OUT, RORY WILLIAMS!

CHAPTER 13 Cover A: Simon Fraser

ONE IMPORTANT [THI]NG TO REMEMBER [AB]OUT MONSTERS...

I HOPE YOU'LL LIKE THIS ONE, DAD. IT HAS *THREE* CHORDS.

"THEY ALL *WANT* SOMETHING.

"NOW, GRANTED, THAT MAY WELL BE 'EAT BRAINS!' OR TO DETONATE THE UNIVERSE WITH A REALITY BOMB.

"BUT JUST THE FACT THAT THEY *WANT* SOMETHING, THAT MAKES THEM TANGIBLE. IT MAKES THEM *REAL*.

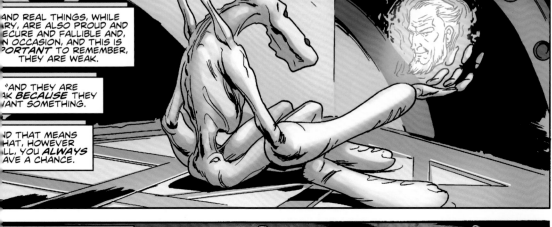

[A]ND REAL THINGS, WHILE [SCA]RY, ARE ALSO PROUD AND [INSE]CURE AND FALLIBLE AND, [O]N OCCASION, AND THIS IS [IM]*PORTANT* TO REMEMBER, THEY ARE WEAK.

"[A]ND THEY ARE [WE]AK *BECAUSE* THEY [W]ANT SOMETHING.

[A]ND THAT MEANS [T]HAT, HOWEVER [SMA]LL, YOU *ALWAYS* [H]AVE A CHANCE.

"BUT HAVING SAID ALL [T]HAT, I WOULD STILL VERY [M]UCH ENCOURAGE YOU TO [BE] SOMEWHAT WARY OF THE [WH]OLE 'EAT BRAINS!' THING."

MONSTERS AND DEVILS APPROACH!

MONSTERS AND DEVILS!

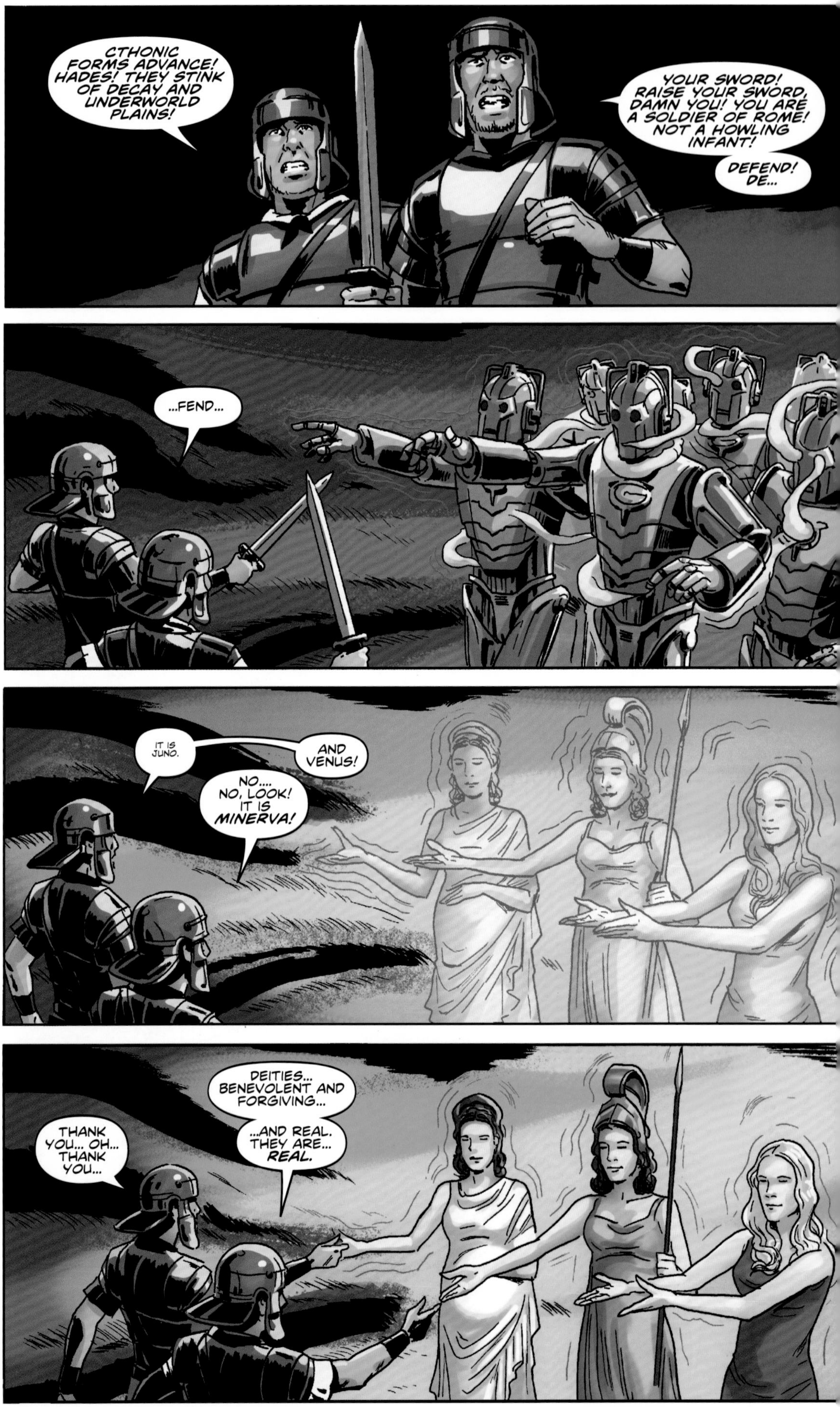
CTHONIC FORMS ADVANCE! HADES! THEY STINK OF DECAY AND UNDERWORLD PLAINS!
YOUR SWORD! RAISE YOUR SWORD, DAMN YOU! YOU ARE A SOLDIER OF ROME! NOT A HOWLING INFANT!
DEFEND! DE...
...FEND...
IT IS JUNO.
AND VENUS!
NO.... NO, LOOK! IT IS MINERVA!
THANK YOU... OH... THANK YOU...
DEITIES... BENEVOLENT AND FORGIVING...
...AND REAL. THEY ARE... REAL.

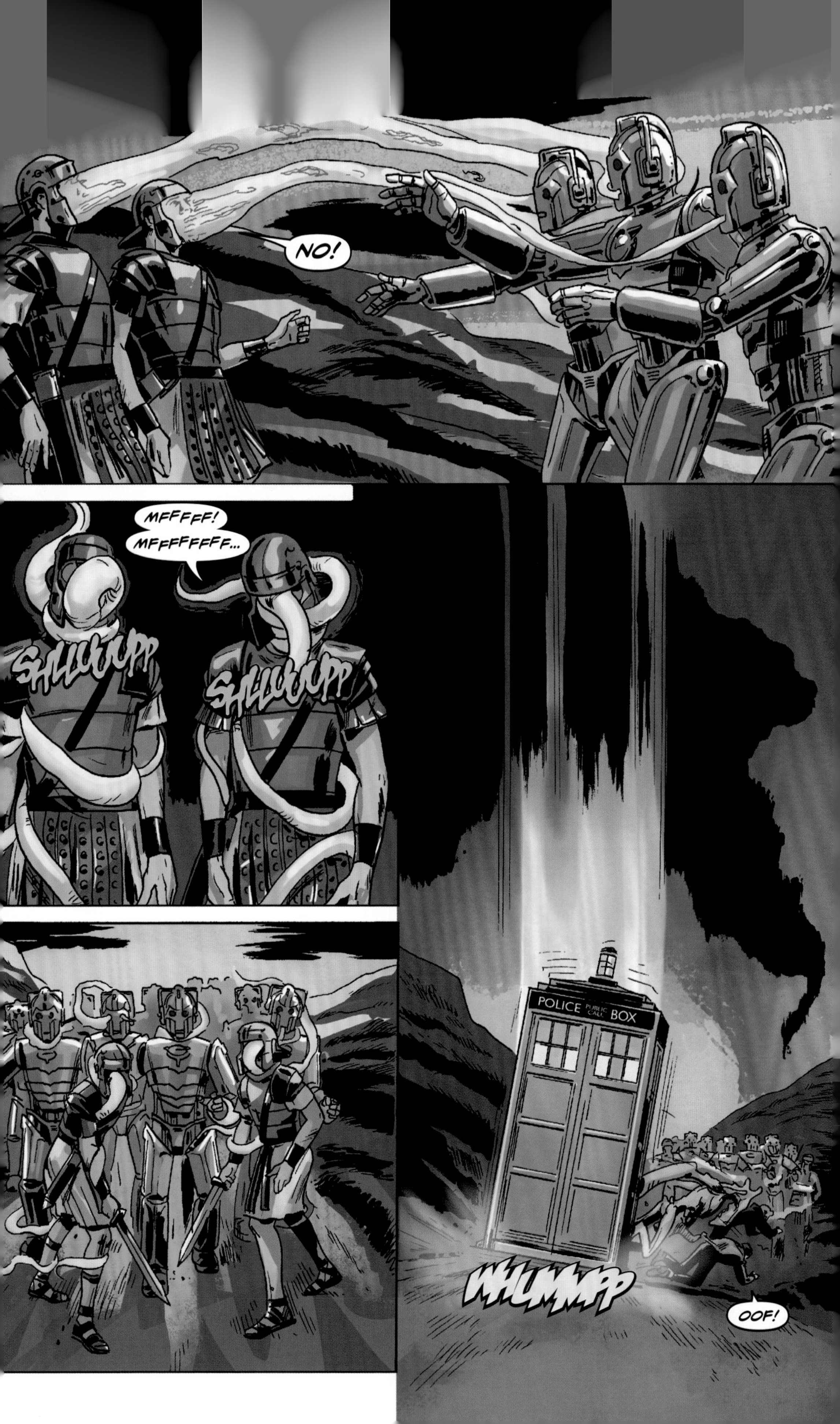
NO!
MFFFFF!
MFFFFFFFF...
SHLLLUUPP
SHLLLUUPP
POLICE PUBLIC CALL BOX
WHUMMPP
OOF!

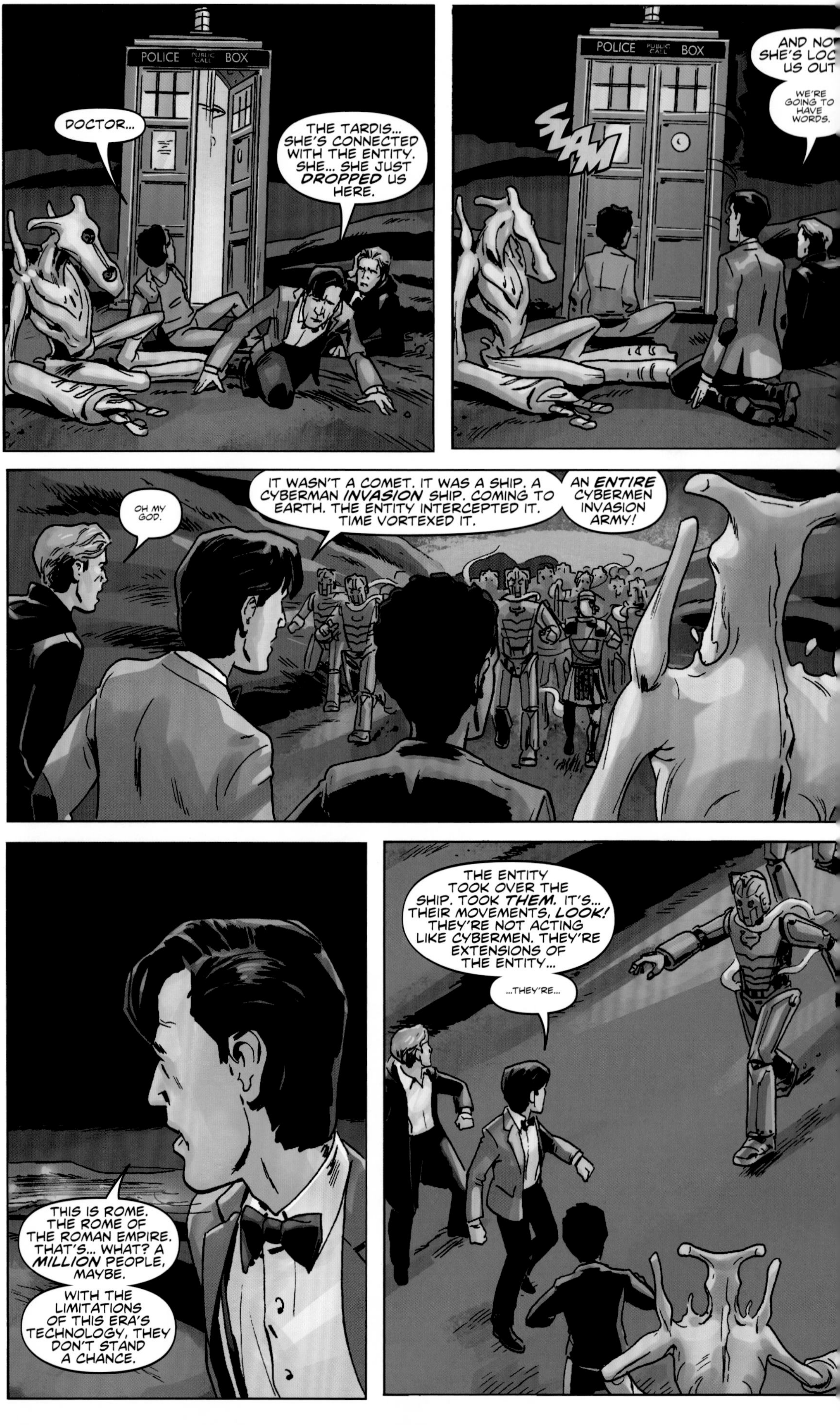
DOCTOR...
THE TARDIS... SHE'S CONNECTED WITH THE ENTITY. SHE... SHE JUST DROPPED US HERE.
SLAM
AND NO SHE'S LOC US OUT
WE'RE GOING TO HAVE WORDS.
OH MY GOD.
IT WASN'T A COMET. IT WAS A SHIP. A CYBERMAN INVASION SHIP. COMING TO EARTH. THE ENTITY INTERCEPTED IT. TIME VORTEXED IT.
AN ENTIRE CYBERMEN INVASION ARMY!
THIS IS ROME. THE ROME OF THE ROMAN EMPIRE. THAT'S... WHAT? A MILLION PEOPLE, MAYBE.
WITH THE LIMITATIONS OF THIS ERA'S TECHNOLOGY, THEY DON'T STAND A CHANCE.
THE ENTITY TOOK OVER THE SHIP. TOOK THEM. IT'S... THEIR MOVEMENTS, LOOK! THEY'RE NOT ACTING LIKE CYBERMEN. THEY'RE EXTENSIONS OF THE ENTITY...
...THEY'RE...

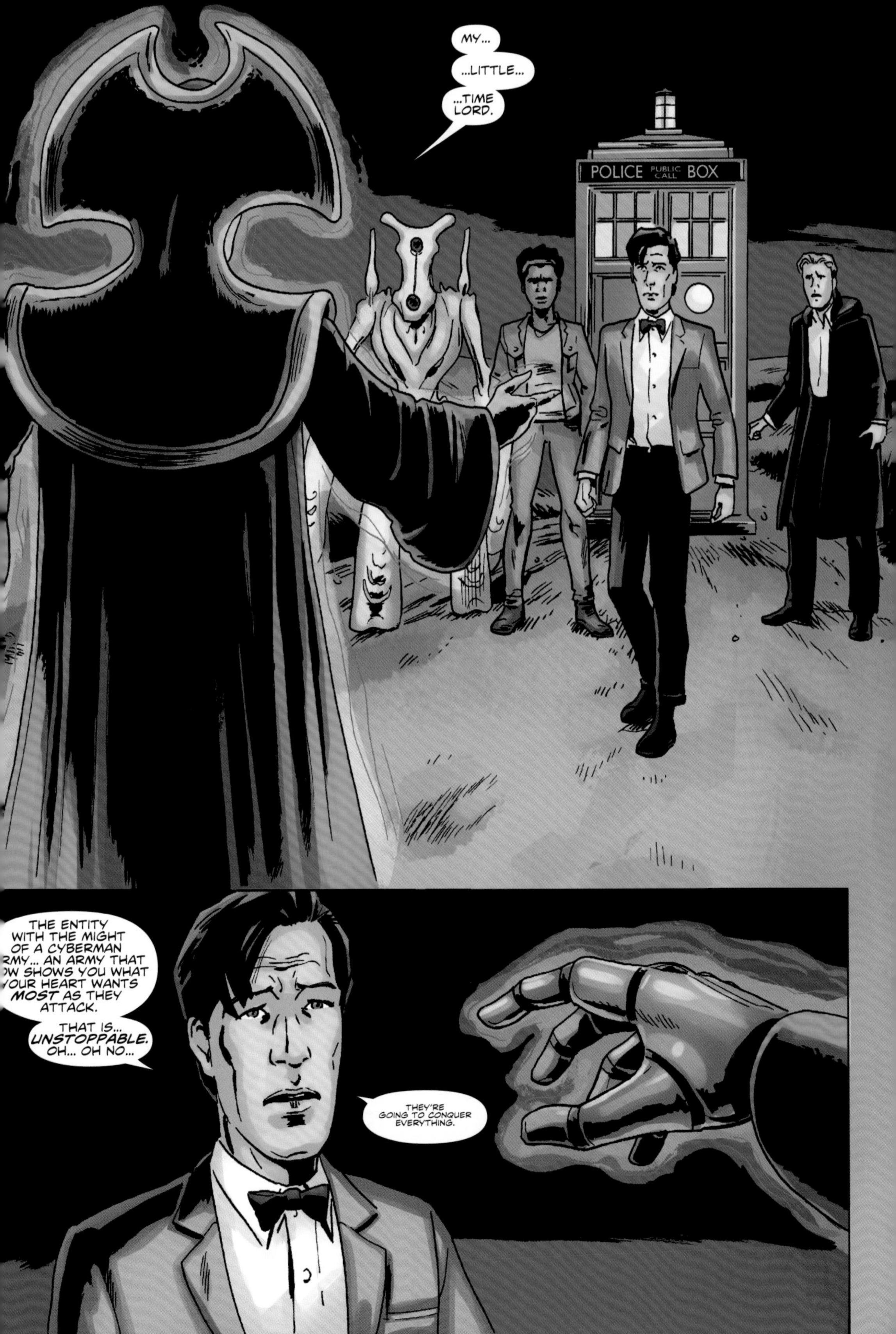

MY...
...LITTLE...
...TIME LORD.
POLICE PUBLIC CALL BOX
THE ENTITY WITH THE MIGHT OF A CYBERMAN RMY... AN ARMY THAT OW SHOWS YOU WHAT YOUR HEART WANTS *MOST* AS THEY ATTACK.
THAT IS... ***UNSTOPPABLE.*** OH... OH NO...
THEY'RE GOING TO CONQUER EVERYTHING.

CHAPTER 13

CONVERSION PART 2

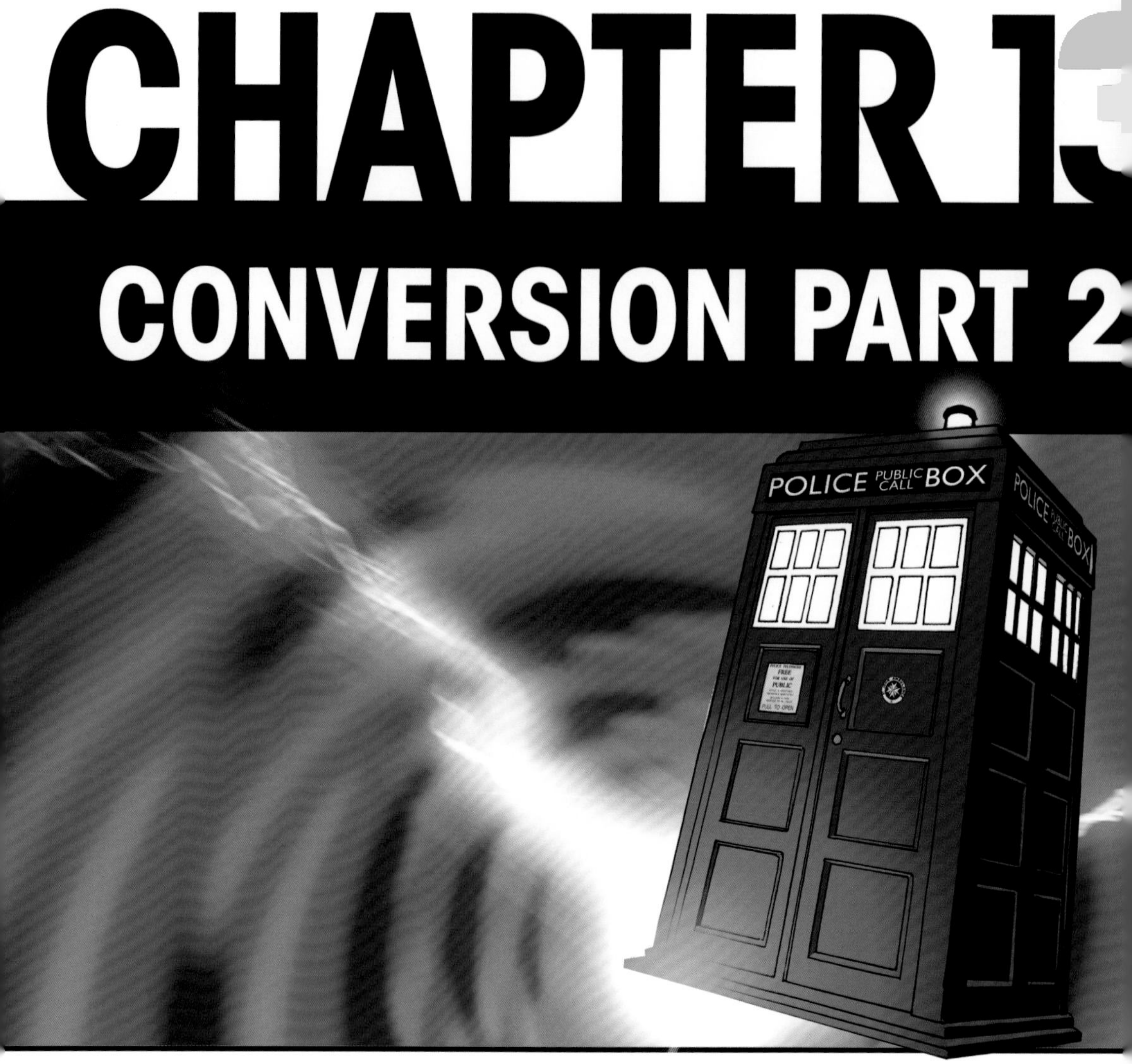
POLICE PUBLIC CALL BOX
POLICE PUBLIC CALL BOX

WRITER
ROB WILLIAMS

ARTIST
WARREN PLEECE

COLORIST
HI-FI

LETTERER
RICHARD STARKINGS AND COMICRAFT'S JIMMY BETANCOURT

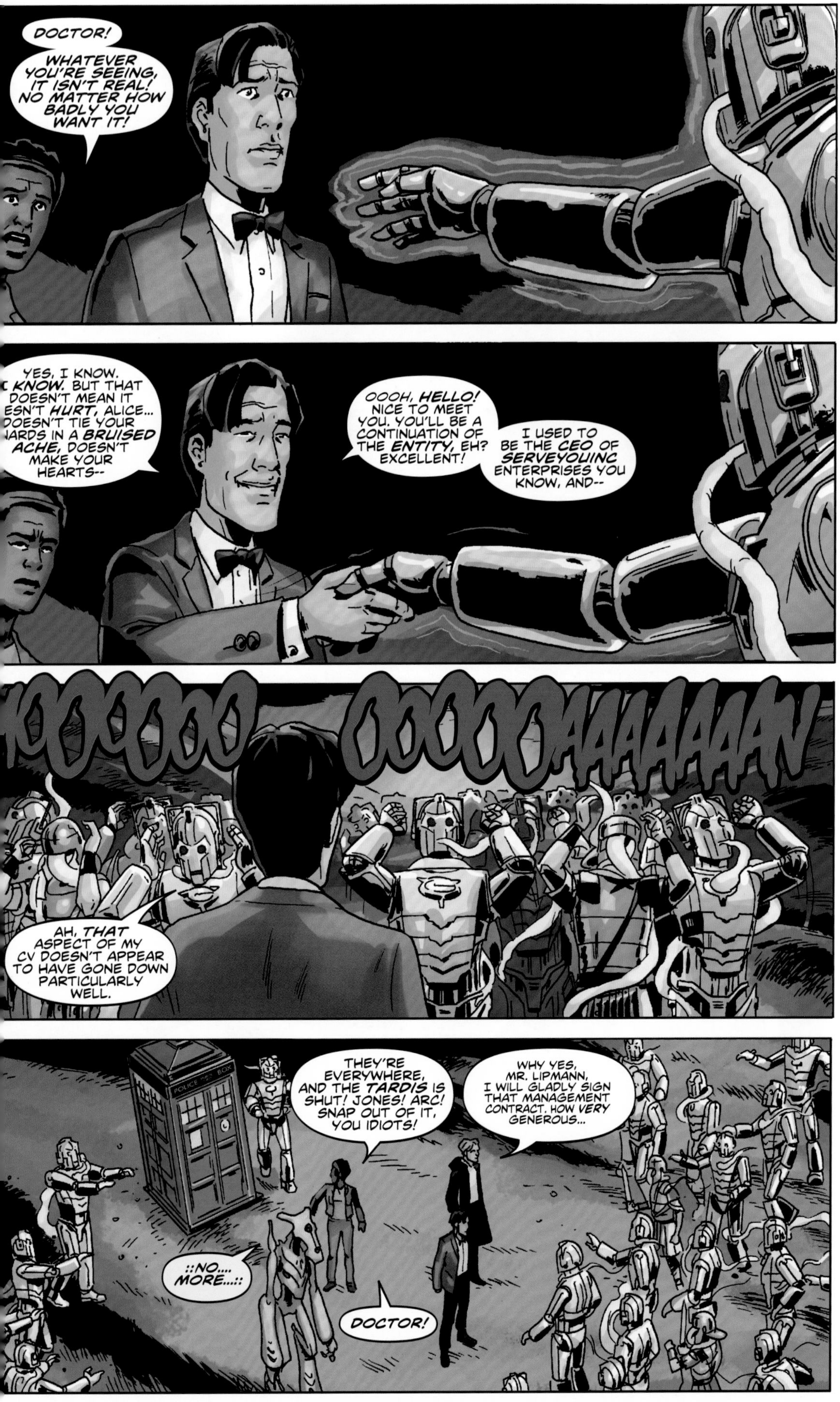
DOCTOR!
WHATEVER YOU'RE SEEING, IT ISN'T REAL! NO MATTER HOW BADLY YOU WANT IT!
YES, I KNOW. I KNOW. BUT THAT DOESN'T MEAN IT DOESN'T HURT, ALICE... DOESN'T TIE YOUR INWARDS IN A BRUISED ACHE, DOESN'T MAKE YOUR HEARTS--
OOOH, HELLO! NICE TO MEET YOU. YOU'LL BE A CONTINUATION OF THE ENTITY, EH? EXCELLENT!
I USED TO BE THE CEO OF SERVEYOUINC ENTERPRISES YOU KNOW, AND--
HOOOOOO OOOOOAAAAAAAN
AH, THAT ASPECT OF MY CV DOESN'T APPEAR TO HAVE GONE DOWN PARTICULARLY WELL.
THEY'RE EVERYWHERE, AND THE TARDIS IS SHUT! JONES! ARC! SNAP OUT OF IT, YOU IDIOTS!
WHY YES, MR. LIPMANN, I WILL GLADLY SIGN THAT MANAGEMENT CONTRACT. HOW VERY GENEROUS...
::NO.... MORE....::
DOCTOR!

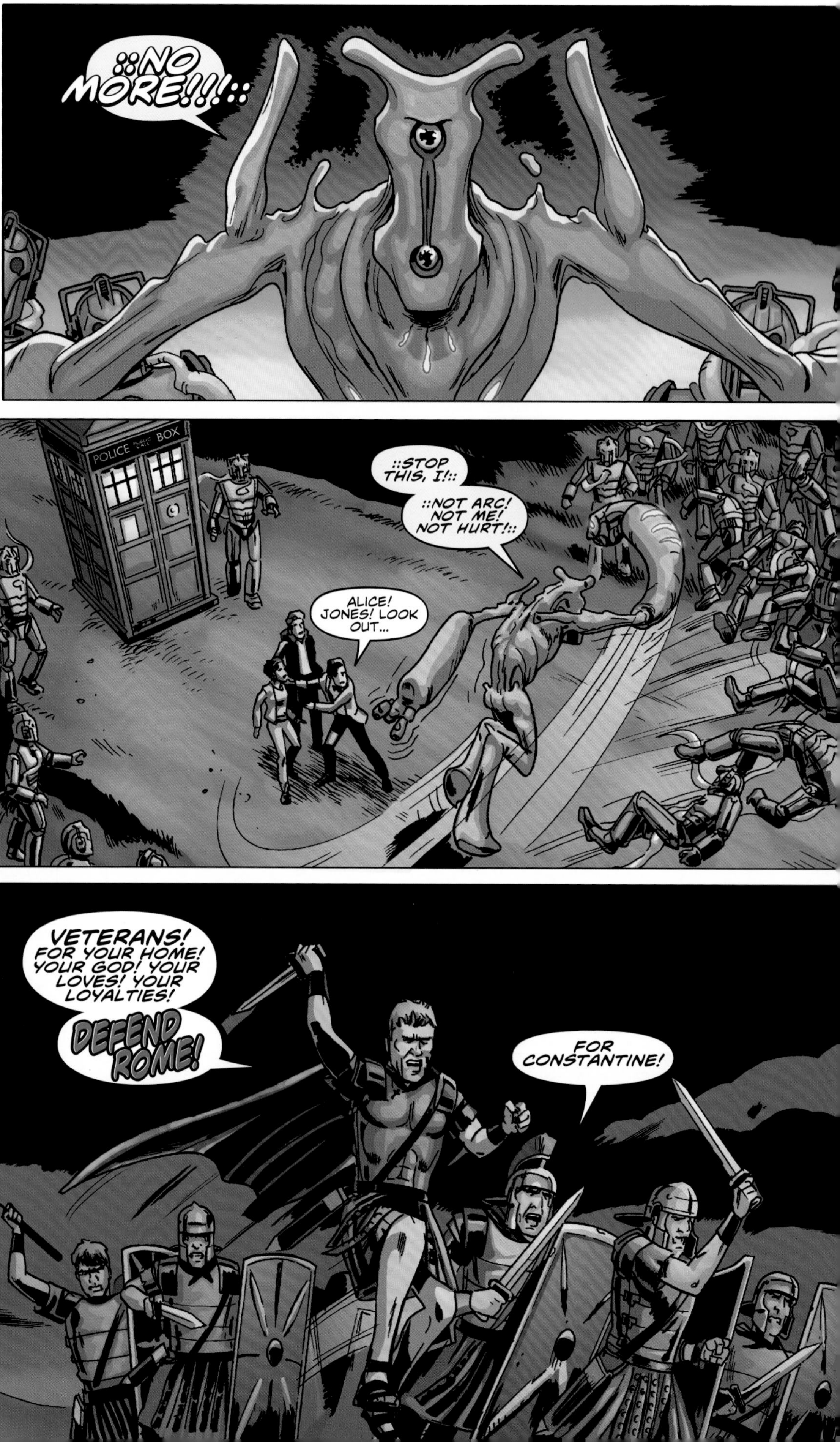
::NO MORE!!!::
::STOP THIS, I!::
::NOT ARC! NOT ME! NOT HURT!::
ALICE! JONES! LOOK OUT...
VETERANS! FOR YOUR HOME! YOUR GOD! YOUR LOVES! YOUR LOYALTIES!
DEFEND ROME!
FOR CONSTANTINE!

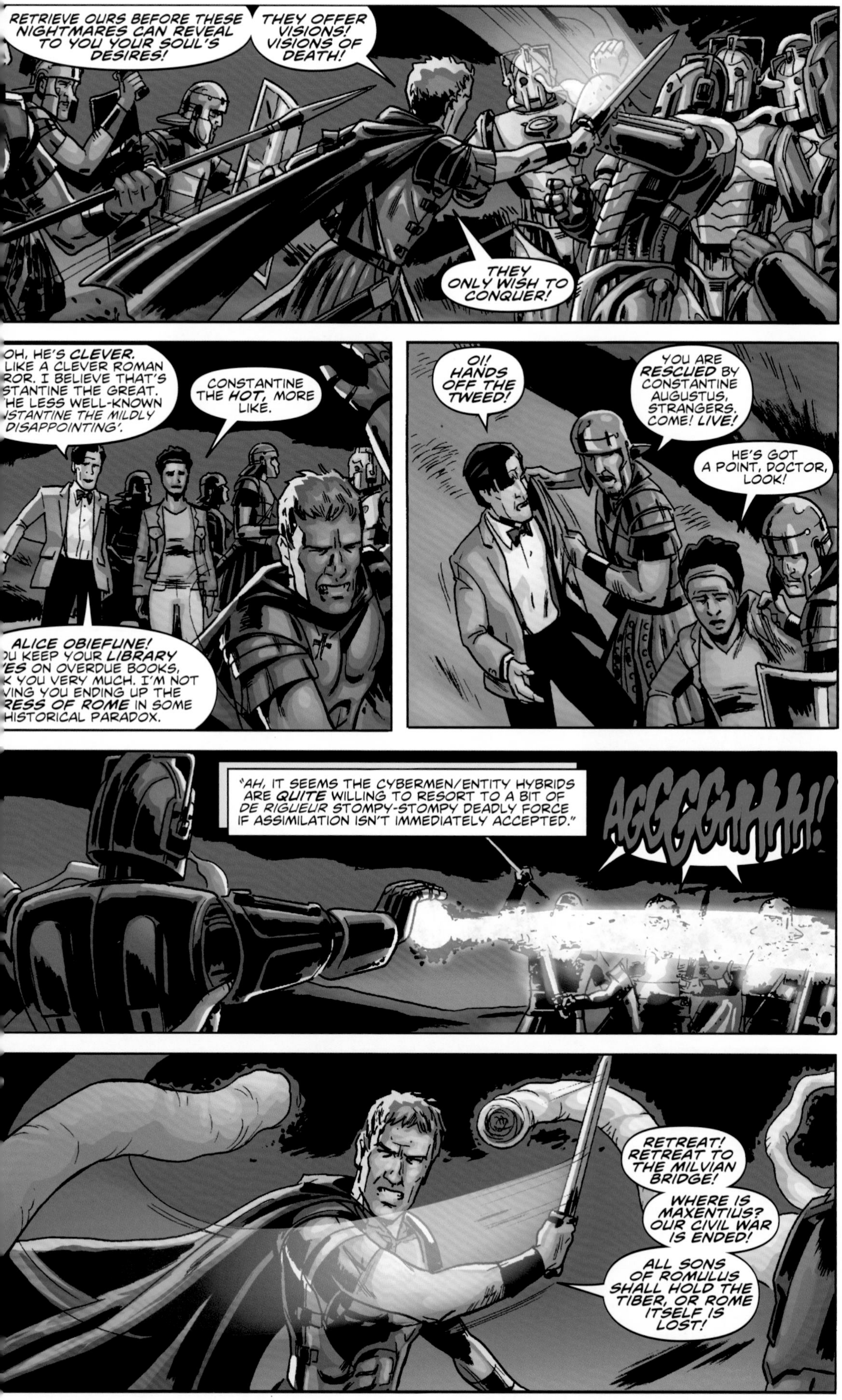
RETRIEVE OURS BEFORE THESE NIGHTMARES CAN REVEAL TO YOU YOUR SOUL'S DESIRES!
THEY OFFER VISIONS! VISIONS OF DEATH!
THEY ONLY WISH TO CONQUER!
OH, HE'S CLEVER. LIKE A CLEVER ROMAN ROR. I BELIEVE THAT'S STANTINE THE GREAT. HE LESS WELL-KNOWN NSTANTINE THE MILDLY DISAPPOINTING'.
CONSTANTINE THE HOT, MORE LIKE.
ALICE OBIEFUNE! OU KEEP YOUR LIBRARY ES ON OVERDUE BOOKS, K YOU VERY MUCH. I'M NOT VING YOU ENDING UP THE RESS OF ROME IN SOME HISTORICAL PARADOX.
OI! HANDS OFF THE TWEED!
YOU ARE RESCUED BY CONSTANTINE AUGUSTUS, STRANGERS. COME! LIVE!
HE'S GOT A POINT, DOCTOR, LOOK!
"AH, IT SEEMS THE CYBERMEN/ENTITY HYBRIDS ARE QUITE WILLING TO RESORT TO A BIT OF DE RIGUEUR STOMPY-STOMPY DEADLY FORCE IF ASSIMILATION ISN'T IMMEDIATELY ACCEPTED."
AGGGGHHHH!
RETREAT! RETREAT TO THE MILVIAN BRIDGE!
WHERE IS MAXENTIUS? OUR CIVIL WAR IS ENDED!
ALL SONS OF ROMULUS SHALL HOLD THE TIBER, OR ROME ITSELF IS LOST!

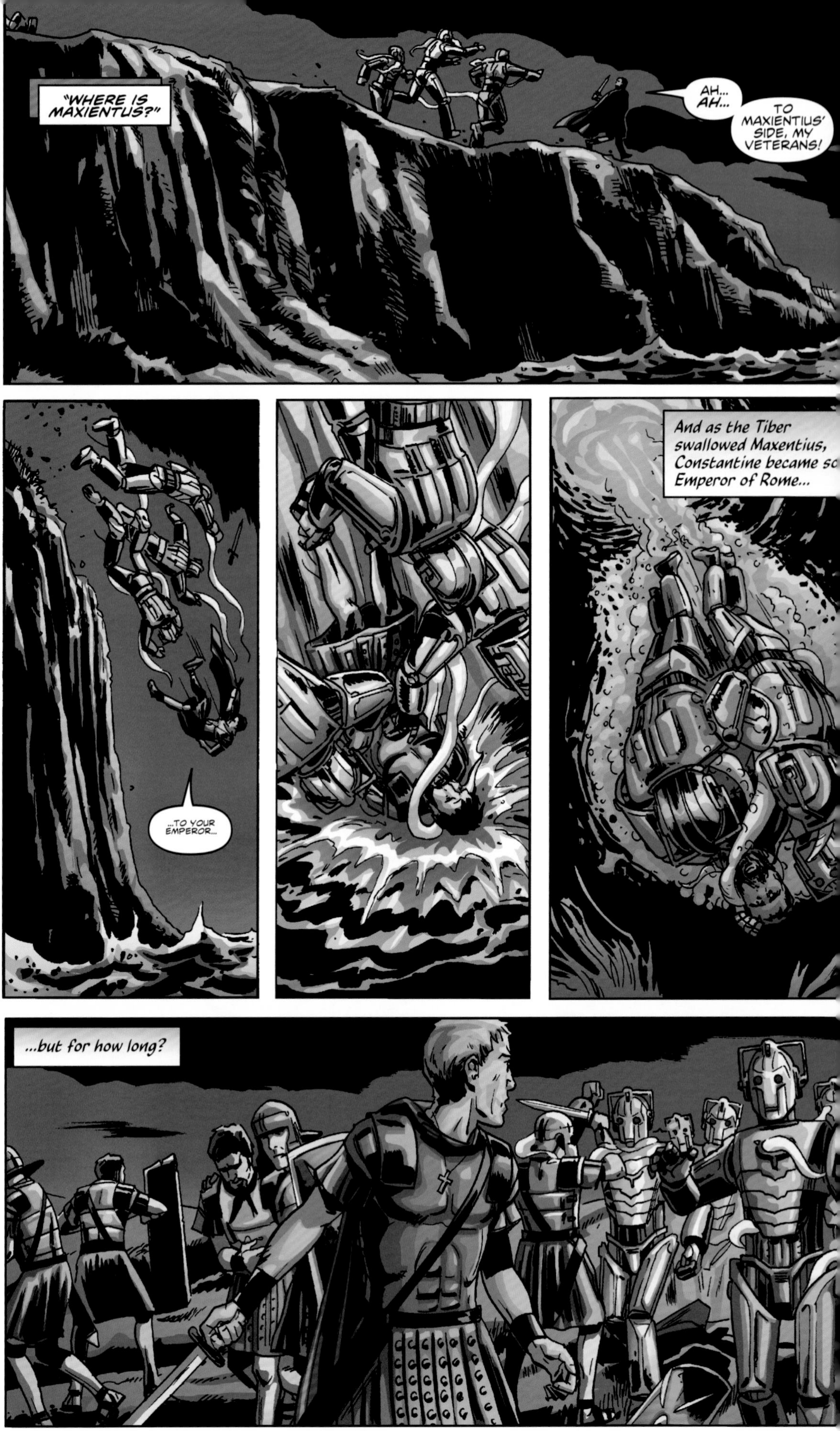
"WHERE IS MAXIENTUS?"
AH... AH...
TO MAXIENTIUS' SIDE, MY VETERANS!
...TO YOUR EMPEROR...
And as the Tiber swallowed Maxentius, Constantine became so Emperor of Rome...
...but for how long?

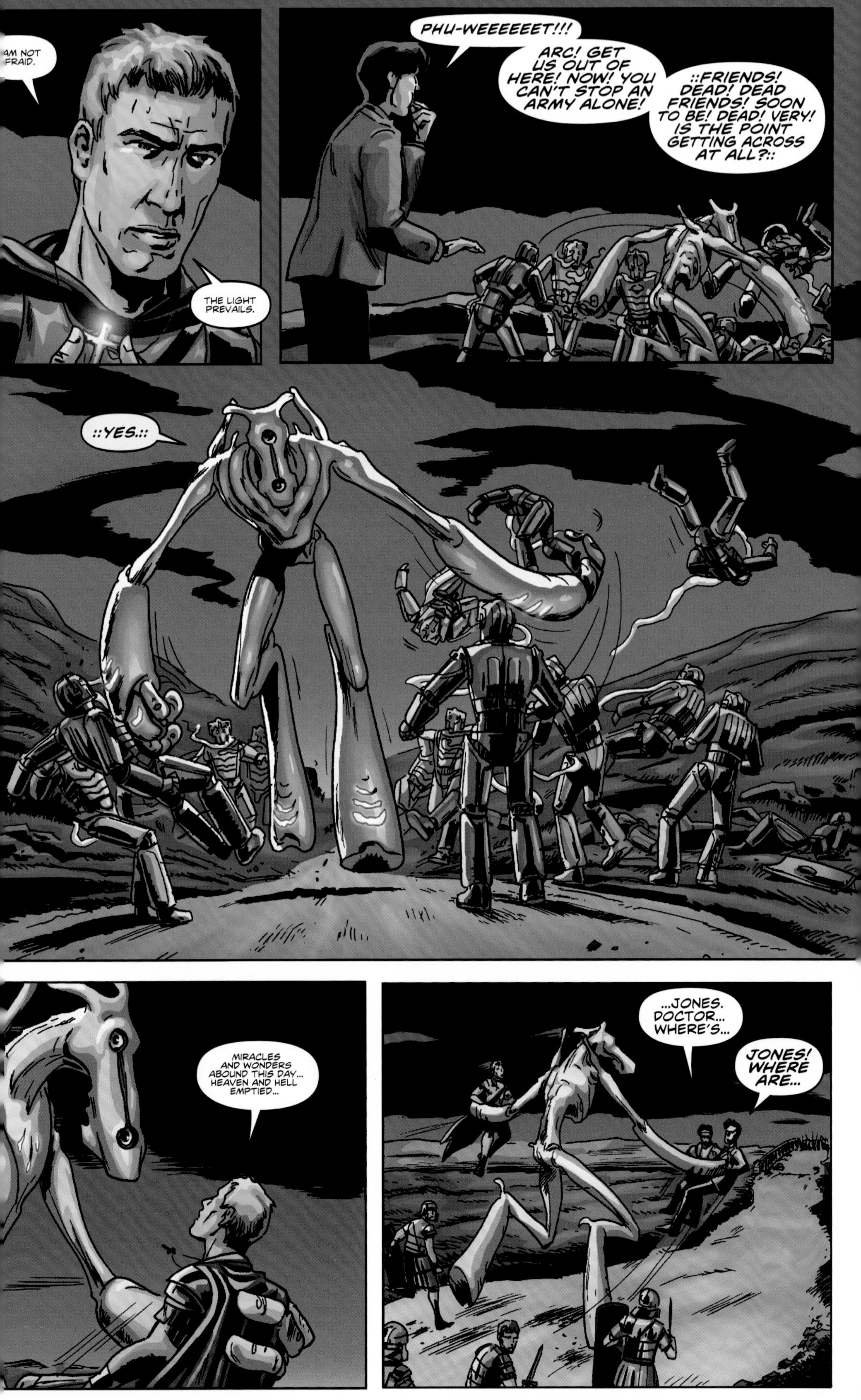

AM NOT FRAID.
THE LIGHT PREVAILS.
PHU-WEEEEEET!!!
ARC! GET US OUT OF HERE! NOW! YOU CAN'T STOP AN ARMY ALONE!
::FRIENDS! DEAD! DEAD FRIENDS! SOON TO BE! DEAD! VERY! IS THE POINT GETTING ACROSS AT ALL?::
::YES.::
MIRACLES AND WONDERS ABOUND THIS DAY... HEAVEN AND HELL EMPTIED...
...JONES. DOCTOR... WHERE'S...
JONES! WHERE ARE...

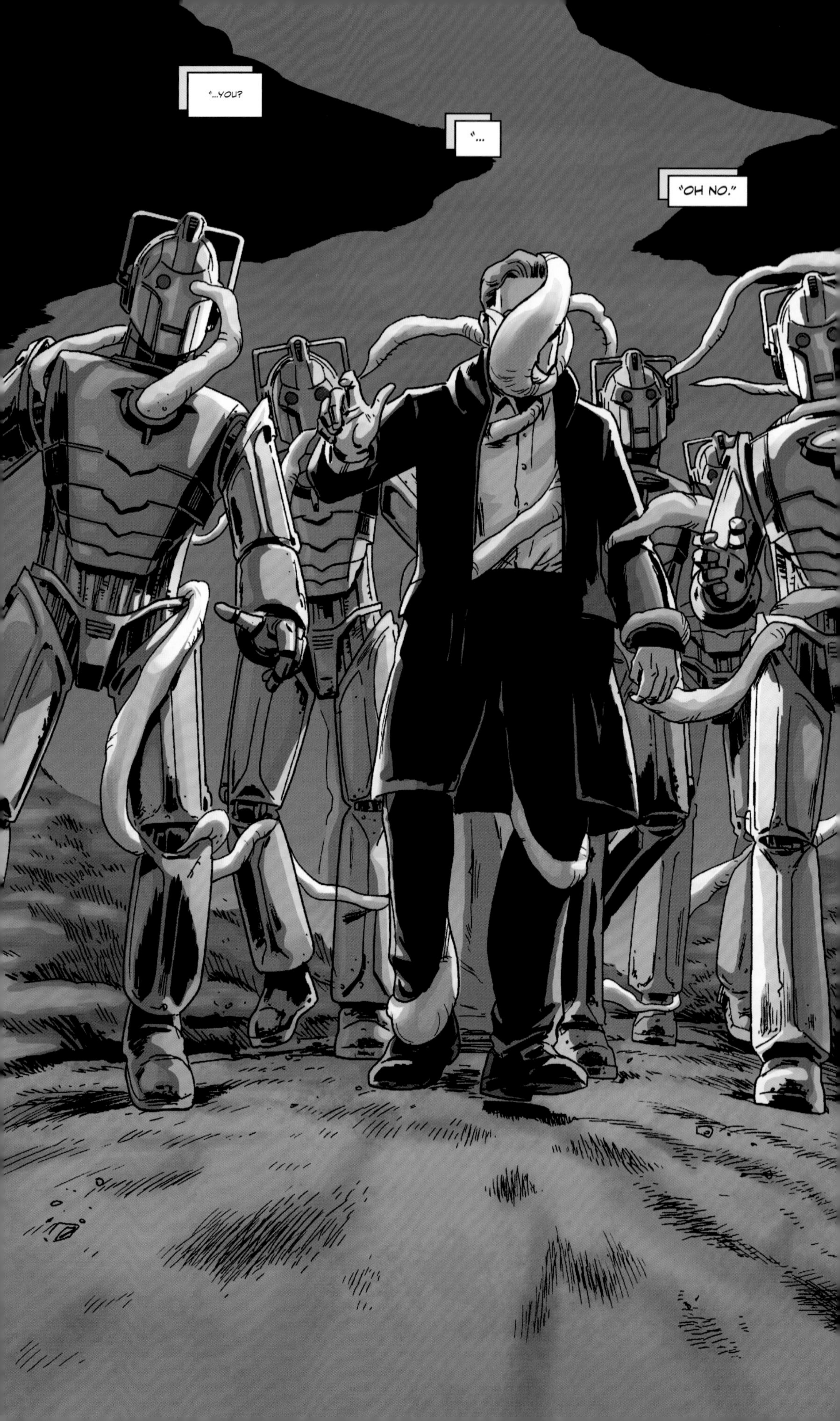
"...YOU?
"...
"OH NO."

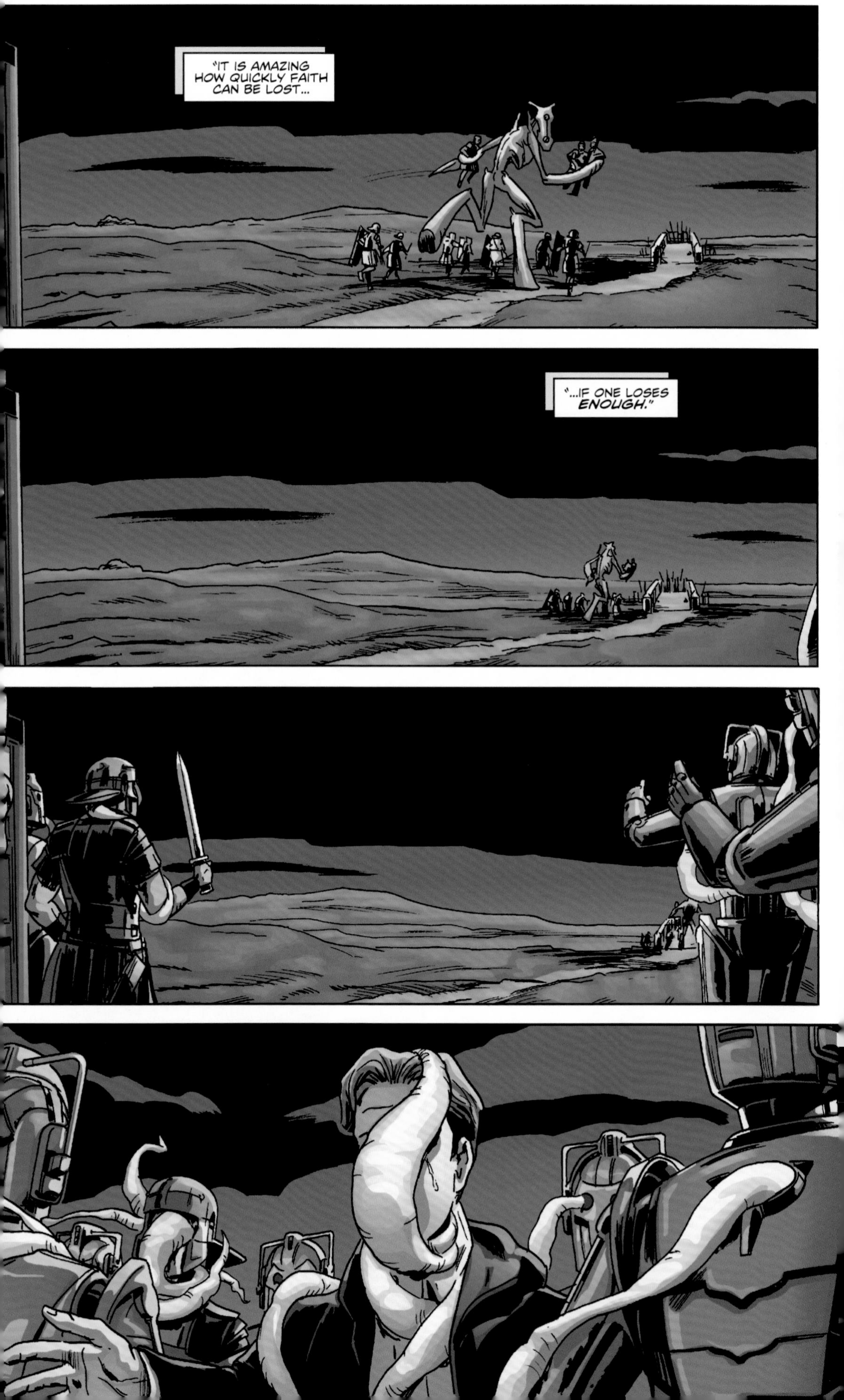
"IT IS AMAZING HOW QUICKLY FAITH CAN BE LOST...
"...IF ONE LOSES ENOUGH."

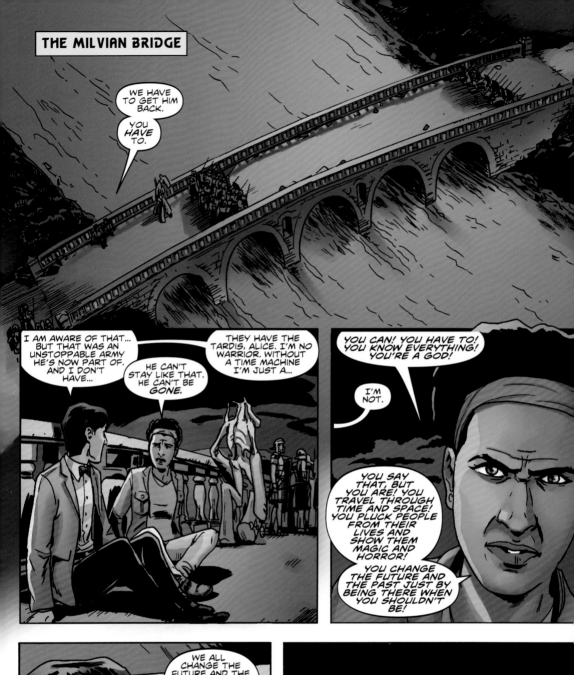

THE MILVIAN BRIDGE

WE HAVE TO GET HIM BACK.

YOU *HAVE* TO.

I AM AWARE OF THAT... BUT THAT WAS AN UNSTOPPABLE ARMY HE'S NOW PART OF. AND I DON'T HAVE...

HE CAN'T STAY LIKE THAT. HE CAN'T BE *GONE*.

THEY HAVE THE TARDIS, ALICE. I'M NO WARRIOR. WITHOUT A TIME MACHINE I'M JUST A...

YOU CAN! YOU HAVE TO! YOU KNOW EVERYTHING! YOU'RE A GOD!

I'M NOT.

YOU SAY THAT, BUT YOU *ARE*! YOU TRAVEL THROUGH TIME AND SPACE! YOU PLUCK PEOPLE FROM THEIR LIVES AND SHOW THEM MAGIC AND HORROR!

YOU CHANGE THE FUTURE AND THE PAST JUST BY BEING THERE WHEN YOU SHOULDN'T BE!

WE ALL CHANGE THE FUTURE AND THE PAST. WITH EVERY STEP, EVERY SUBJECTIVE READING OF A MEMORY.

THIS ISN'T ABOUT YOUR MUM, ALICE.

JONES IS REAL. JOHN JONES. POOR JOHN JONES.

YOU'RE RIGHT.

ALL I COULD THINK OF WA THAT HE'S MU... *FAVORITE A...* HOW CAN H... DEAD? THEN H... WON'T MAKE... THOSE ALBUM... SHE LOVED.

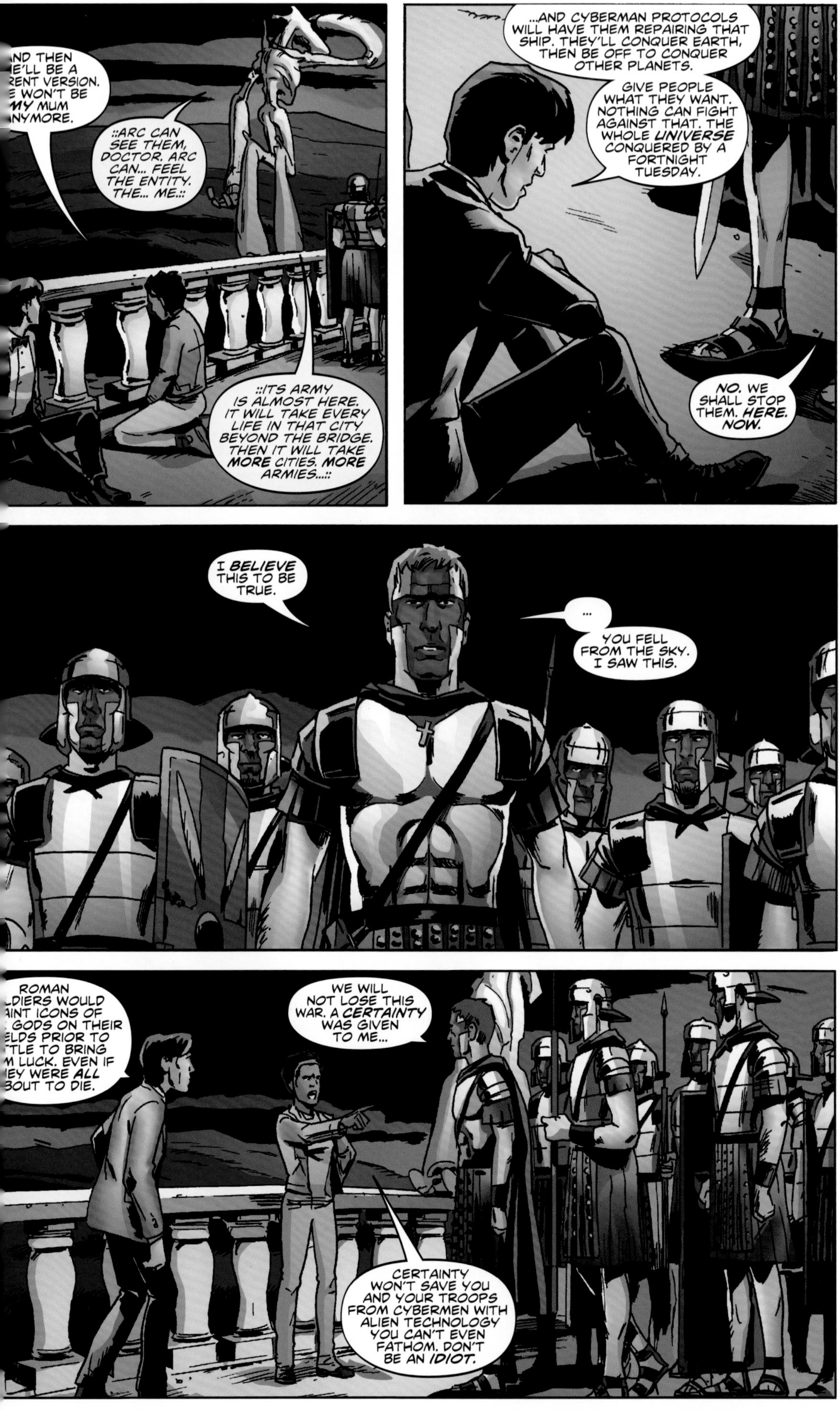
ND THEN E'LL BE A RENT VERSION. E WON'T BE MY MUM NYMORE.
::ARC CAN SEE THEM, DOCTOR. ARC CAN... FEEL THE ENTITY. THE... ME.::
::ITS ARMY IS ALMOST HERE. IT WILL TAKE EVERY LIFE IN THAT CITY BEYOND THE BRIDGE. THEN IT WILL TAKE MORE CITIES. MORE ARMIES...::
...AND CYBERMAN PROTOCOLS WILL HAVE THEM REPAIRING THAT SHIP. THEY'LL CONQUER EARTH, THEN BE OFF TO CONQUER OTHER PLANETS.
GIVE PEOPLE WHAT THEY WANT. NOTHING CAN FIGHT AGAINST THAT. THE WHOLE UNIVERSE CONQUERED BY A FORTNIGHT TUESDAY.
NO. WE SHALL STOP THEM. HERE. NOW.
I BELIEVE THIS TO BE TRUE.
...
YOU FELL FROM THE SKY. I SAW THIS.
ROMAN LDIERS WOULD AINT ICONS OF GODS ON THEIR ELDS PRIOR TO TTLE TO BRING M LUCK. EVEN IF EY WERE ALL BOUT TO DIE.
WE WILL NOT LOSE THIS WAR. A CERTAINTY WAS GIVEN TO ME...
CERTAINTY WON'T SAVE YOU AND YOUR TROOPS FROM CYBERMEN WITH ALIEN TECHNOLOGY YOU CAN'T EVEN FATHOM. DON'T BE AN IDIOT.

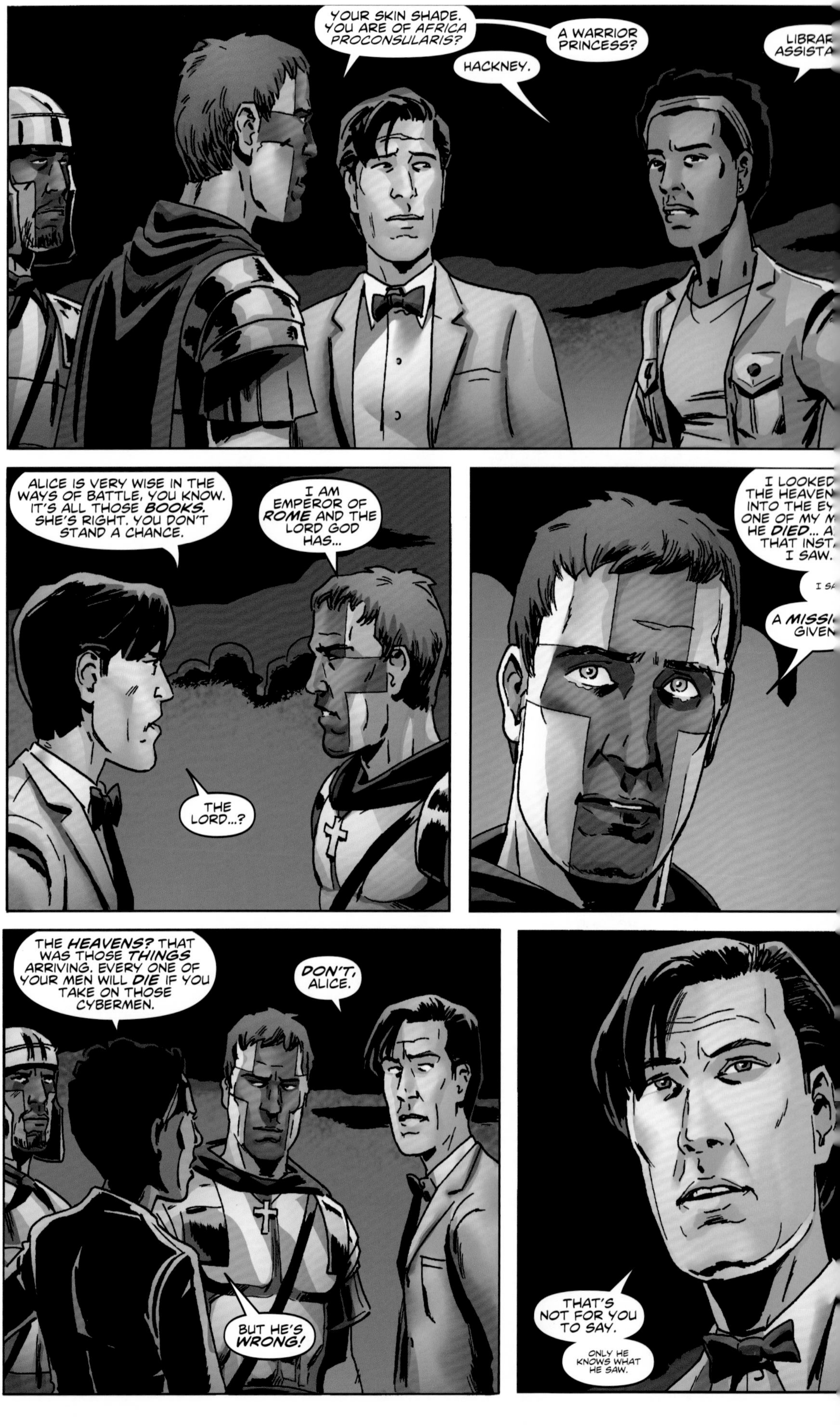

YOUR SKIN SHADE. YOU ARE OF *AFRICA PROCONSULARIS?*
HACKNEY.
A WARRIOR PRINCESS?
LIBRAR ASSISTA
ALICE IS VERY WISE IN THE WAYS OF BATTLE, YOU KNOW. IT'S ALL THOSE ***BOOKS.*** SHE'S RIGHT. YOU DON'T STAND A CHANCE.
I AM EMPEROR OF ***ROME*** AND THE LORD GOD HAS...
THE LORD...?
I LOOKED THE HEAVEN INTO THE EY ONE OF MY M HE ***DIED***... A THAT INST I SAW.
I S
A ***MISSI*** GIVEN
THE ***HEAVENS?*** THAT WAS THOSE ***THINGS*** ARRIVING. EVERY ONE OF YOUR MEN WILL ***DIE*** IF YOU TAKE ON THOSE CYBERMEN.
DON'T, ALICE.
BUT HE'S ***WRONG!***
THAT'S NOT FOR YOU TO SAY.
ONLY HE KNOWS WHAT HE SAW.

RIGHT THEN, CONSTANTINE AUGUSTUS! YOU SAW ME FALL FROM THE HEAVENS, CORRECT?

I DID.

YOU LOOK ME IN THE EYES AND YOU RECOGNIZE... A FELLOW GENERAL, AM I RIGHT? A STRATEGIAN OF THE STARS! A MAN OF POWER!

I RECOGNIZE IN YOU THE WEIGHT OF LOSS. OF EVERY LIFE YOU HAVE SACRIFICED IN WAR VIA YOUR ORDERS.

WE ARE KINDRED IN GUILT... GENERAL.

YES.

I HAVE A PLAN. PLEASE, TAKE MY ASSOCIATE PRISONER.

KEEP HER HERE. ENSURE NO HARM COMES TO HER OR I WILL BE VERY ANGRY. AND YOU DO NOT WANT TO MAKE ME ANGRY, TRUST ME.

WHAT?

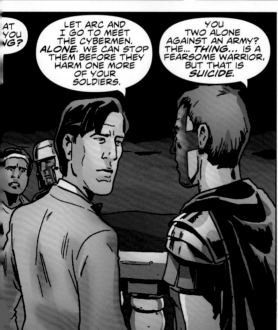

AT YOU NG?

LET ARC AND I GO TO MEET THE CYBERMEN. ALONE. WE CAN STOP THEM BEFORE THEY HARM ONE MORE OF YOUR SOLDIERS.

YOU TWO ALONE AGAINST AN ARMY? THE... THING... IS A FEARSOME WARRIOR, BUT THAT IS SUICIDE.

NOT SUICIDE...

...SACRIFICE.

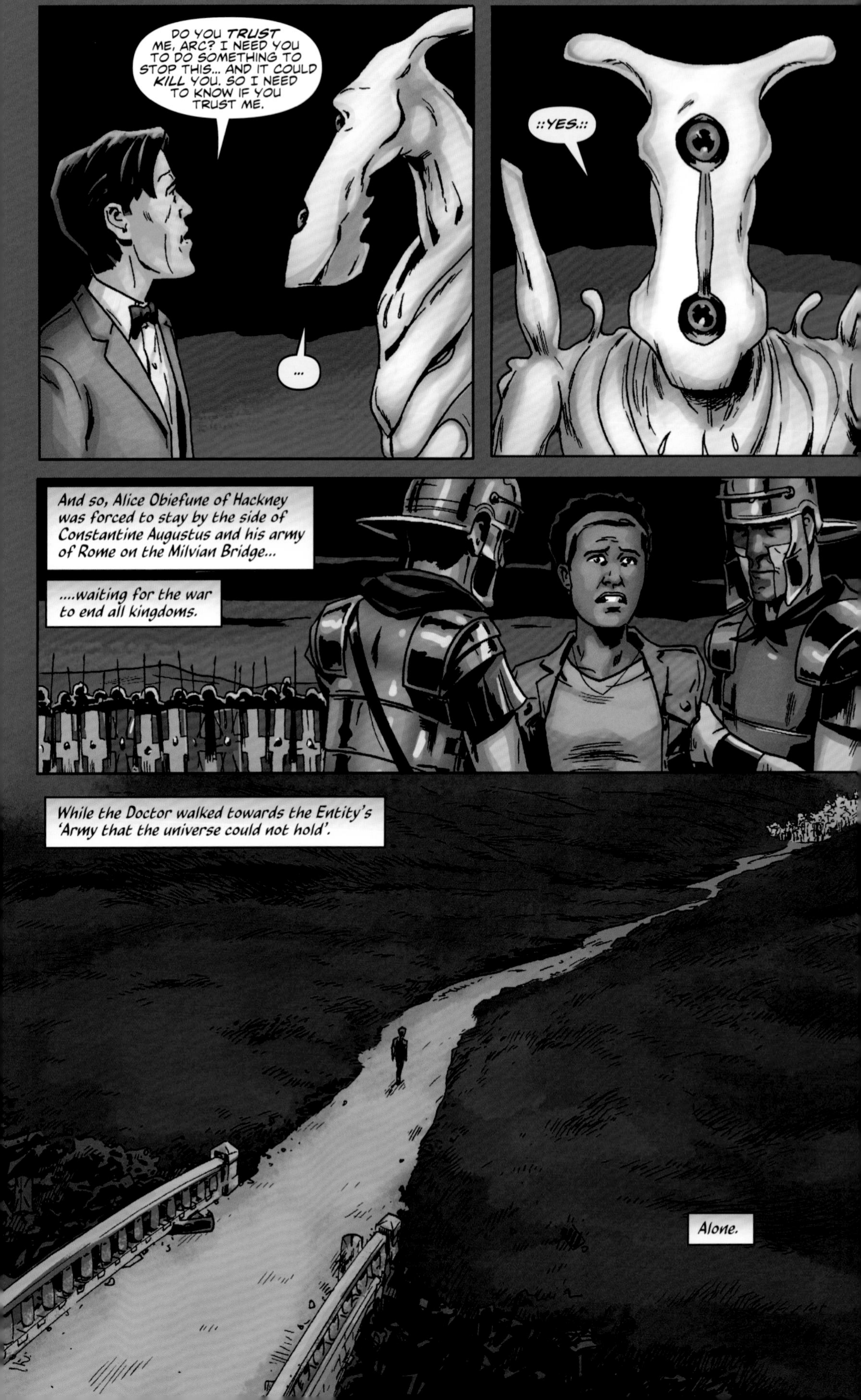
DO YOU TRUST ME, ARC? I NEED YOU TO DO SOMETHING TO STOP THIS... AND IT COULD KILL YOU. SO I NEED TO KNOW IF YOU TRUST ME.
...
::YES.::
And so, Alice Obiefune of Hackney was forced to stay by the side of Constantine Augustus and his army of Rome on the Milvian Bridge...
....waiting for the war to end all kingdoms.
While the Doctor walked towards the Entity's 'Army that the universe could not hold'.
Alone.

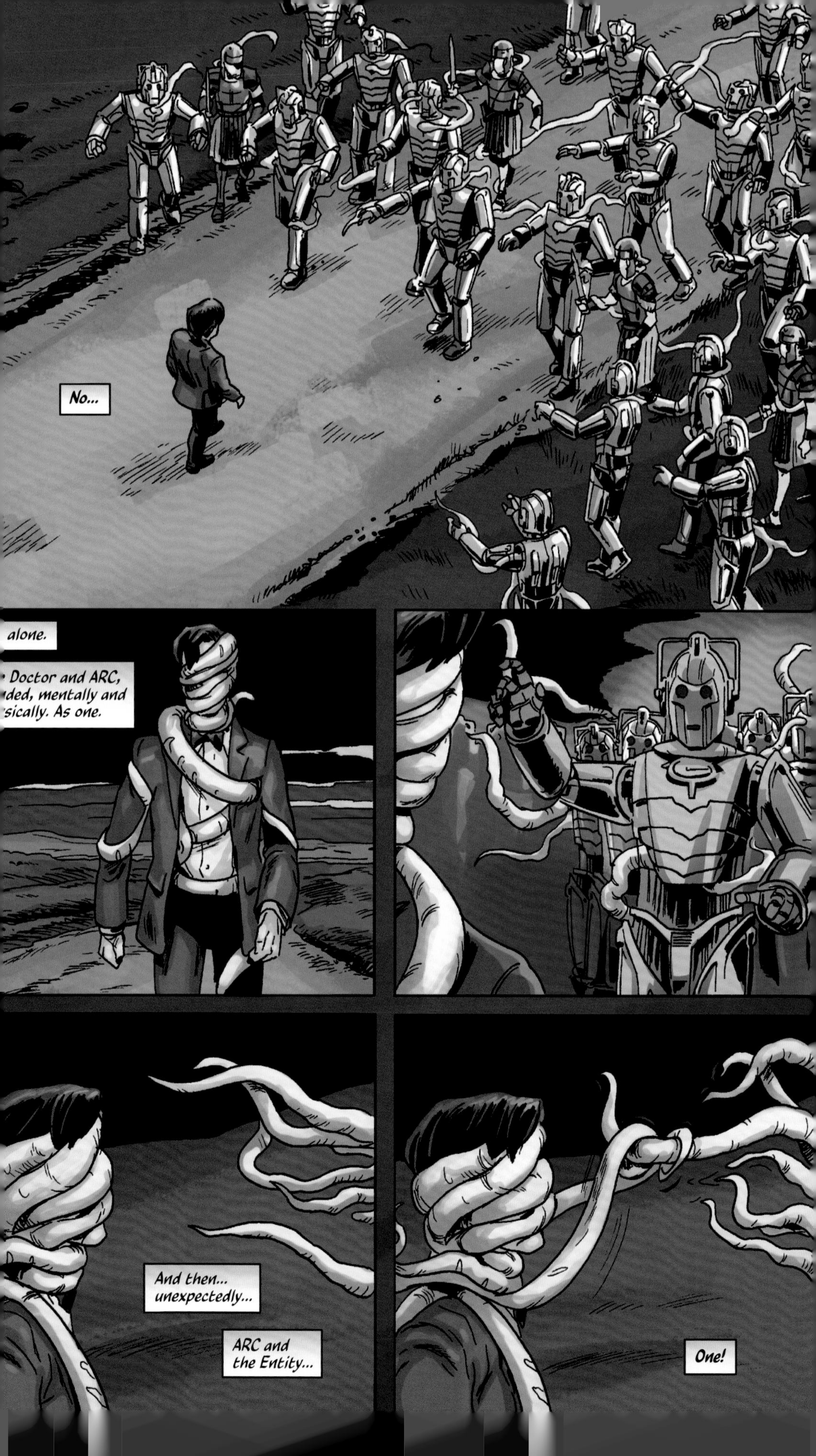
No...
alone.
Doctor and ARC,
ded, mentally and
sically. As one.
And then...
unexpectedly...
ARC and
the Entity...
One!

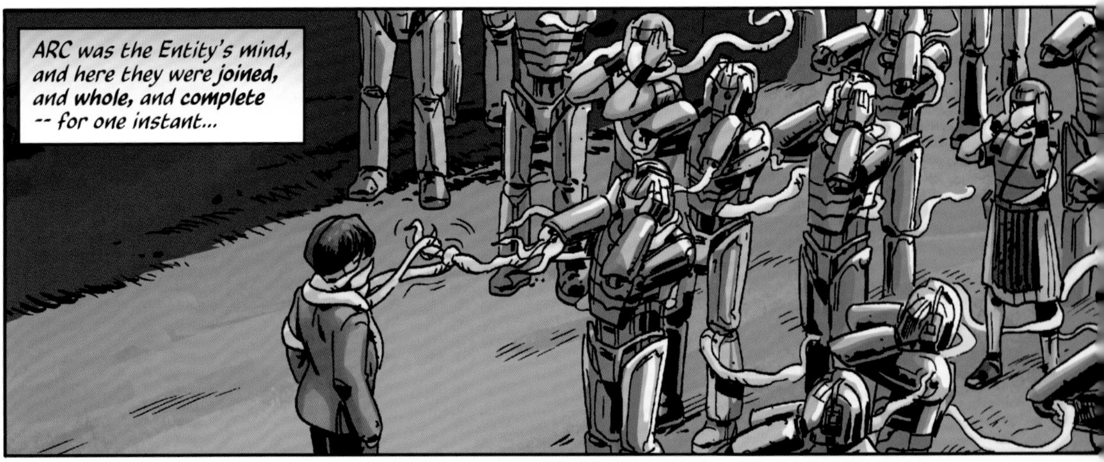
ARC was the Entity's mind, and here they were joined, and whole, and complete -- for one instant...

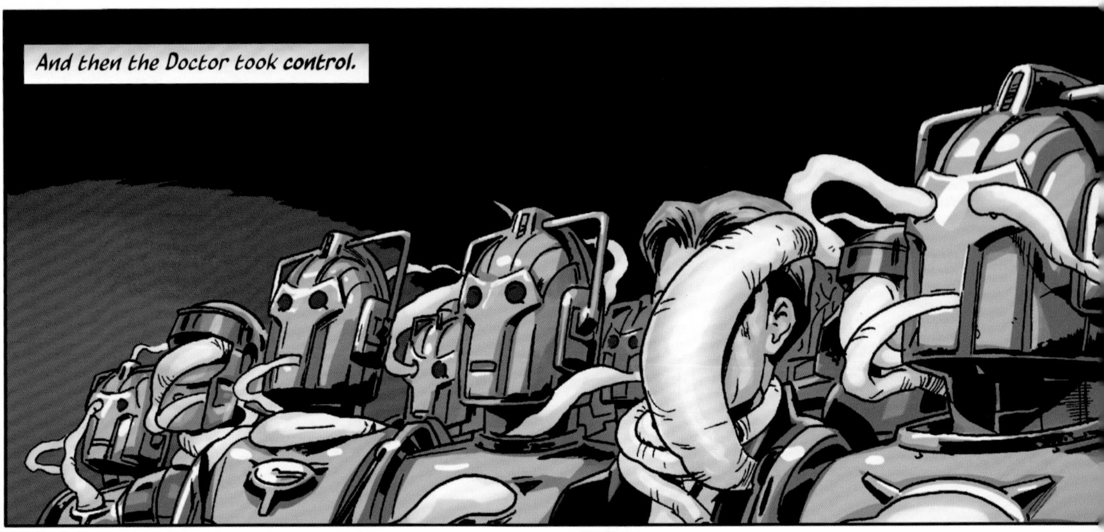
And then the Doctor took control.

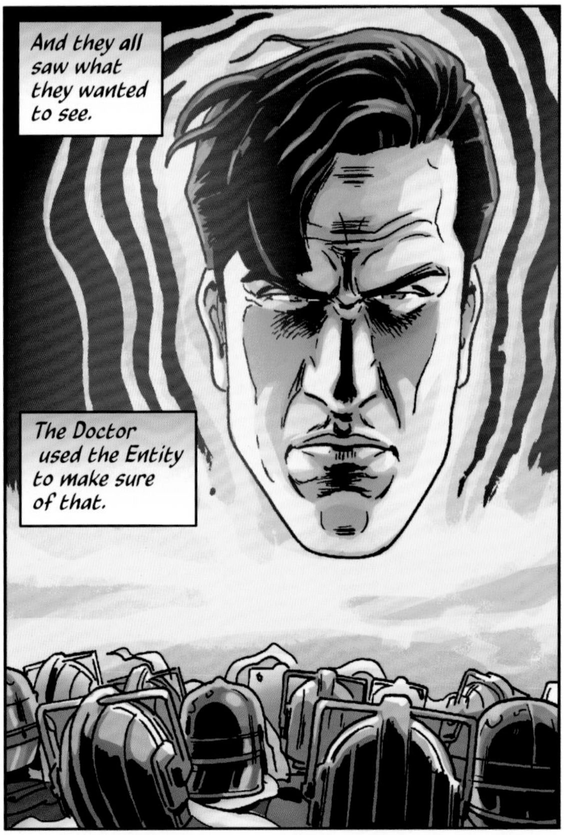
And they all saw what they wanted to see.
The Doctor used the Entity to make sure of that.

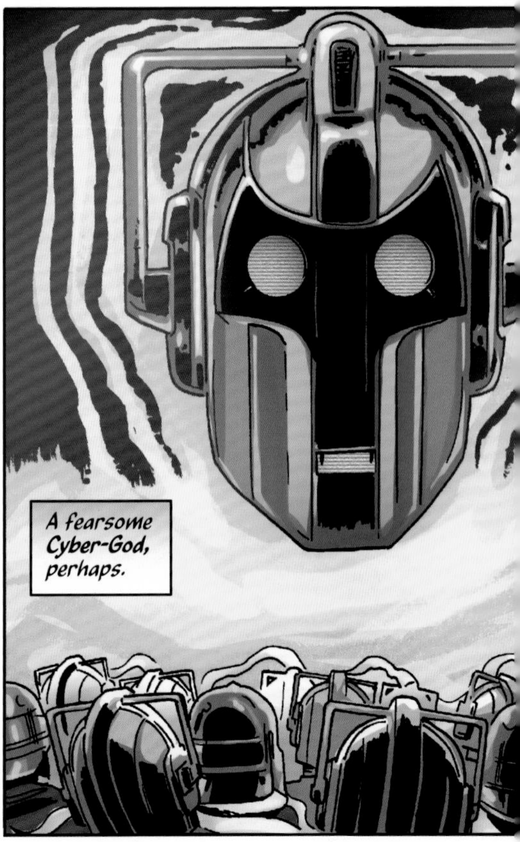
A fearsome Cyber-God, perhaps.

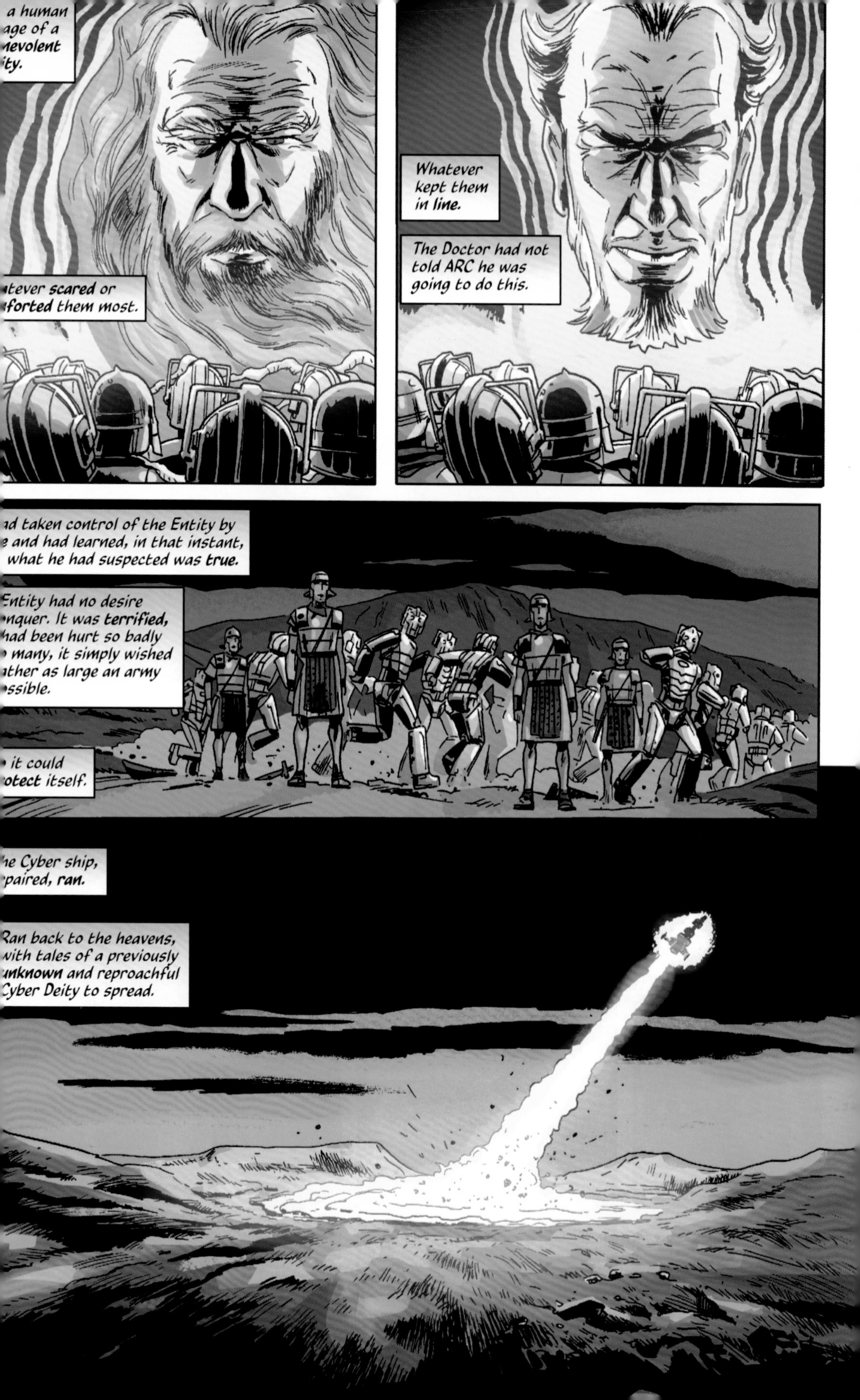
a human
age of a
nevolent
ity.
tever scared or
forted them most.
Whatever
kept them
in line.
The Doctor had not
told ARC he was
going to do this.
d taken control of the Entity by
e and had learned, in that instant,
what he had suspected was true.
Entity had no desire
nquer. It was terrified,
had been hurt so badly
many, it simply wished
ther as large an army
ssible.
it could
otect itself.
he Cyber ship,
paired, ran.
Ran back to the heavens,
with tales of a previously
unknown and reproachful
Cyber Deity to spread.

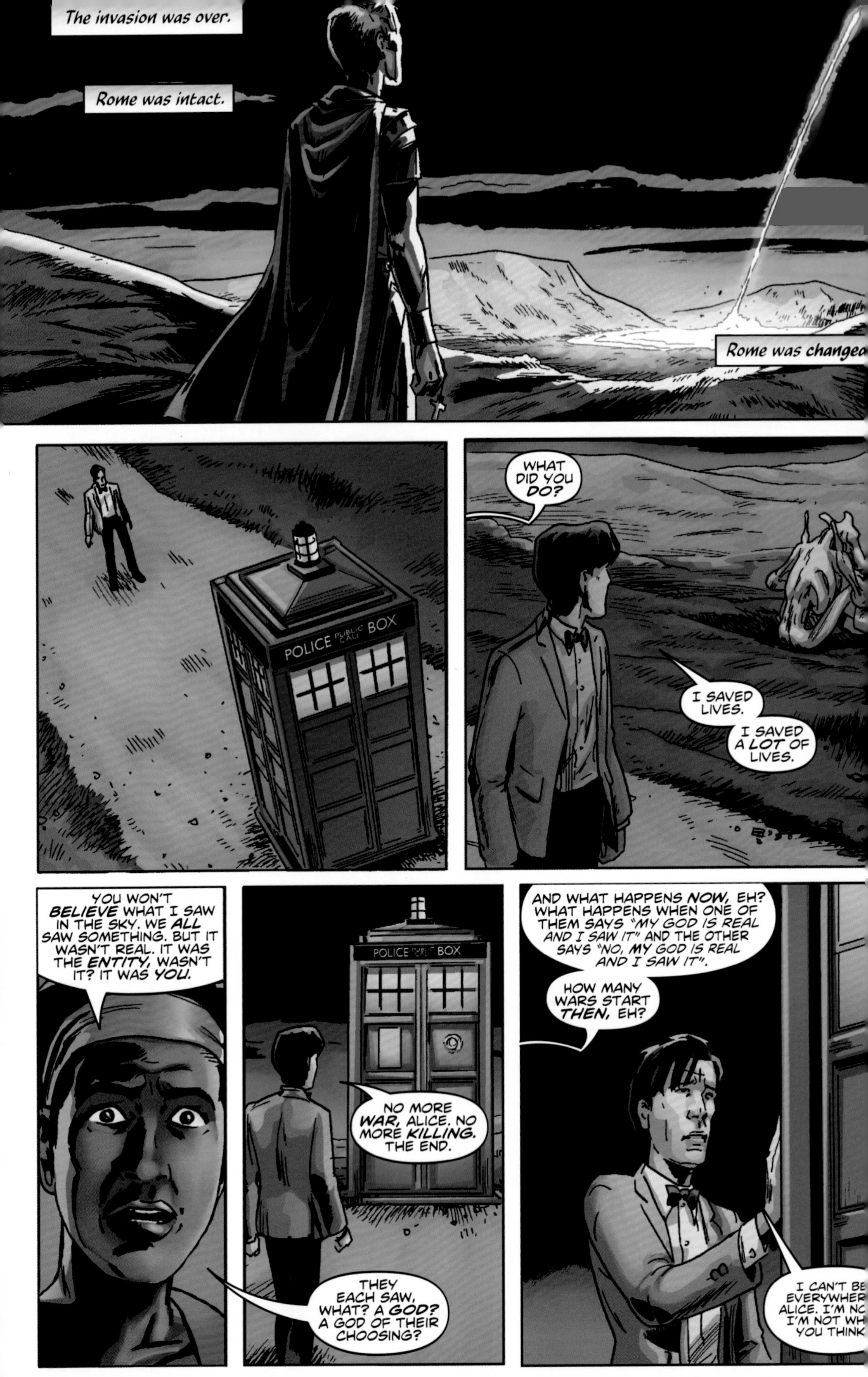
The invasion was over.
Rome was intact.
Rome was changed
POLICE PUBLIC CALL BOX
WHAT DID YOU DO?
I SAVED LIVES.
I SAVED A LOT OF LIVES.
YOU WON'T BELIEVE WHAT I SAW IN THE SKY. WE ALL SAW SOMETHING. BUT IT WASN'T REAL. IT WAS THE ENTITY, WASN'T IT? IT WAS YOU.
POLICE BOX
NO MORE WAR, ALICE. NO MORE KILLING. THE END.
THEY EACH SAW, WHAT? A GOD? A GOD OF THEIR CHOOSING?
AND WHAT HAPPENS NOW, EH? WHAT HAPPENS WHEN ONE OF THEM SAYS "MY GOD IS REAL AND I SAW IT" AND THE OTHER SAYS "NO, MY GOD IS REAL AND I SAW IT".
HOW MANY WARS START THEN, EH?
I CAN'T BE EVERYWHER ALICE. I'M NO I'M NOT WH YOU THINK

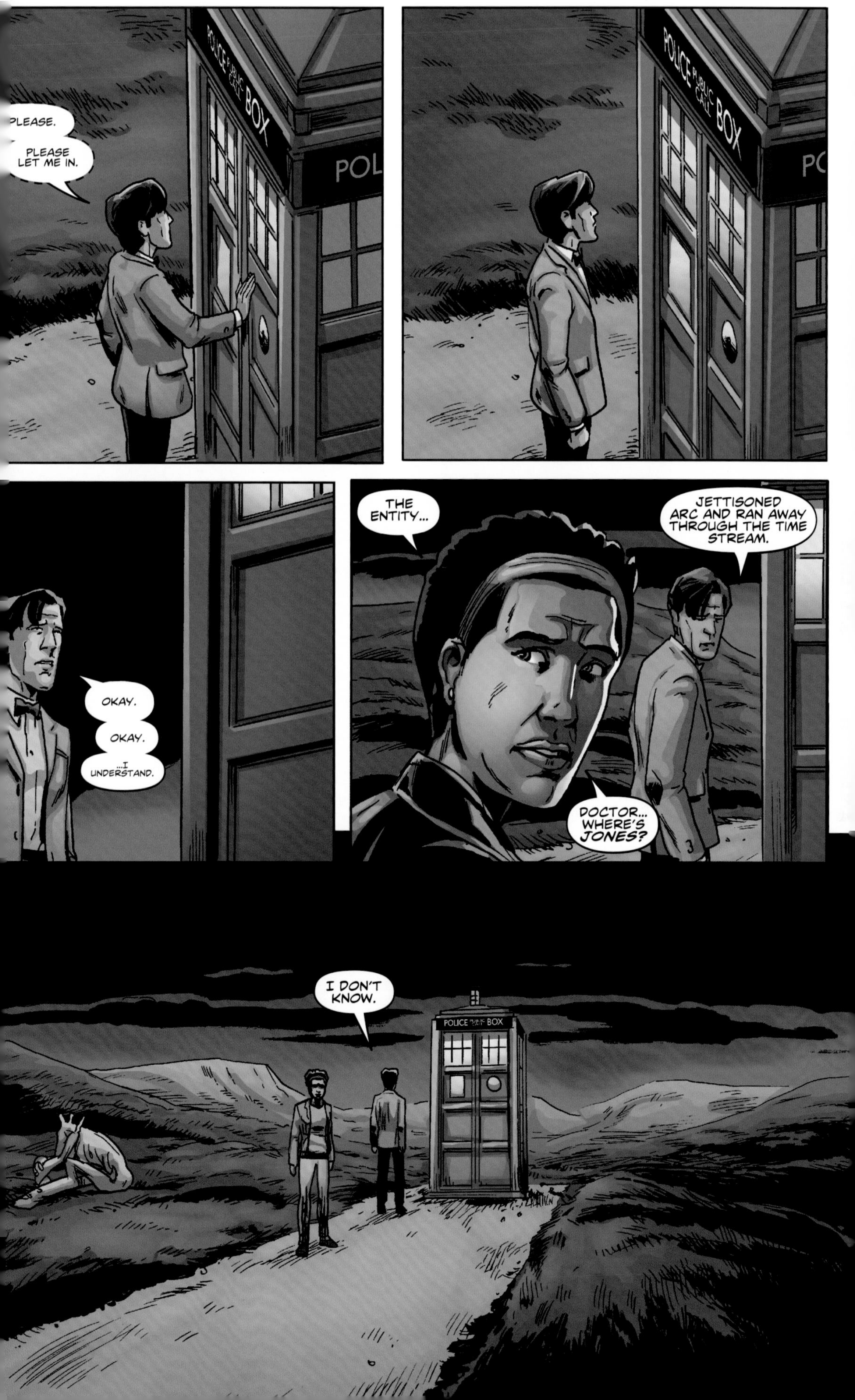
PLEASE.
PLEASE LET ME IN.
POLICE PUBLIC CALL BOX
POL
POLICE PUBLIC CALL BOX
OKAY.
OKAY.
...I UNDERSTAND.
THE ENTITY...
JETTISONED ARC AND RAN AWAY THROUGH THE TIME STREAM.
DOCTOR... WHERE'S JONES?
I DON'T KNOW.
POLICE BOX

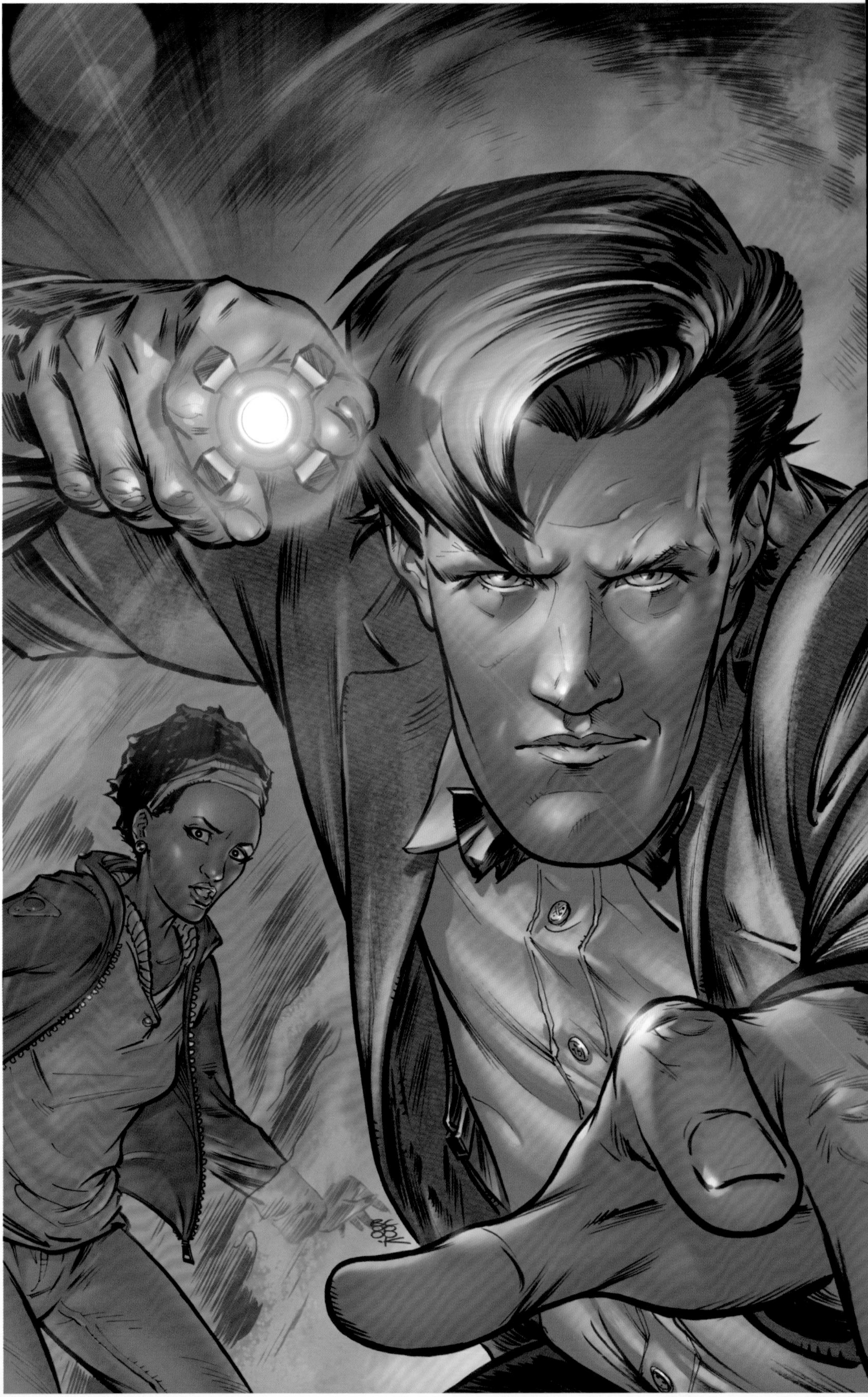

CHAPTER 14

Cover A: Boo Cook

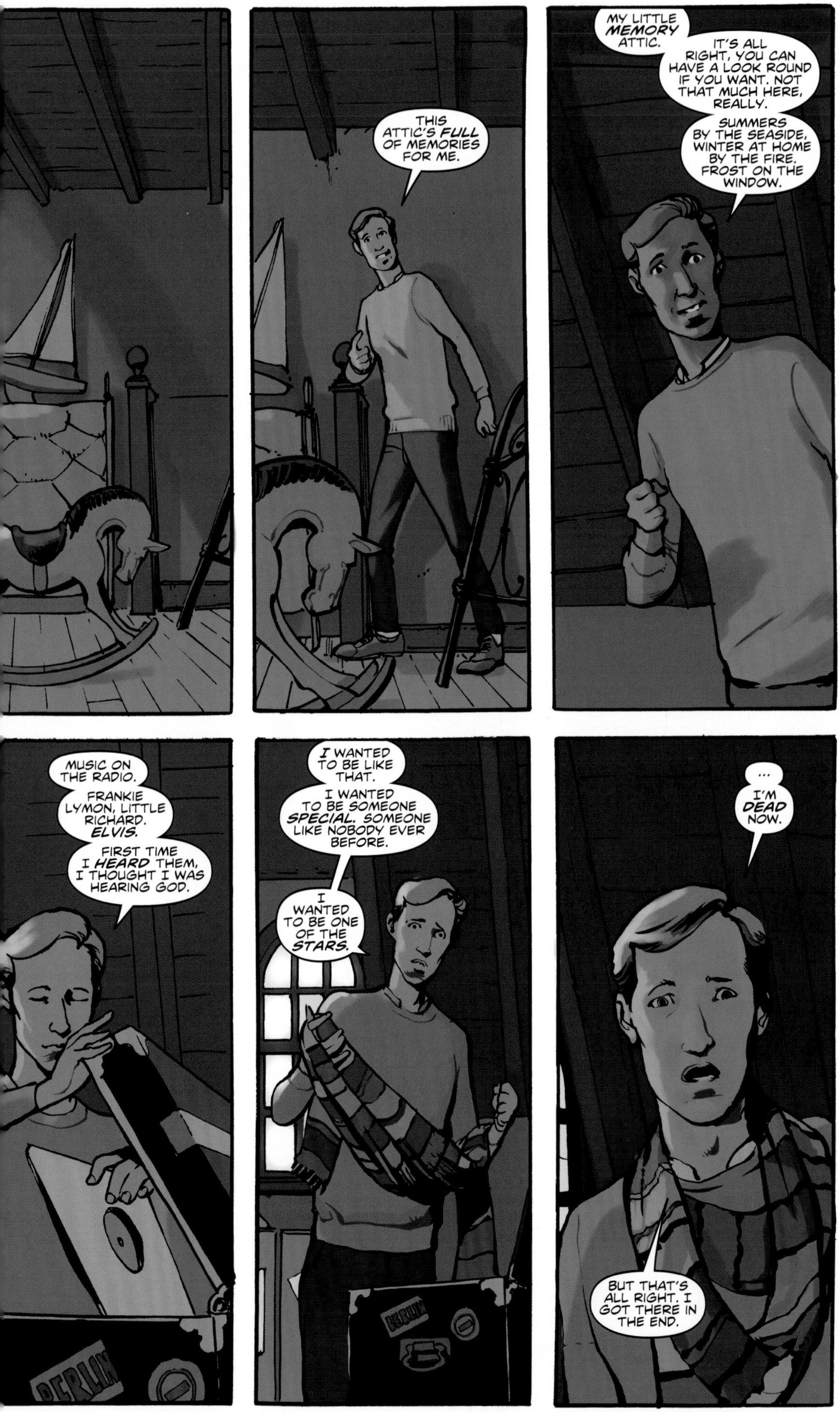
THIS ATTIC'S FULL OF MEMORIES FOR ME.
MY LITTLE MEMORY ATTIC.
IT'S ALL RIGHT, YOU CAN HAVE A LOOK ROUND IF YOU WANT. NOT THAT MUCH HERE, REALLY.
SUMMERS BY THE SEASIDE, WINTER AT HOME BY THE FIRE. FROST ON THE WINDOW.
MUSIC ON THE RADIO.
FRANKIE LYMON, LITTLE RICHARD. ELVIS.
FIRST TIME I HEARD THEM, I THOUGHT I WAS HEARING GOD.
I WANTED TO BE LIKE THAT.
I WANTED TO BE SOMEONE SPECIAL. SOMEONE LIKE NOBODY EVER BEFORE.
I WANTED TO BE ONE OF THE STARS.
...
I'M DEAD NOW.
BUT THAT'S ALL RIGHT. I GOT THERE IN THE END.

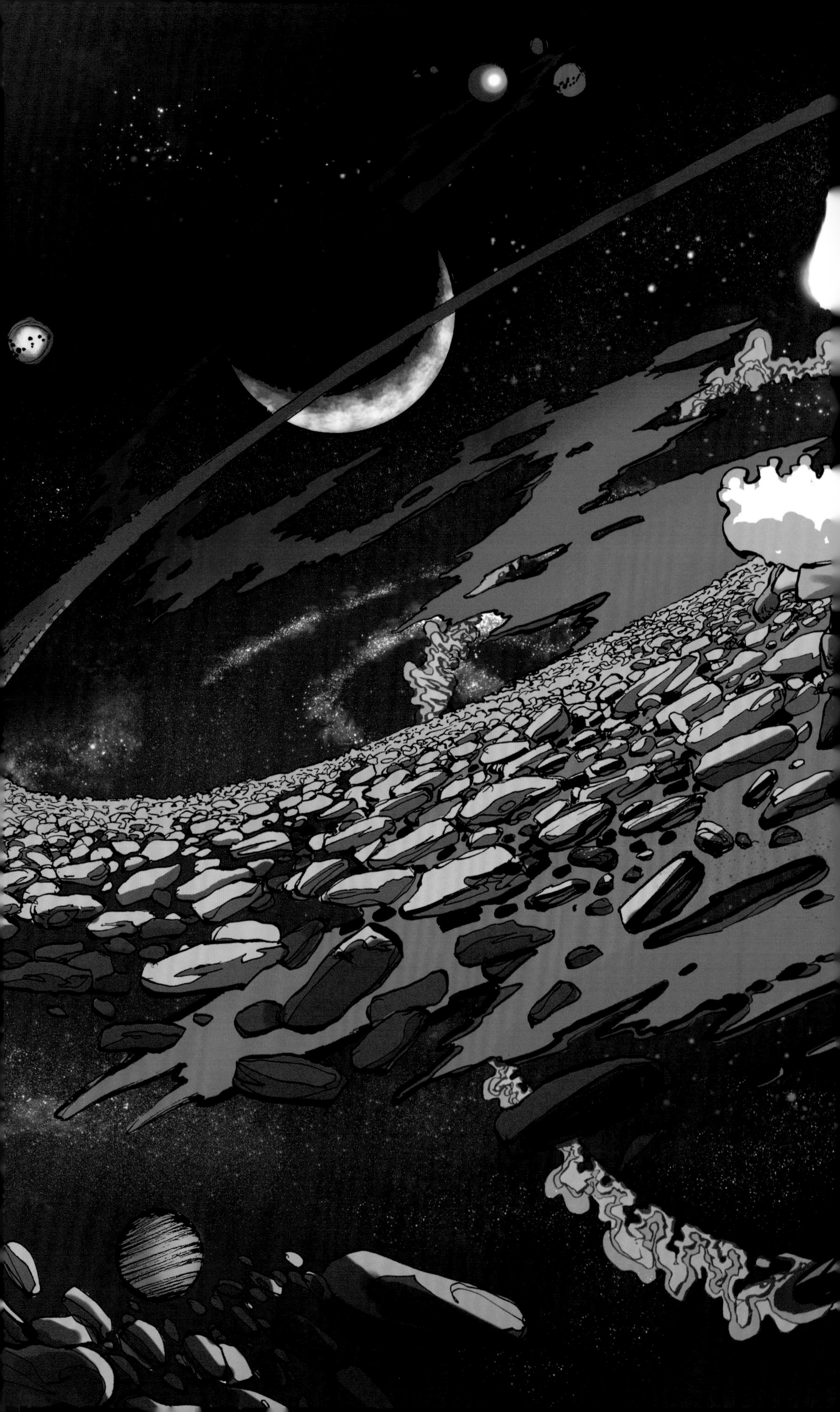

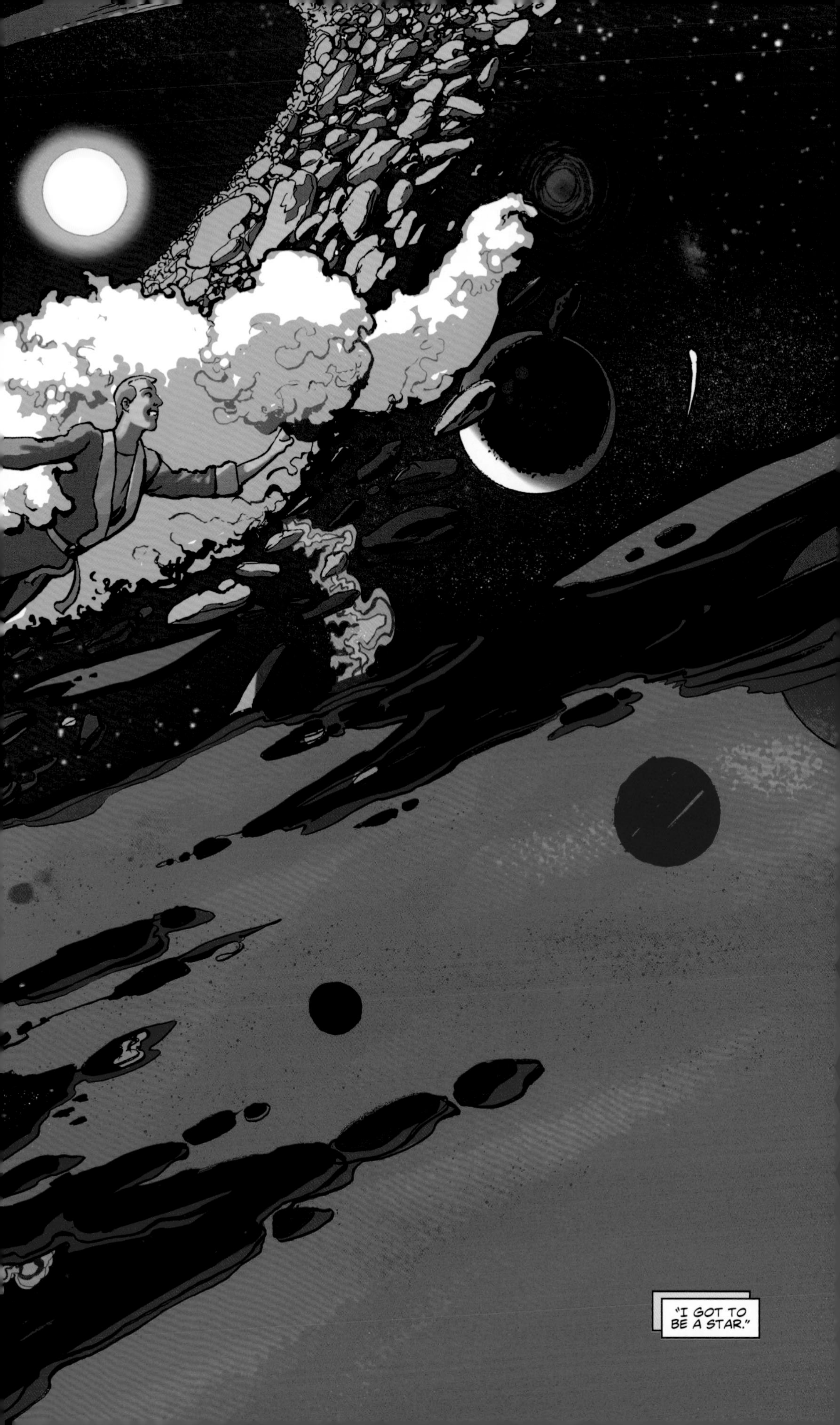
"I GOT TO BE A STAR."

CHAPTER 14

THE COMFORT OF THE GOOD PART 1

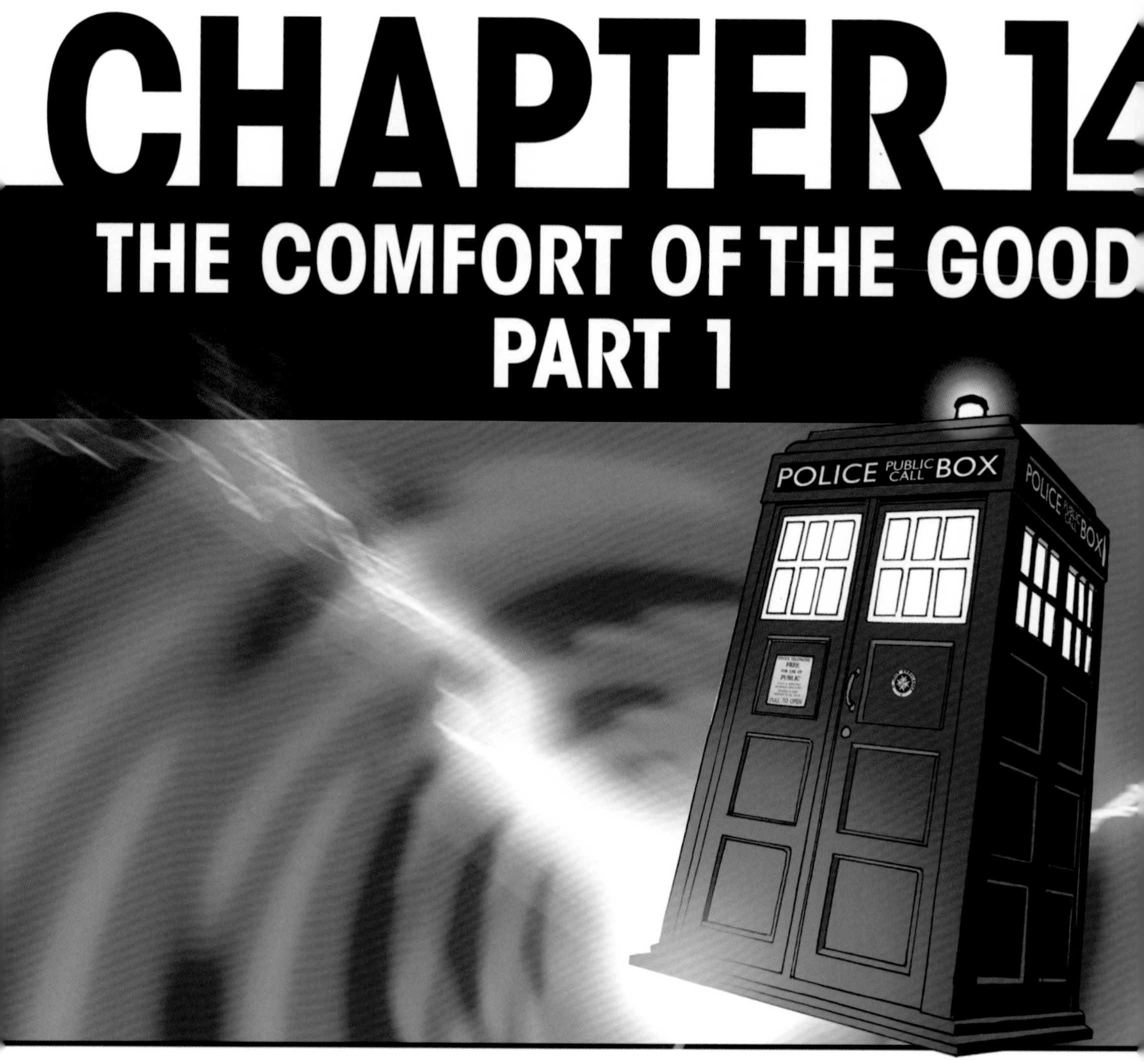
POLICE PUBLIC CALL BOX
POLICE PUBLIC CALL BOX

WRITERS
AL EWINGS & ROB WILLIAMS

ARTIST
SIMON FRASER

COLORIST
GARY CALDWELL

LETTERER
RICHARD STARKINGS AND COMICRAFT'S JIMMY BETANCOURT

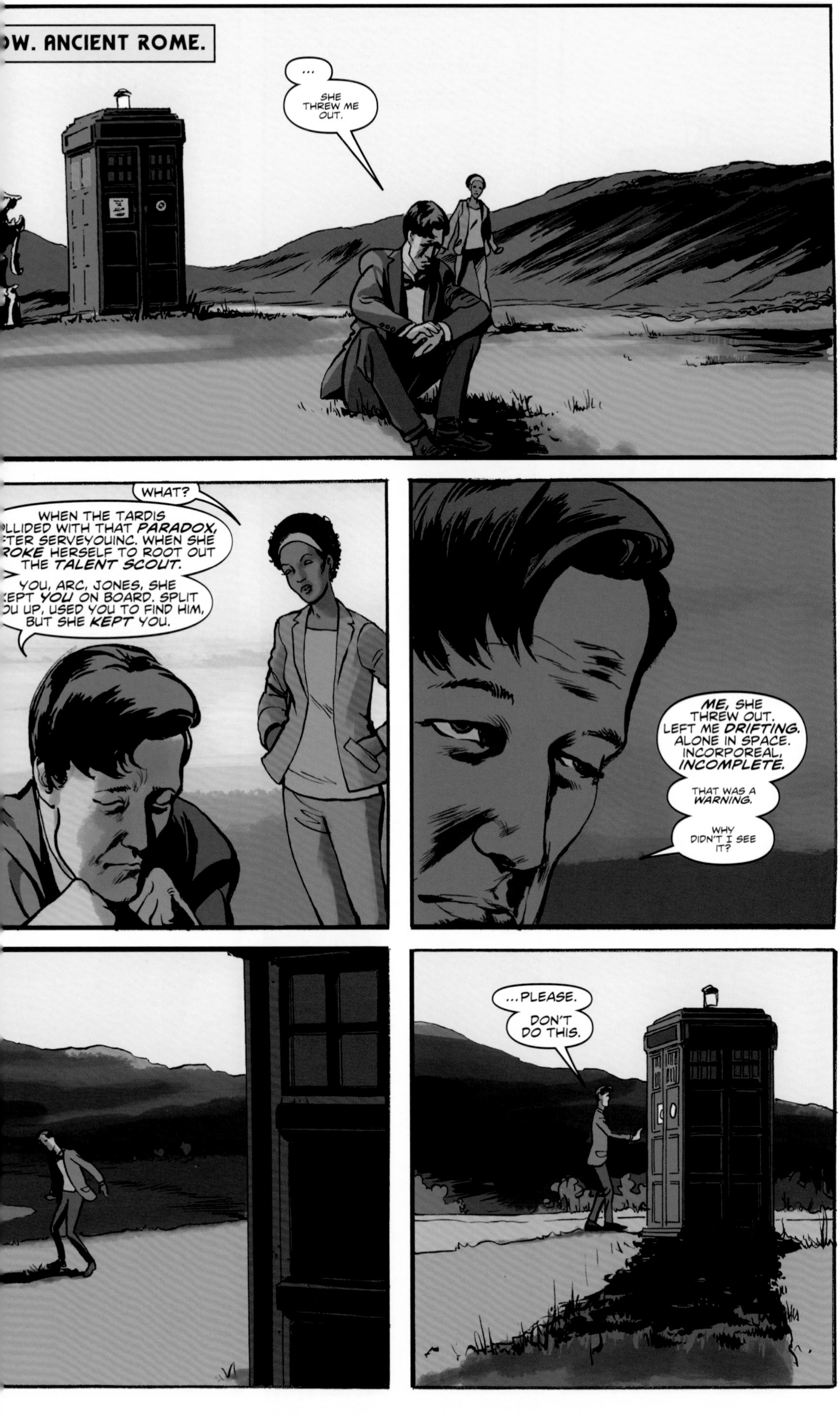

OW. ANCIENT ROME.
...
SHE THREW ME OUT.
WHAT?
WHEN THE TARDIS OLLIDED WITH THAT PARADOX, FTER SERVEYOUINC. WHEN SHE ROKE HERSELF TO ROOT OUT THE TALENT SCOUT.
YOU, ARC, JONES, SHE KEPT YOU ON BOARD. SPLIT OU UP, USED YOU TO FIND HIM, BUT SHE KEPT YOU.
ME, SHE THREW OUT. LEFT ME DRIFTING. ALONE IN SPACE. INCORPOREAL, INCOMPLETE.
THAT WAS A WARNING.
WHY DIDN'T I SEE IT?
...PLEASE.
DON'T DO THIS.

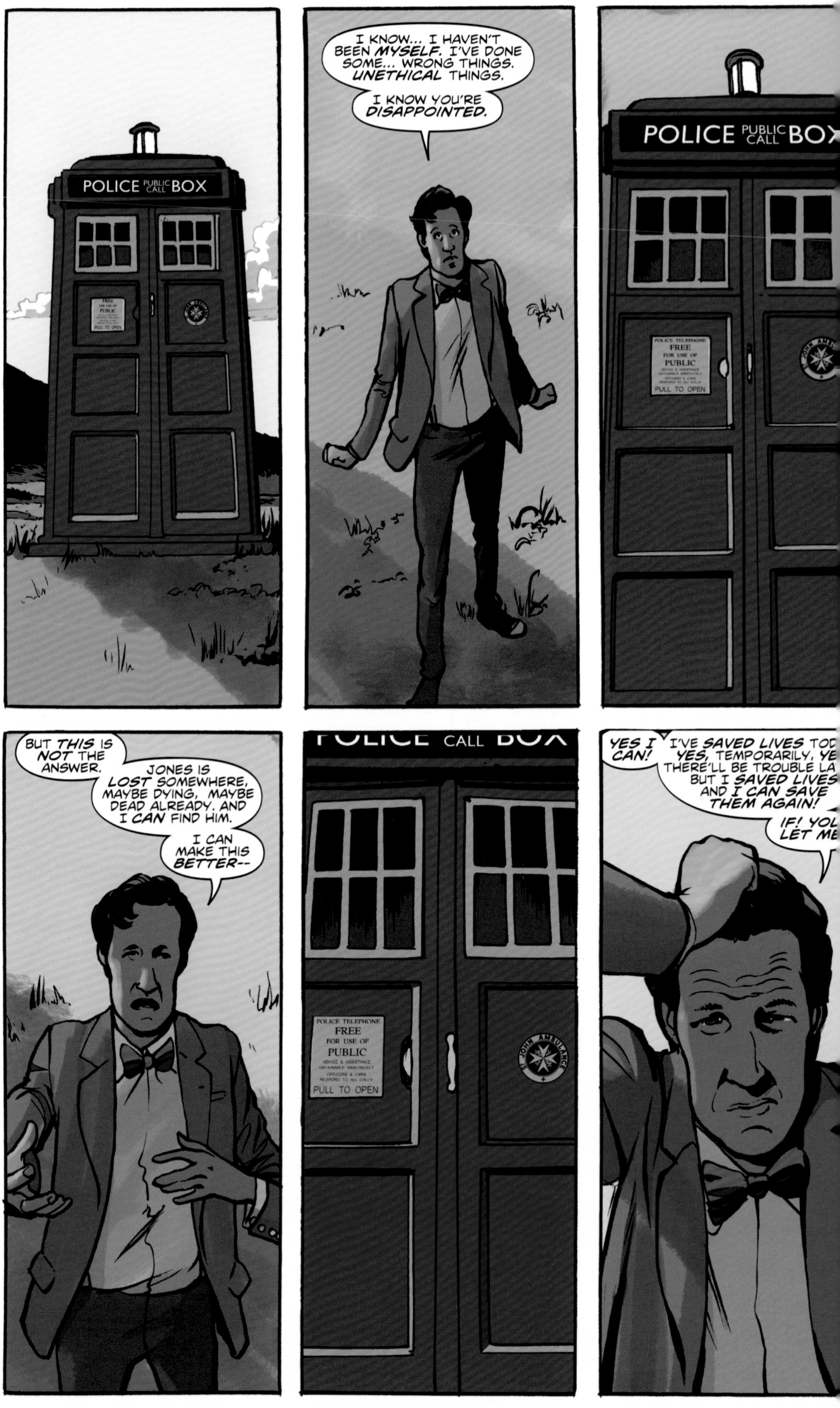
I KNOW... I HAVEN'T BEEN *MYSELF*. I'VE DONE SOME... WRONG THINGS. *UNETHICAL* THINGS.
I KNOW YOU'RE *DISAPPOINTED.*
BUT *THIS* IS *NOT* THE ANSWER.
JONES IS *LOST* SOMEWHERE, MAYBE DYING, MAYBE DEAD ALREADY. AND I *CAN* FIND HIM.
I CAN MAKE THIS *BETTER--*
YES I CAN!
I'VE *SAVED LIVES* TOD
YES, TEMPORARILY, YE
THERE'LL BE TROUBLE LA
BUT I *SAVED LIVES*
AND *I CAN SAVE THEM AGAIN!*
IF! YOU LET ME

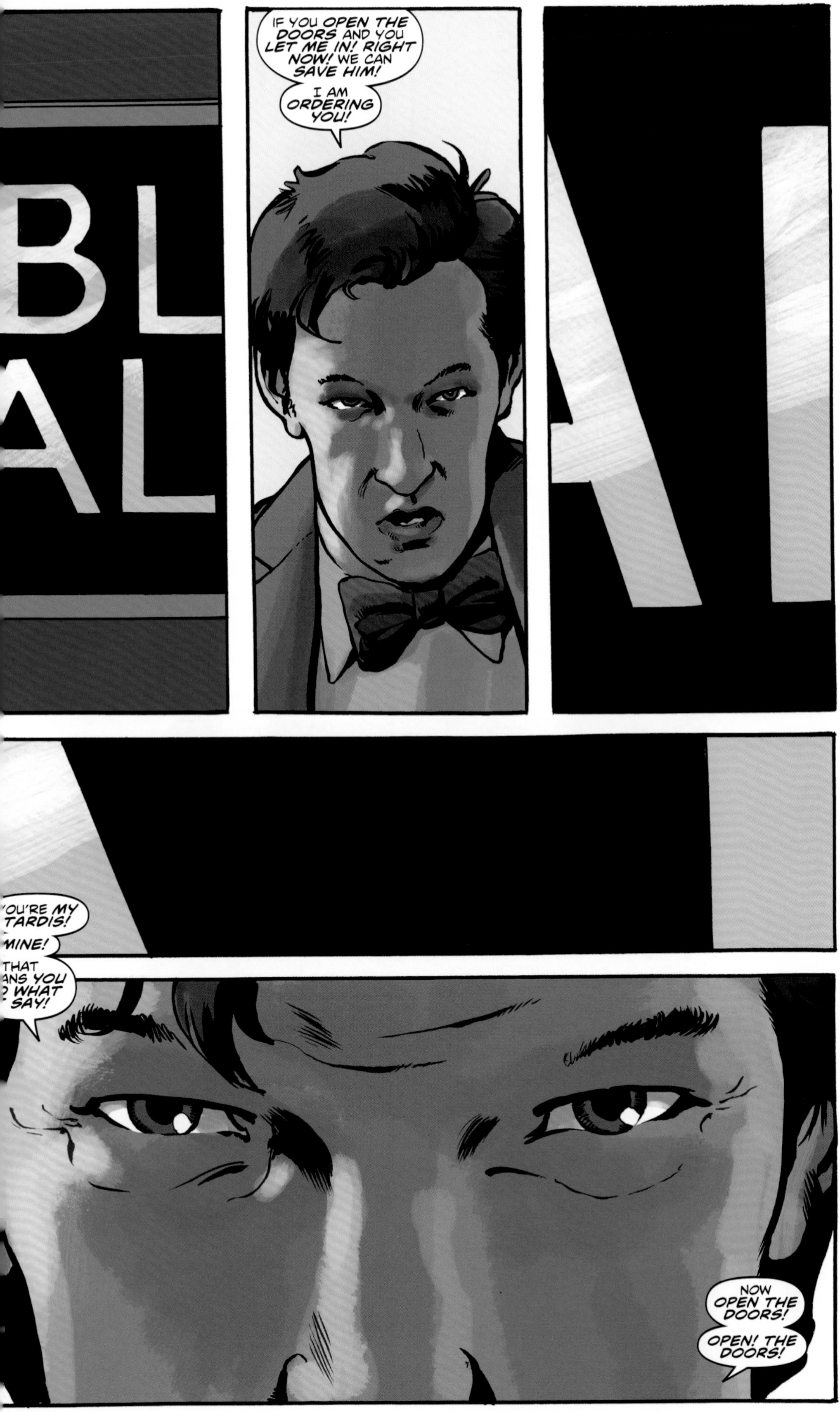
IF YOU OPEN THE DOORS AND YOU LET ME IN! RIGHT NOW! WE CAN SAVE HIM!
I AM ORDERING YOU!
OU'RE MY TARDIS!
MINE!
NOW OPEN THE DOORS!
OPEN! THE DOORS!

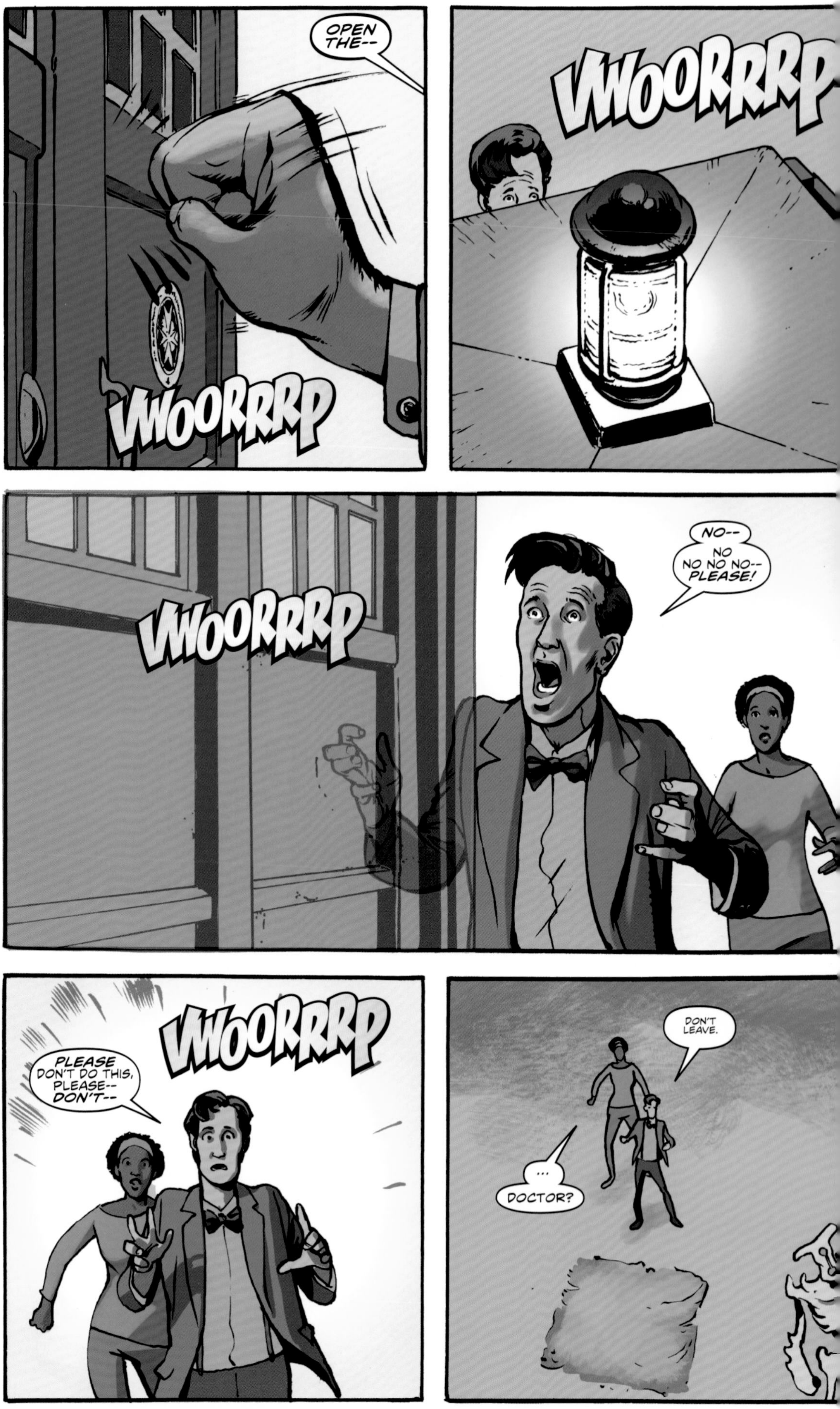
OPEN THE--
VWOORRRP
VWOORRRP
VWOORRRP
NO--
NO NO NO NO--
PLEASE!
VWOORRRP
PLEASE DON'T DO THIS, PLEASE-- DON'T--
DON'T LEAVE.
... DOCTOR?

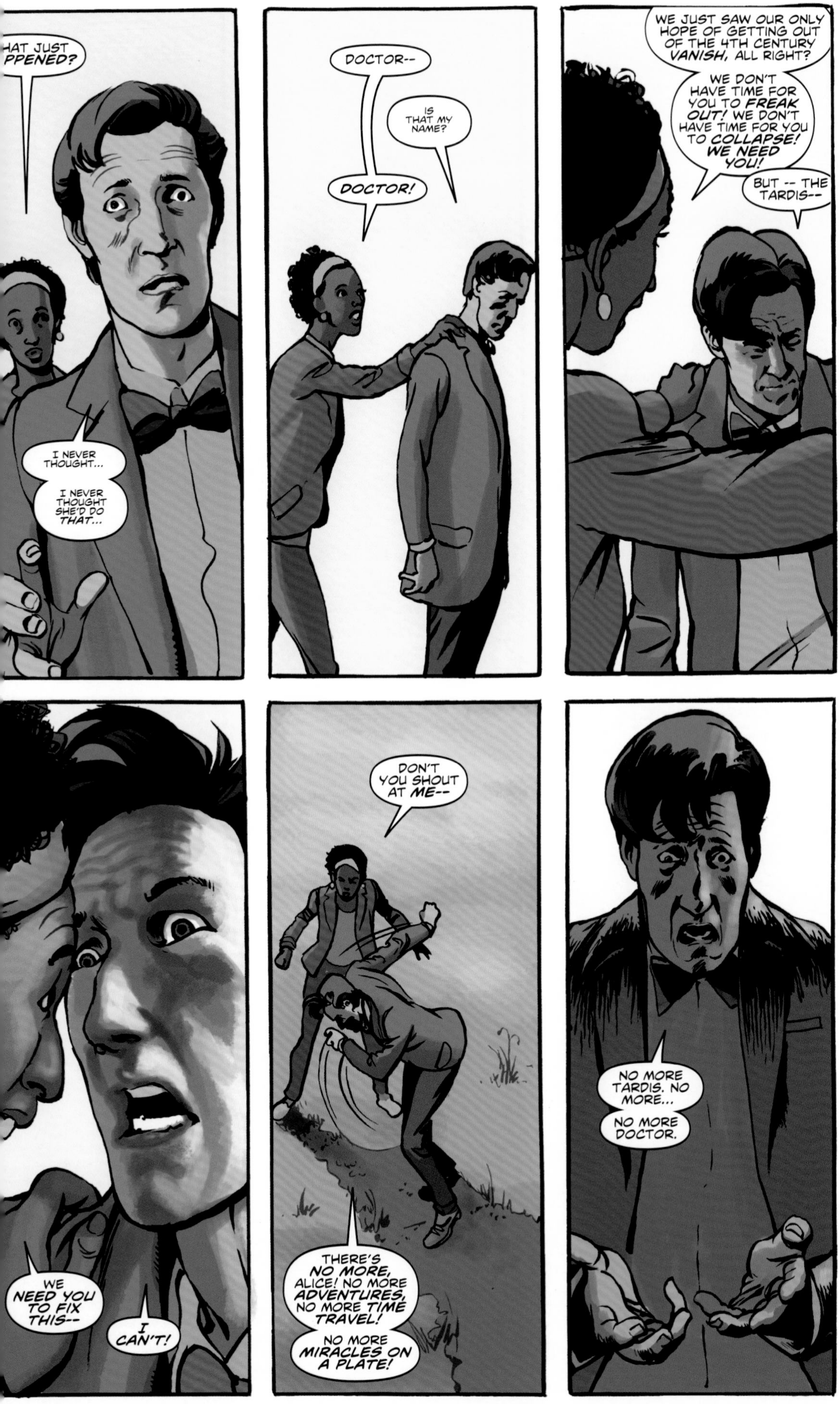
HAT JUST
PPENED?
I NEVER THOUGHT...
I NEVER THOUGHT SHE'D DO *THAT*...
DOCTOR--
IS THAT MY NAME?
DOCTOR!
WE JUST SAW OUR ONLY HOPE OF GETTING OUT OF THE 4TH CENTURY *VANISH*, ALL RIGHT?
WE DON'T HAVE TIME FOR YOU TO ***FREAK OUT!*** WE DON'T HAVE TIME FOR YOU TO ***COLLAPSE! WE NEED YOU!***
BUT -- THE TARDIS--
WE *NEED YOU* TO FIX THIS--
I CAN'T!
DON'T YOU SHOUT AT ***ME***--
THERE'S ***NO MORE***, ALICE! NO MORE ***ADVENTURES***, NO MORE *TIME TRAVEL!*
NO MORE ***MIRACLES ON A PLATE!***
NO MORE TARDIS. NO MORE...
NO MORE DOCTOR.

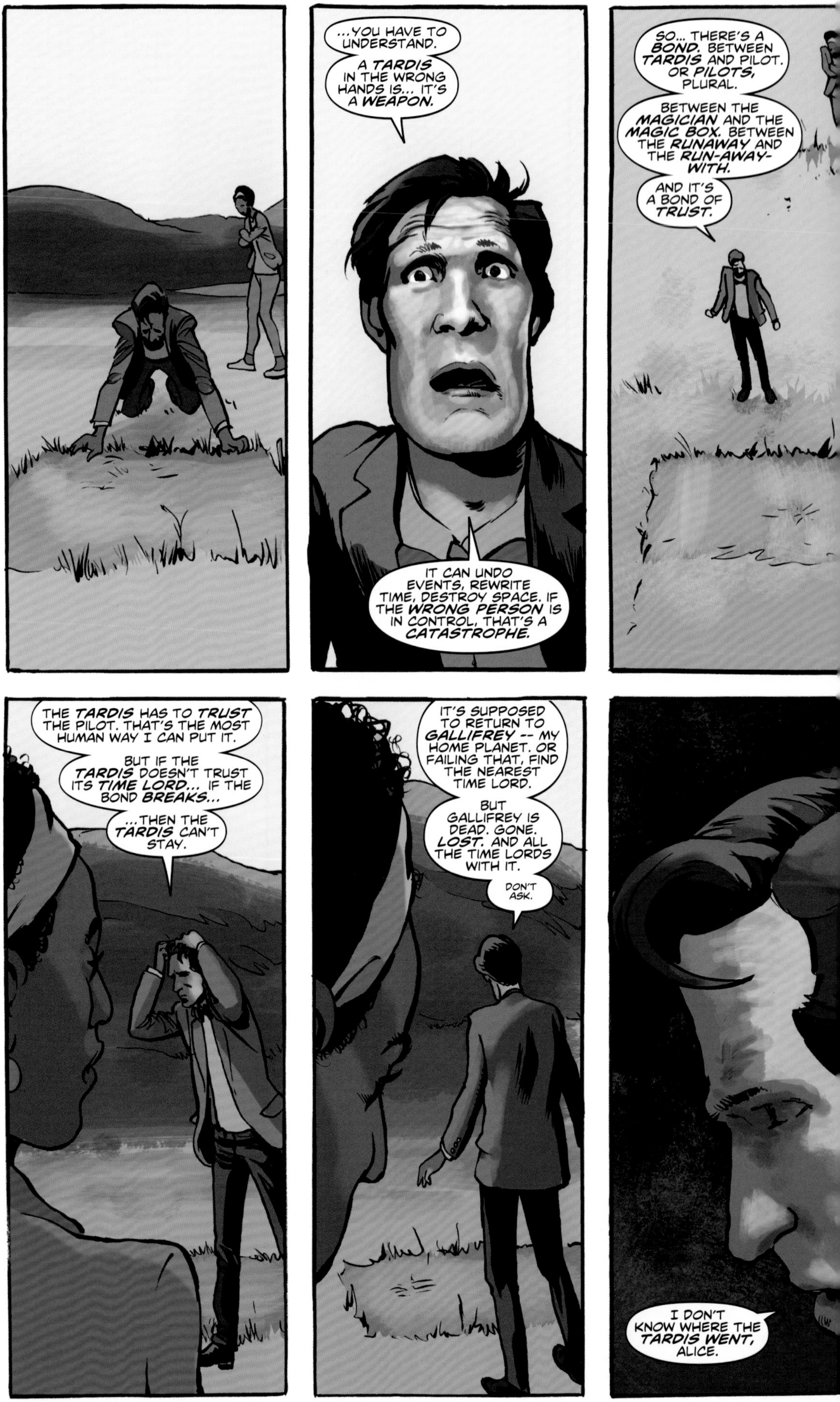
...YOU HAVE TO UNDERSTAND.
A TARDIS IN THE WRONG HANDS IS... IT'S A WEAPON.
IT CAN UNDO EVENTS, REWRITE TIME, DESTROY SPACE. IF THE WRONG PERSON IS IN CONTROL, THAT'S A CATASTROPHE.
SO... THERE'S A BOND. BETWEEN TARDIS AND PILOT. OR PILOTS, PLURAL.
BETWEEN THE MAGICIAN AND THE MAGIC BOX. BETWEEN THE RUNAWAY AND THE RUN-AWAY-WITH.
AND IT'S A BOND OF TRUST.
THE TARDIS HAS TO TRUST THE PILOT. THAT'S THE MOST HUMAN WAY I CAN PUT IT.
BUT IF THE TARDIS DOESN'T TRUST ITS TIME LORD... IF THE BOND BREAKS...
...THEN THE TARDIS CAN'T STAY.
IT'S SUPPOSED TO RETURN TO GALLIFREY -- MY HOME PLANET. OR FAILING THAT, FIND THE NEAREST TIME LORD.
BUT GALLIFREY IS DEAD. GONE. LOST. AND ALL THE TIME LORDS WITH IT.
DON'T ASK.
I DON'T KNOW WHERE THE TARDIS WENT, ALICE.

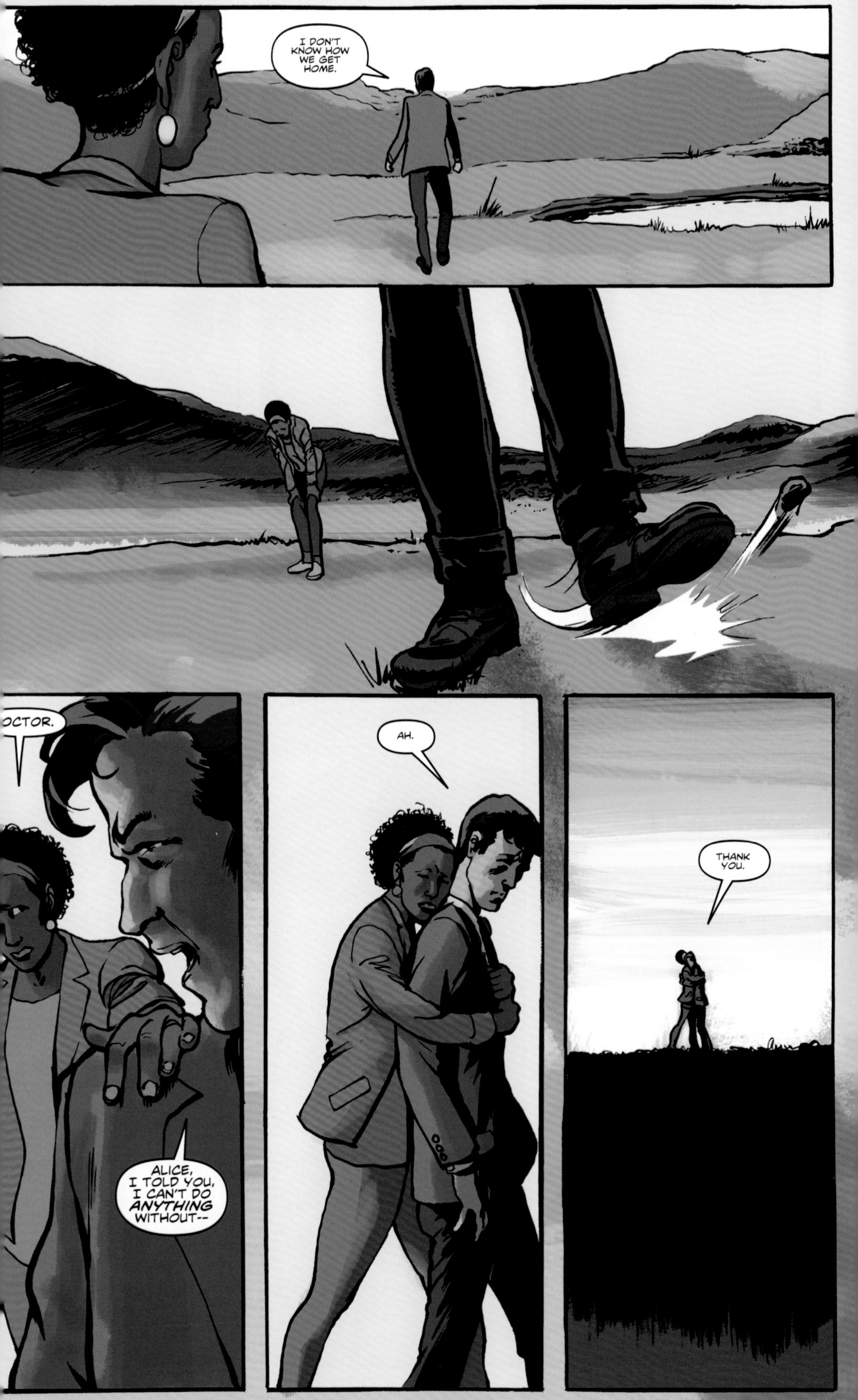
I DON'T KNOW HOW WE GET HOME.
OCTOR.
ALICE, I TOLD YOU, I CAN'T DO *ANYTHING* WITHOUT--
AH.
THANK YOU.

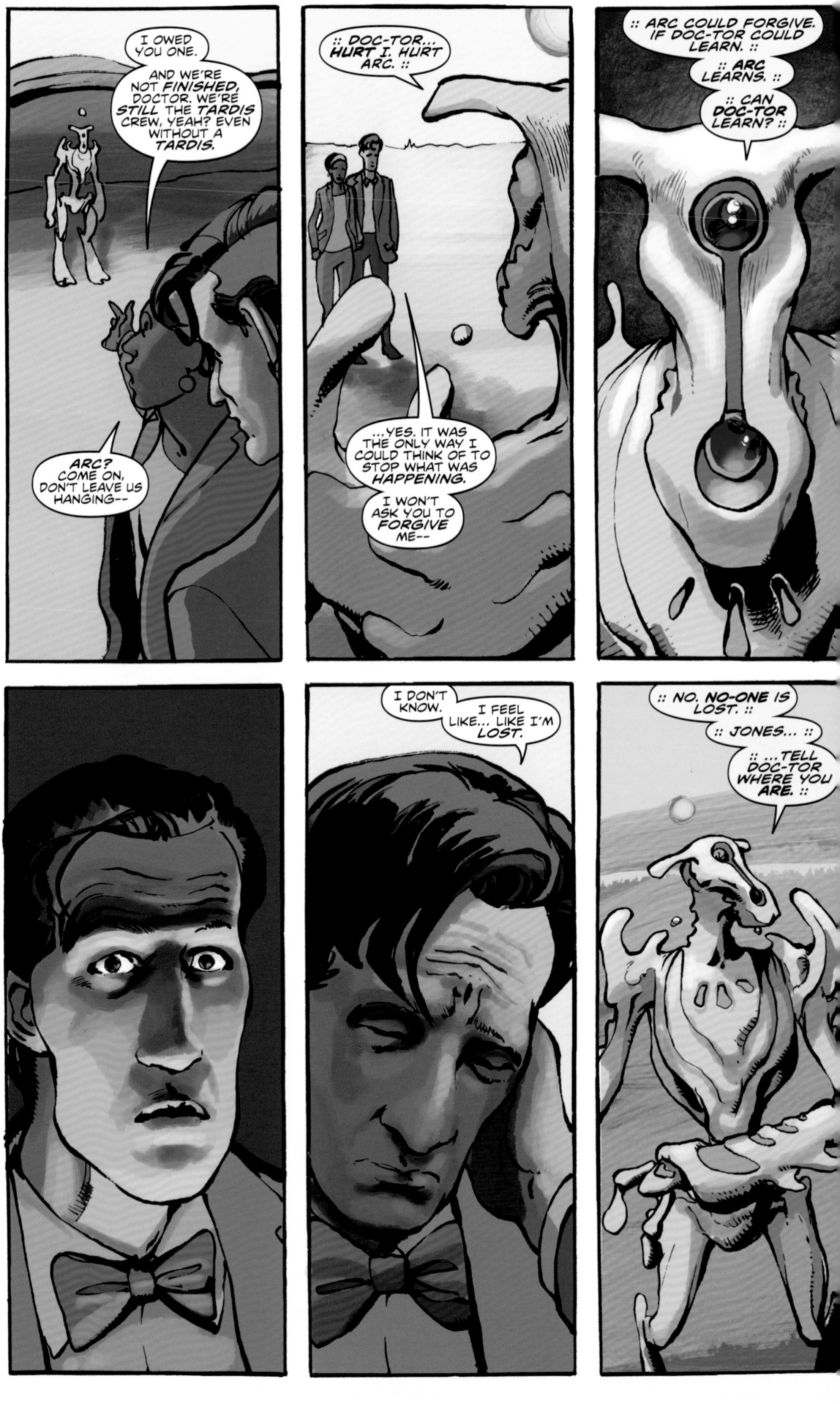
I OWED YOU ONE.
AND WE'RE NOT FINISHED, DOCTOR. WE'RE STILL THE TARDIS CREW, YEAH? EVEN WITHOUT A TARDIS.
ARC? COME ON, DON'T LEAVE US HANGING--
:: DOC-TOR... HURT I. HURT ARC. ::
...YES. IT WAS THE ONLY WAY I COULD THINK OF TO STOP WHAT WAS HAPPENING.
I WON'T ASK YOU TO FORGIVE ME--
:: ARC COULD FORGIVE. IF DOC-TOR COULD LEARN. ::
:: ARC LEARNS. ::
:: CAN DOC-TOR LEARN? ::
I DON'T KNOW.
I FEEL LIKE... LIKE I'M LOST.
:: NO. NO-ONE IS LOST. ::
:: JONES... ::
:: ...TELL DOC-TOR WHERE YOU ARE. ::

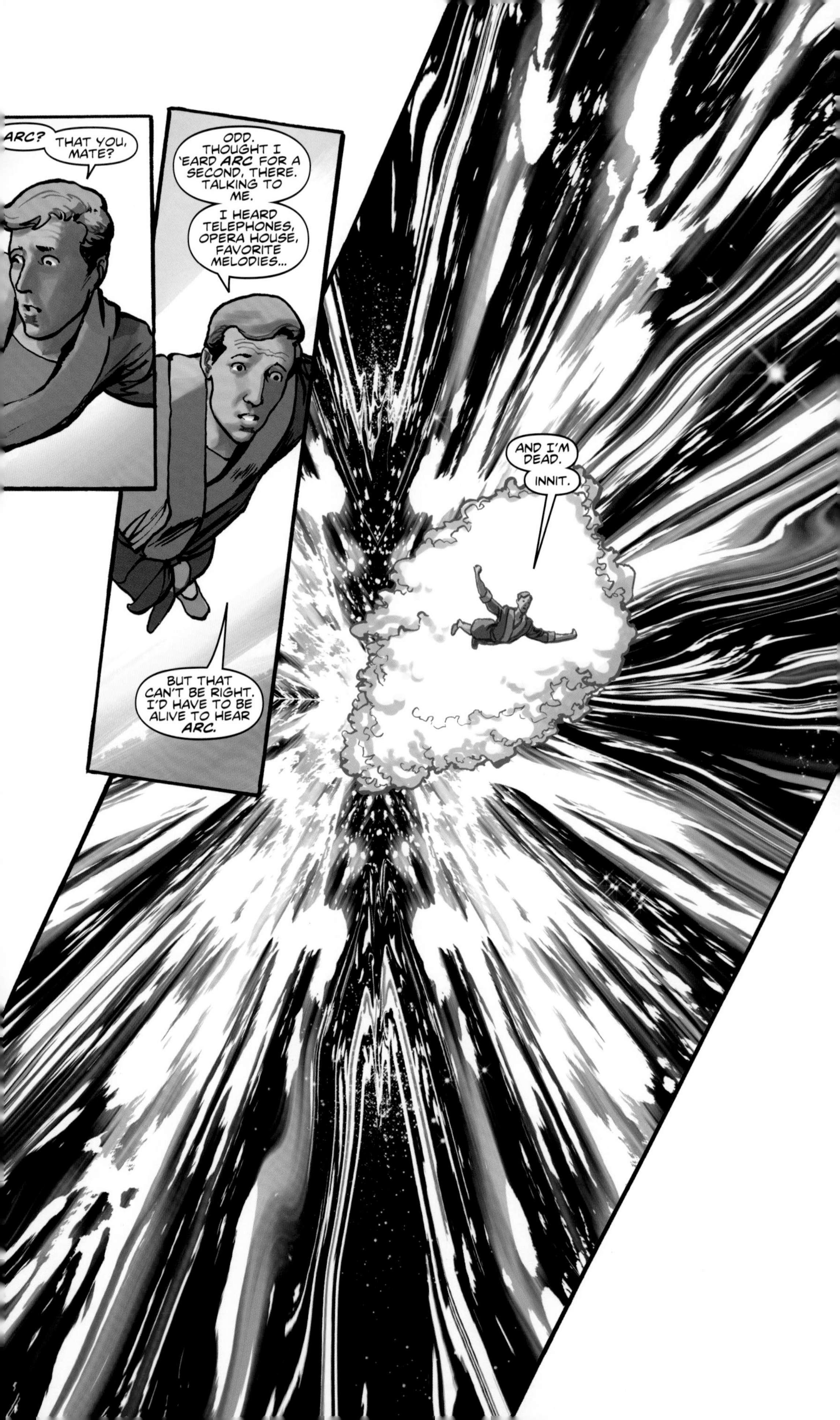
ARC? THAT YOU, MATE?
ODD. THOUGHT I 'EARD ARC FOR A SECOND, THERE. TALKING TO ME.
I HEARD TELEPHONES, OPERA HOUSE, FAVORITE MELODIES...
BUT THAT CAN'T BE RIGHT. I'D HAVE TO BE ALIVE TO HEAR ARC.
AND I'M DEAD.
INNIT.

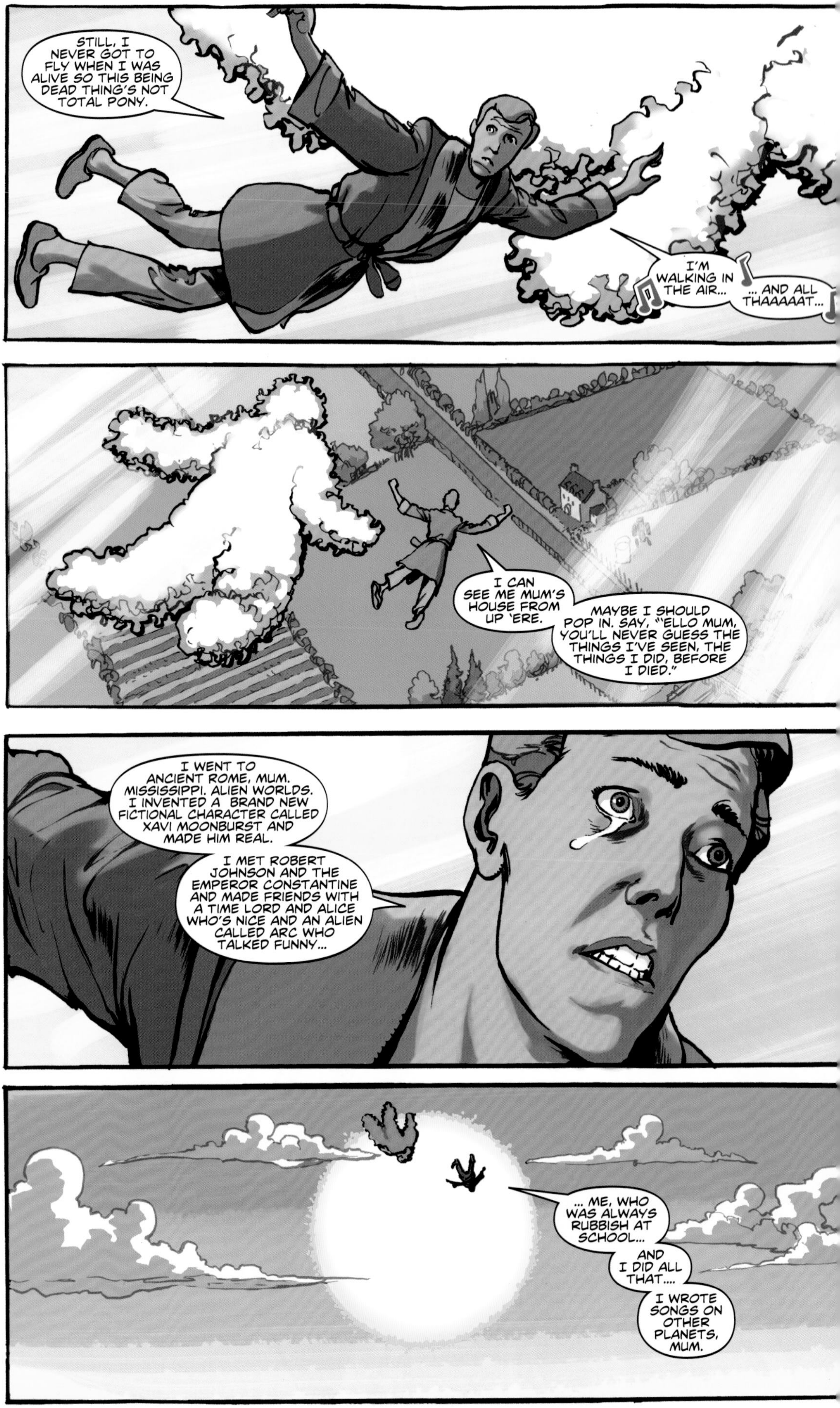
STILL, I NEVER GOT TO FLY WHEN I WAS ALIVE SO THIS BEING DEAD THING'S NOT TOTAL PONY.
I'M WALKING IN THE AIR...
... AND ALL THAAAAAT...
I CAN SEE ME MUM'S HOUSE FROM UP 'ERE.
MAYBE I SHOULD POP IN. SAY, "'ELLO MUM, YOU'LL NEVER GUESS THE THINGS I'VE SEEN, THE THINGS I DID, BEFORE I DIED."
I WENT TO ANCIENT ROME, MUM. MISSISSIPPI. ALIEN WORLDS. I INVENTED A BRAND NEW FICTIONAL CHARACTER CALLED XAVI MOONBURST AND MADE HIM REAL.
I MET ROBERT JOHNSON AND THE EMPEROR CONSTANTINE AND MADE FRIENDS WITH A TIME LORD AND ALICE WHO'S NICE AND AN ALIEN CALLED ARC WHO TALKED FUNNY...
... ME, WHO WAS ALWAYS RUBBISH AT SCHOOL...
AND I DID ALL THAT....
I WROTE SONGS ON OTHER PLANETS, MUM.

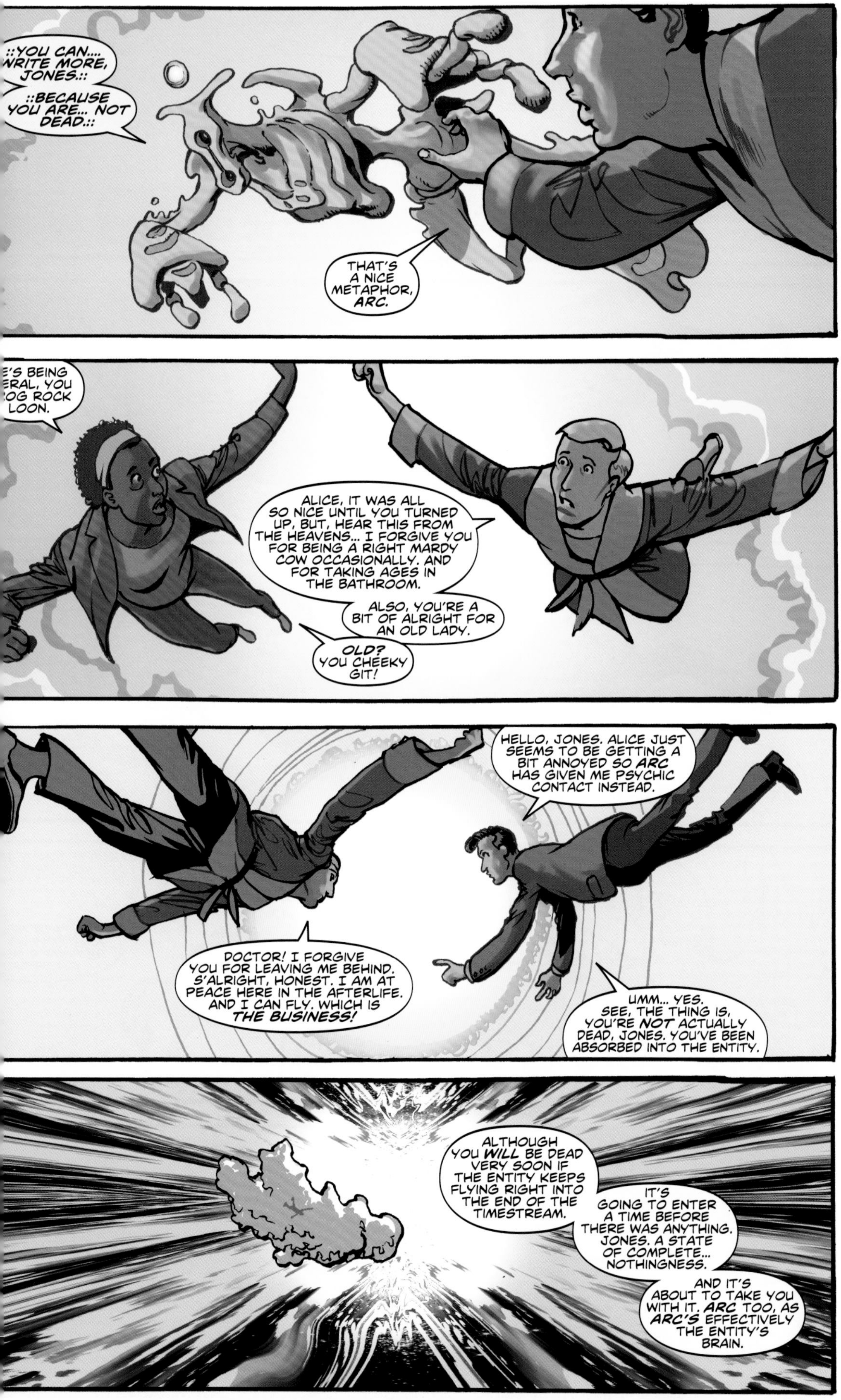
::YOU CAN.... WRITE MORE, JONES.::
::BECAUSE YOU ARE... NOT DEAD.::
THAT'S A NICE METAPHOR, ARC.
'S BEING ERAL, YOU OG ROCK LOON.
ALICE, IT WAS ALL SO NICE UNTIL YOU TURNED UP, BUT, HEAR THIS FROM THE HEAVENS... I FORGIVE YOU FOR BEING A RIGHT MARDY COW OCCASIONALLY. AND FOR TAKING AGES IN THE BATHROOM.
ALSO, YOU'RE A BIT OF ALRIGHT FOR AN OLD LADY.
OLD? YOU CHEEKY GIT!
HELLO, JONES. ALICE JUST SEEMS TO BE GETTING A BIT ANNOYED SO ARC HAS GIVEN ME PSYCHIC CONTACT INSTEAD.
DOCTOR! I FORGIVE YOU FOR LEAVING ME BEHIND. S'ALRIGHT, HONEST. I AM AT PEACE HERE IN THE AFTERLIFE. AND I CAN FLY. WHICH IS THE BUSINESS!
UMM... YES. SEE, THE THING IS, YOU'RE NOT ACTUALLY DEAD, JONES. YOU'VE BEEN ABSORBED INTO THE ENTITY.
ALTHOUGH YOU WILL BE DEAD VERY SOON IF THE ENTITY KEEPS FLYING RIGHT INTO THE END OF THE TIMESTREAM.
IT'S GOING TO ENTER A TIME BEFORE THERE WAS ANYTHING. JONES. A STATE OF COMPLETE... NOTHINGNESS.
AND IT'S ABOUT TO TAKE YOU WITH IT. ARC TOO, AS ARC'S EFFECTIVELY THE ENTITY'S BRAIN.

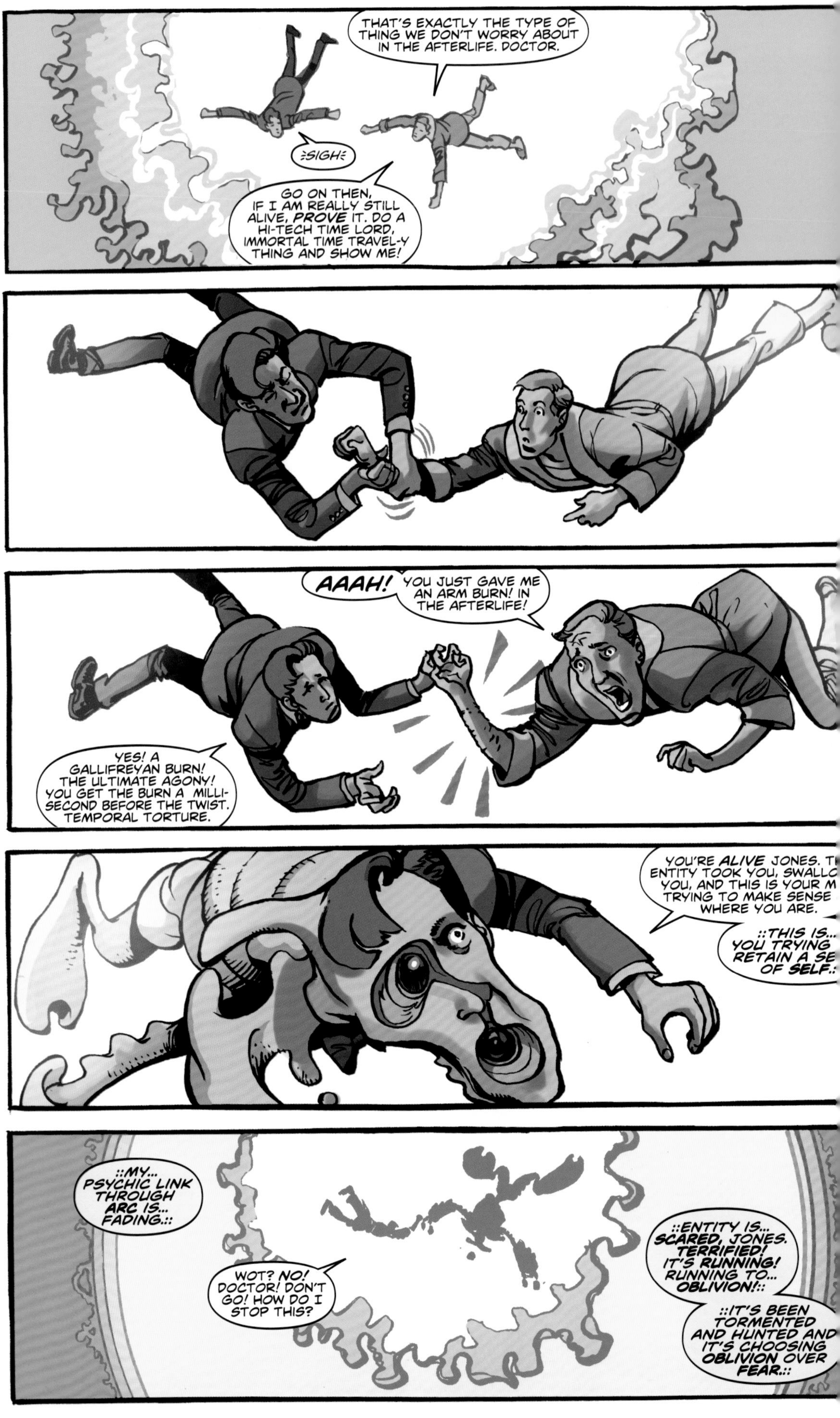

THAT'S EXACTLY THE TYPE OF THING WE DON'T WORRY ABOUT IN THE AFTERLIFE. DOCTOR.
SIGH
GO ON THEN, IF I AM REALLY STILL ALIVE, PROVE IT. DO A HI-TECH TIME LORD, IMMORTAL TIME TRAVEL-Y THING AND SHOW ME!
AAAH!
YOU JUST GAVE ME AN ARM BURN! IN THE AFTERLIFE!
YES! A GALLIFREYAN BURN! THE ULTIMATE AGONY! YOU GET THE BURN A MILLI-SECOND BEFORE THE TWIST. TEMPORAL TORTURE.
YOU'RE ALIVE JONES. ENTITY TOOK YOU, YOU, AND THIS IS YOUR TRYING TO MAKE SENSE WHERE YOU ARE.
::THIS IS... YOU TRYING RETAIN A OF SELF.::
::MY... PSYCHIC LINK THROUGH ARC IS... FADING.::
WOT? NO! DOCTOR! DON'T GO! HOW DO I STOP THIS?
::ENTITY IS... SCARED, JONES. TERRIFIED! IT'S RUNNING! RUNNING TO... OBLIVION!::
::IT'S BEEN TORMENTED AND HUNTED AND IT'S CHOOSING OBLIVION OVER FEAR.::

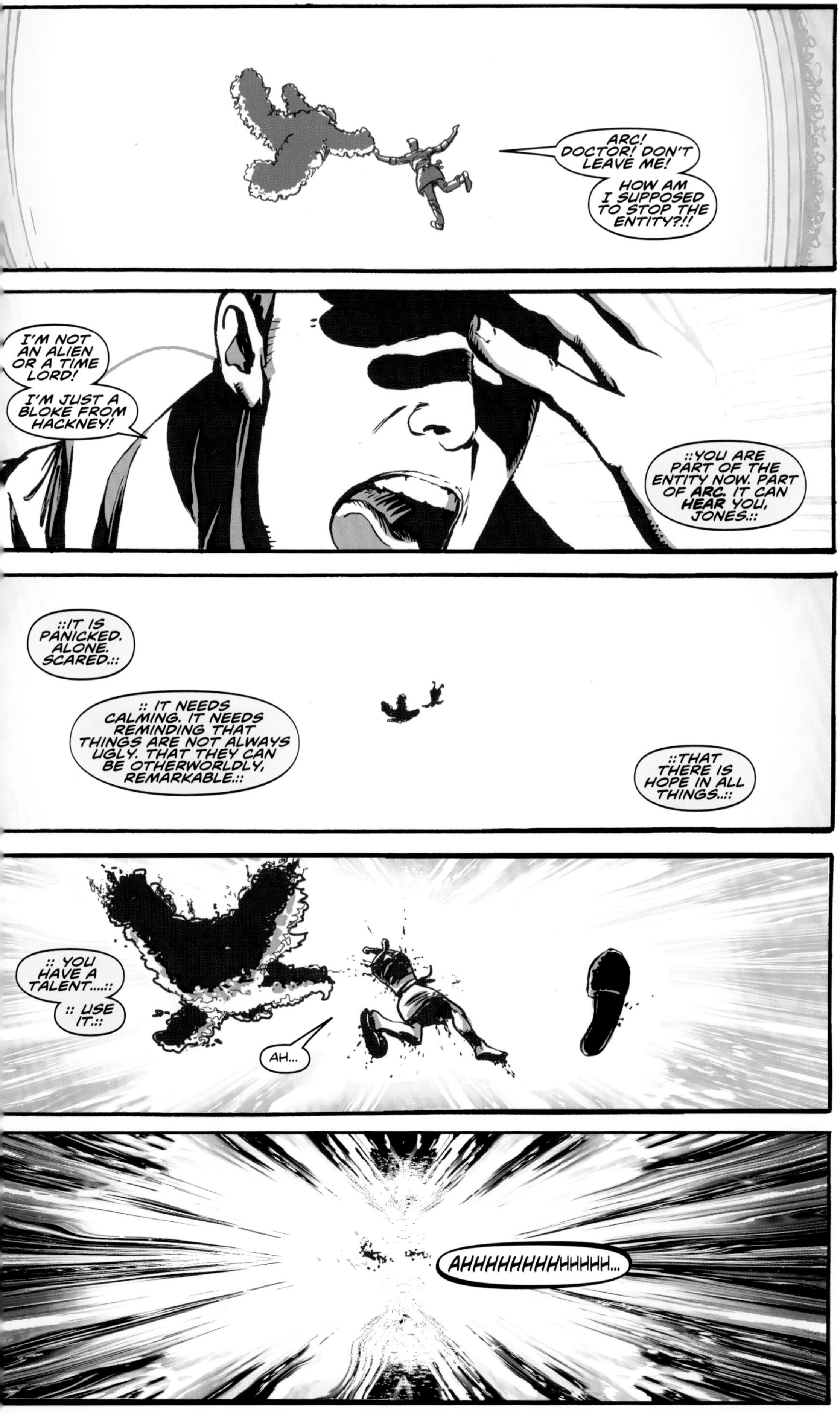
ARC! DOCTOR! DON'T LEAVE ME!
HOW AM I SUPPOSED TO STOP THE ENTITY?!!
I'M NOT AN ALIEN OR A TIME LORD!
I'M JUST A BLOKE FROM HACKNEY!
::YOU ARE PART OF THE ENTITY NOW. PART OF ARC. IT CAN HEAR YOU, JONES.::
::IT IS PANICKED. ALONE. SCARED.::
:: IT NEEDS CALMING. IT NEEDS REMINDING THAT THINGS ARE NOT ALWAYS UGLY. THAT THEY CAN BE OTHERWORLDLY, REMARKABLE.::
::THAT THERE IS HOPE IN ALL THINGS...::
:: YOU HAVE A TALENT....::
:: USE IT.::
AH...
AHHHHHHHHHHHHH...

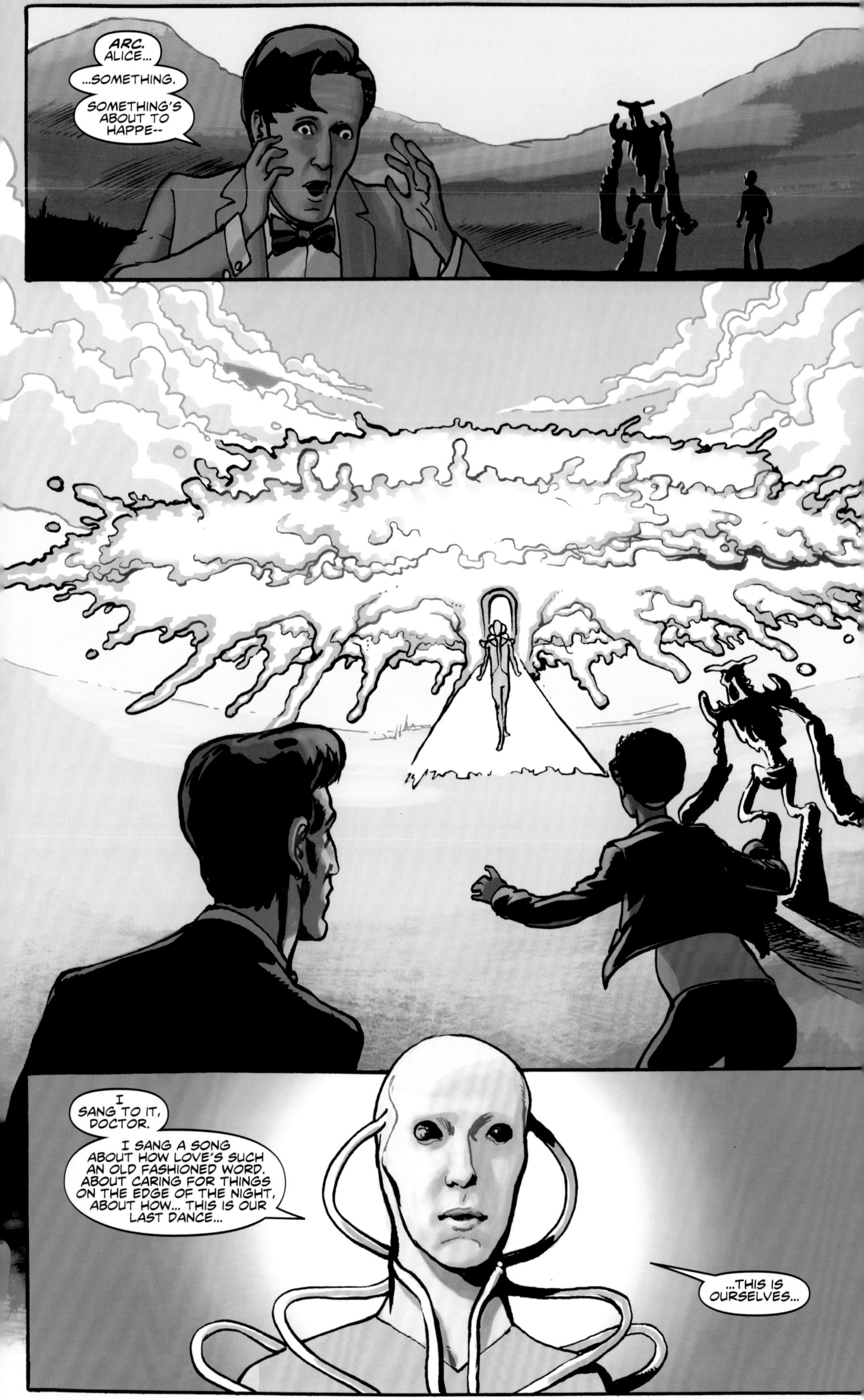
ARC. ALICE...
...SOMETHING.
SOMETHING'S ABOUT TO HAPPE--
I SANG TO IT, DOCTOR.
I SANG A SONG ABOUT HOW LOVE'S SUCH AN OLD FASHIONED WORD. ABOUT CARING FOR THINGS ON THE EDGE OF THE NIGHT, ABOUT HOW... THIS IS OUR LAST DANCE...
...THIS IS OURSELVES...

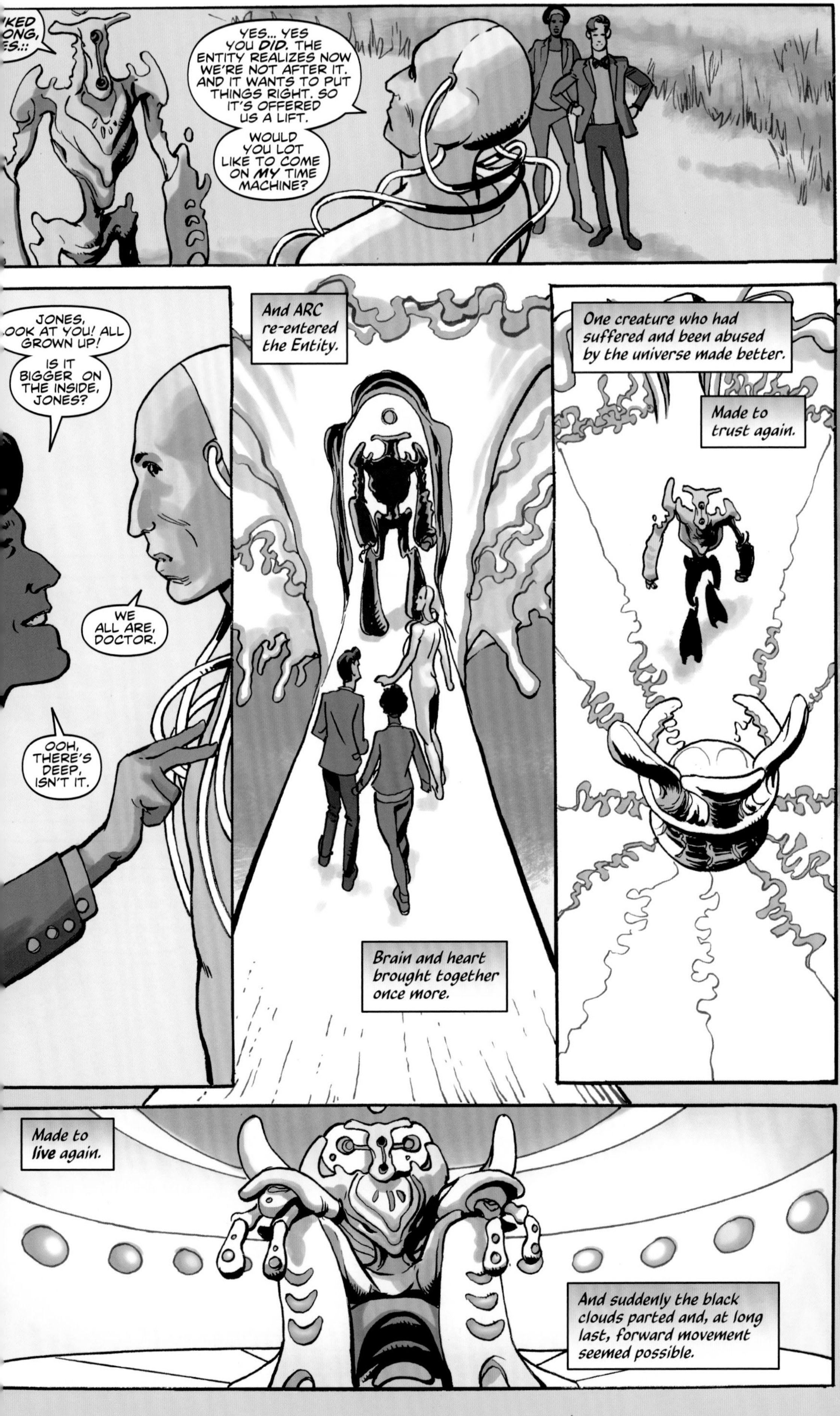

YES... YES YOU DID. THE ENTITY REALIZES NOW WE'RE NOT AFTER IT. AND IT WANTS TO PUT THINGS RIGHT. SO IT'S OFFERED US A LIFT.
WOULD YOU LOT LIKE TO COME ON MY TIME MACHINE?
IS IT BIGGER ON THE INSIDE, JONES?
WE ALL ARE, DOCTOR.
OOH, THERE'S DEEP, ISN'T IT.
And ARC re-entered the Entity.
Brain and heart brought together once more.
One creature who had suffered and been abused by the universe made better.
Made to trust again.
Made to live again.
And suddenly the black clouds parted and, at long last, forward movement seemed possible.

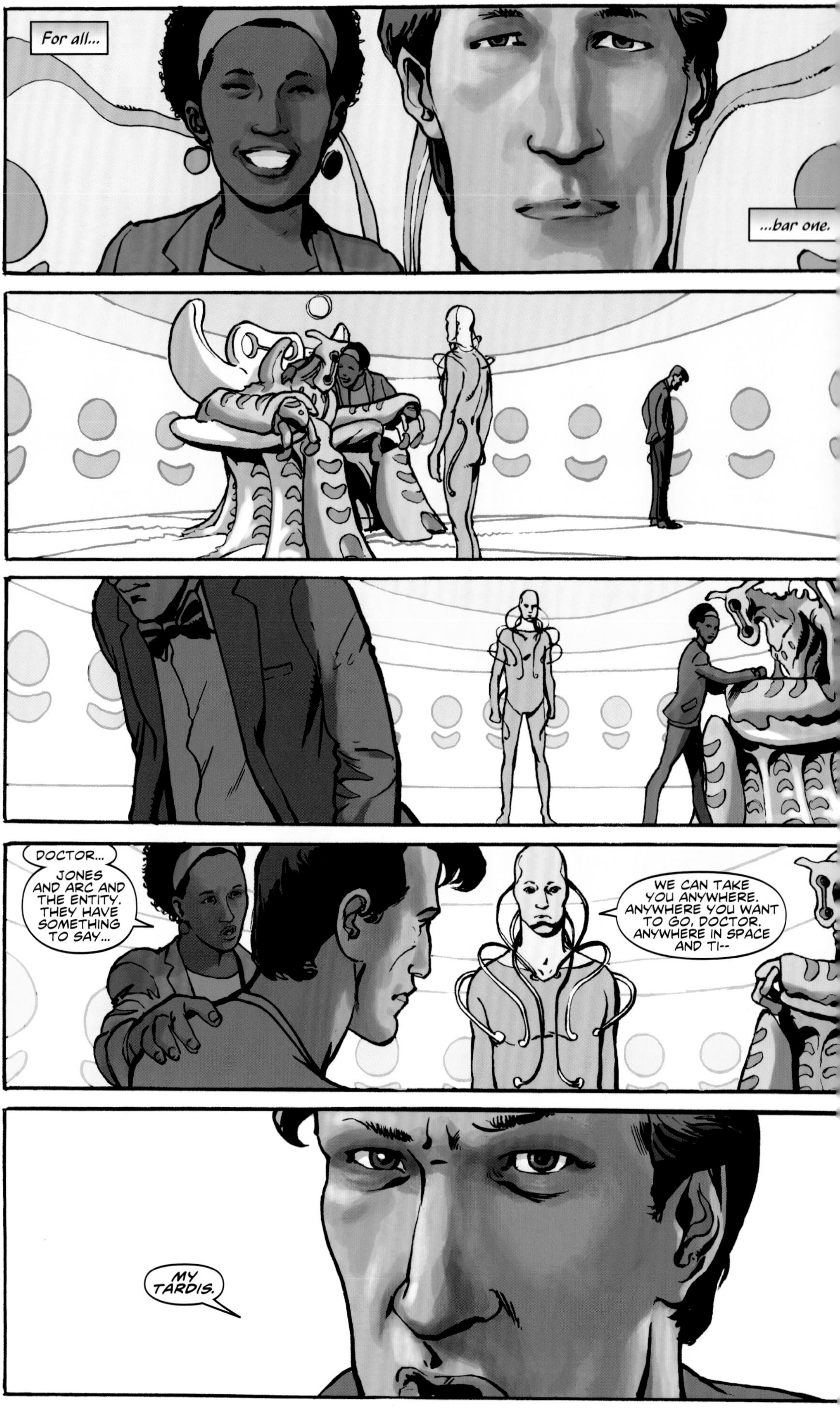
For all...
...bar one.
DOCTOR...
JONES AND ARC AND THE ENTITY. THEY HAVE SOMETHING TO SAY...
WE CAN TAKE YOU ANYWHERE. ANYWHERE YOU WANT TO GO, DOCTOR. ANYWHERE IN SPACE AND TI--
MY TARDIS.

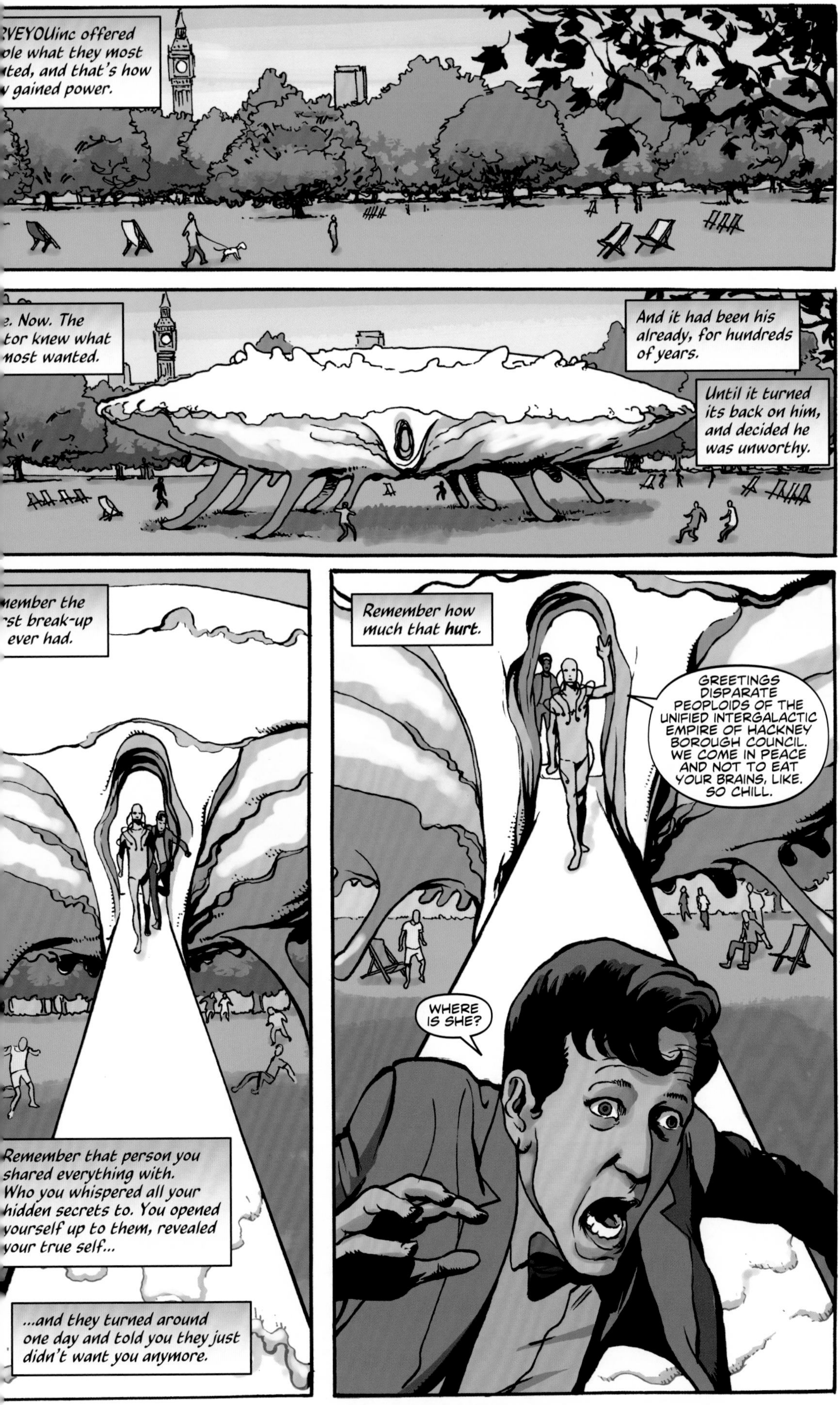

RVEYOUinc offered
ple what they most
nted, and that's how
y gained power.
. Now. The
tor knew what
most wanted.
And it had been his already, for hundreds of years.
Until it turned its back on him, and decided he was unworthy.
member the
rst break-up
ever had.
Remember that person you shared everything with. Who you whispered all your hidden secrets to. You opened yourself up to them, revealed your true self...
...and they turned around one day and told you they just didn't want you anymore.
Remember how much that hurt.
GREETINGS DISPARATE PEOPLOIDS OF THE UNIFIED INTERGALACTIC EMPIRE OF HACKNEY BOROUGH COUNCIL. WE COME IN PEACE AND NOT TO EAT YOUR BRAINS, LIKE. SO CHILL.
WHERE IS SHE?

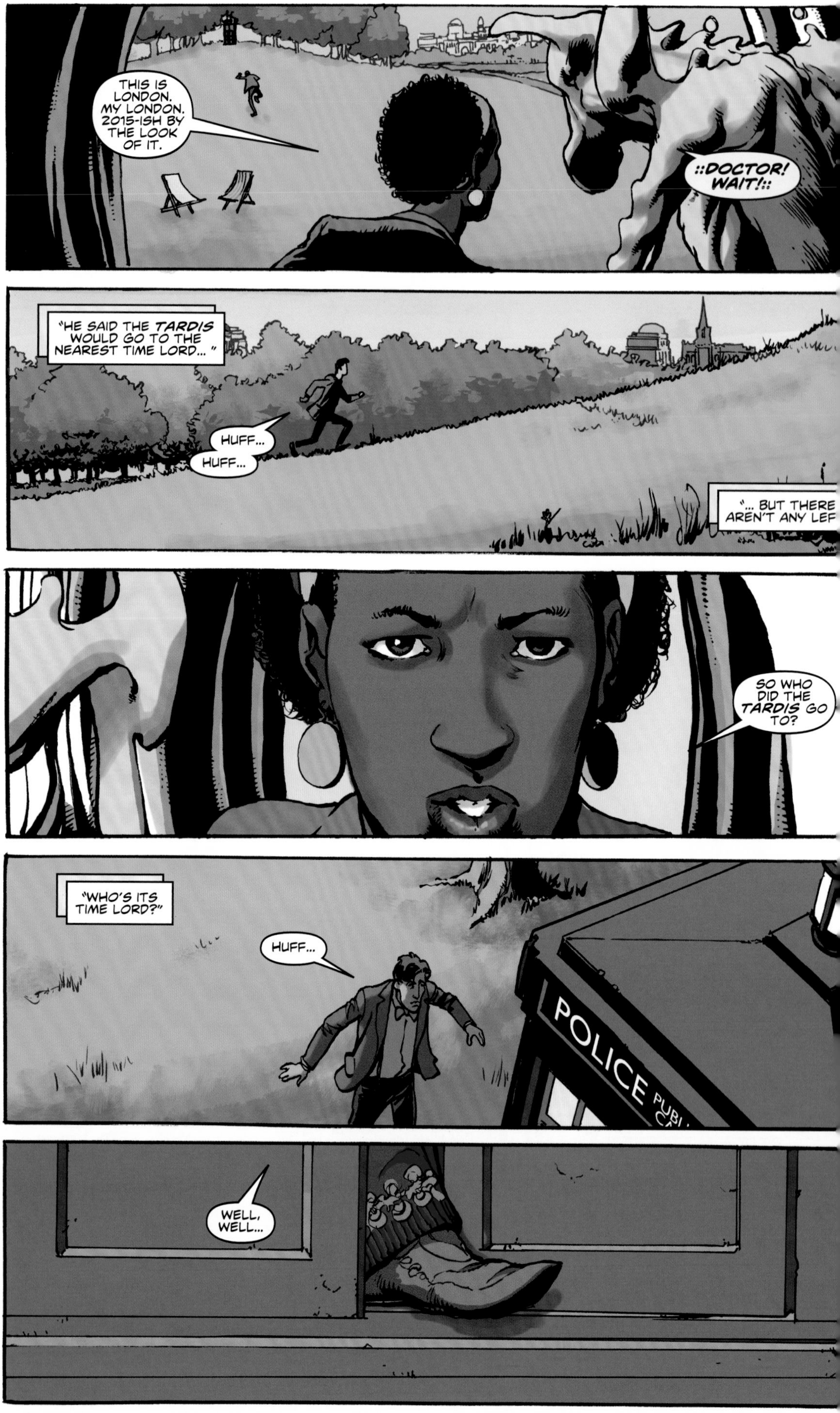
THIS IS LONDON. MY LONDON. 2015-ISH BY THE LOOK OF IT.
::DOCTOR! WAIT!::
"HE SAID THE TARDIS WOULD GO TO THE NEAREST TIME LORD..."
HUFF...
HUFF...
"... BUT THERE AREN'T ANY LEF
SO WHO DID THE TARDIS GO TO?
"WHO'S ITS TIME LORD?"
HUFF...
POLICE
WELL, WELL...

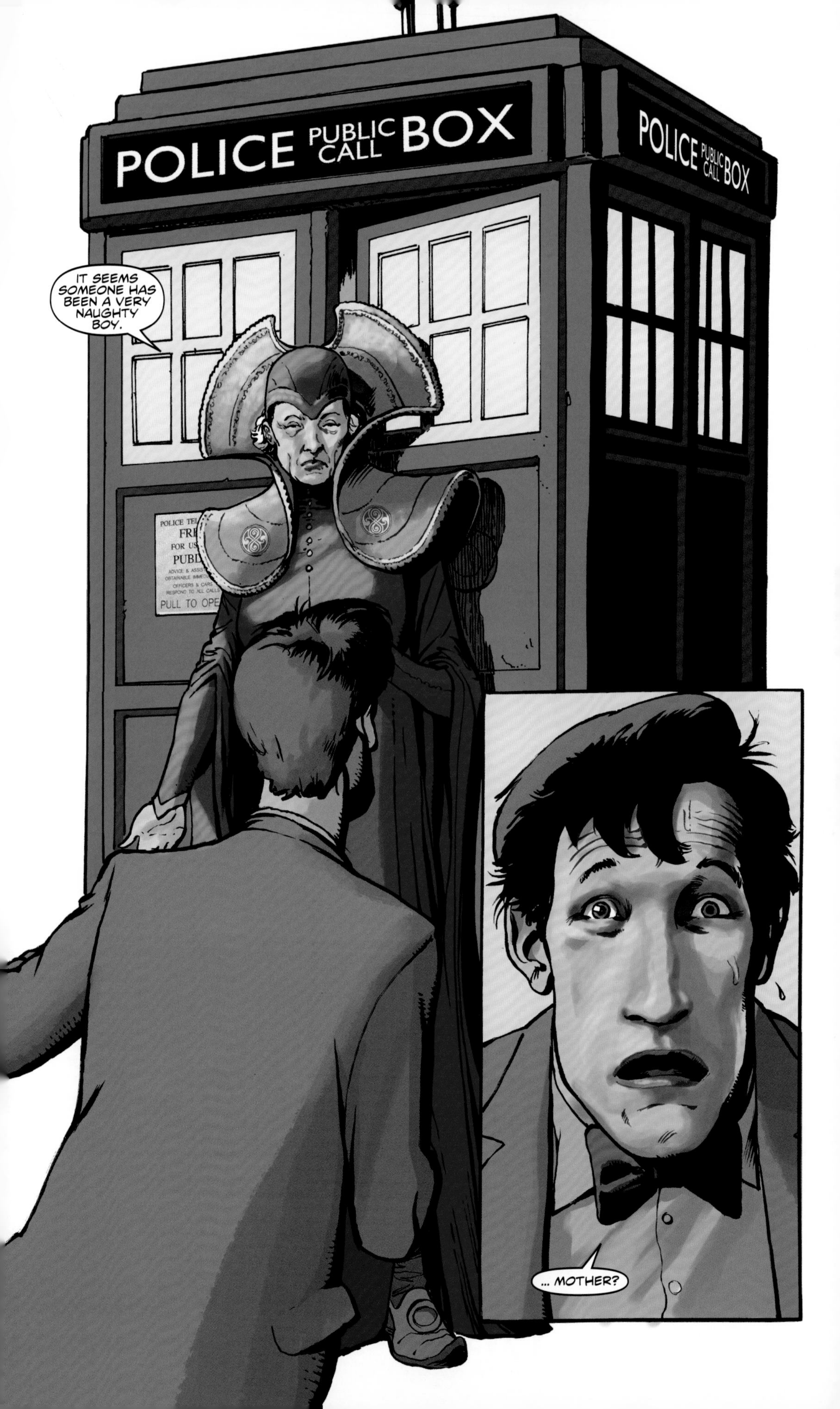
POLICE PUBLIC CALL BOX
POLICE PUBLIC CALL BOX
IT SEEMS SOMEONE HAS BEEN A VERY NAUGHTY BOY.
PULL TO OPE
... MOTHER?

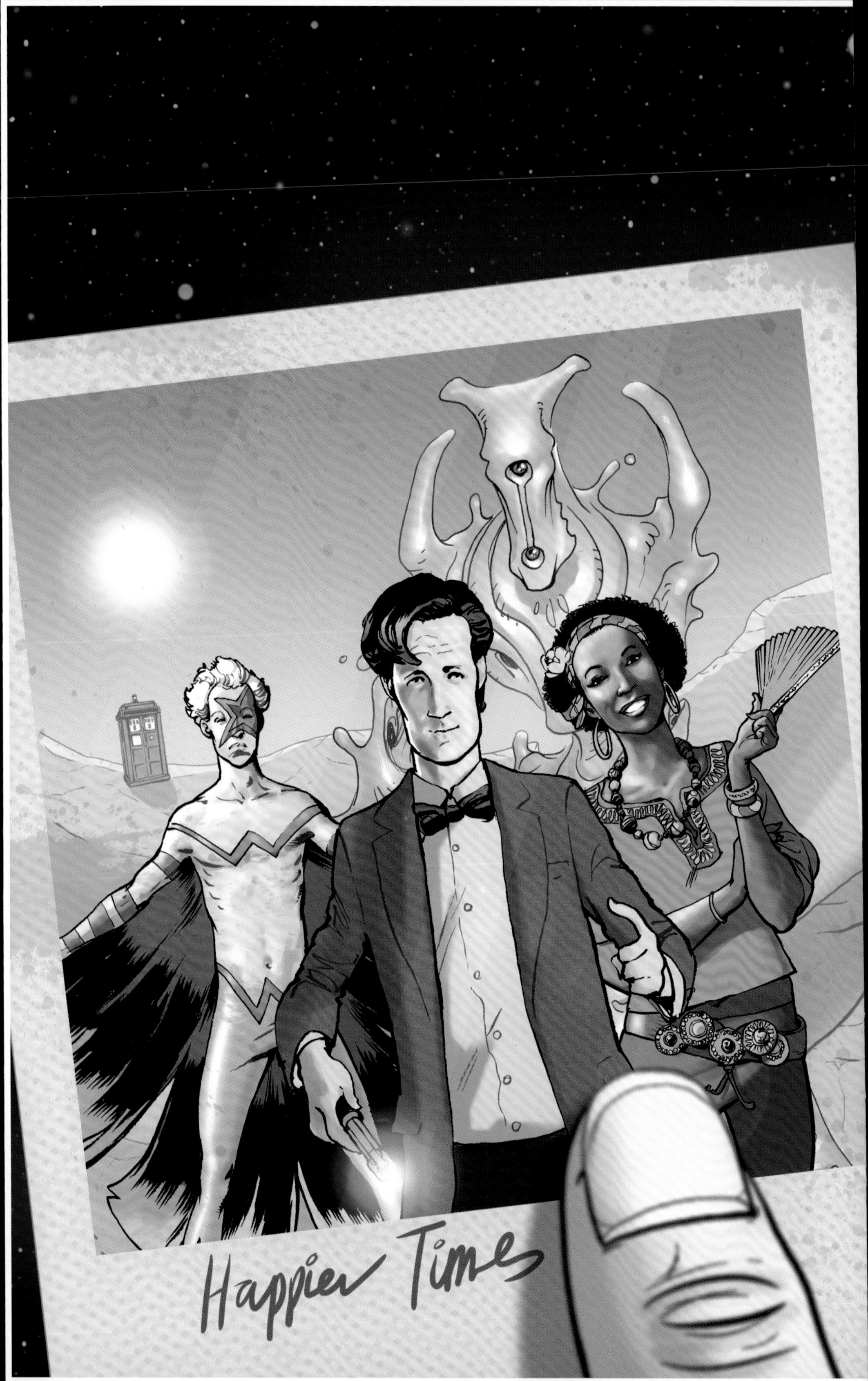
Happier Times

CHAPTER 15

Cover A: Simon Fraser / Boo Cook

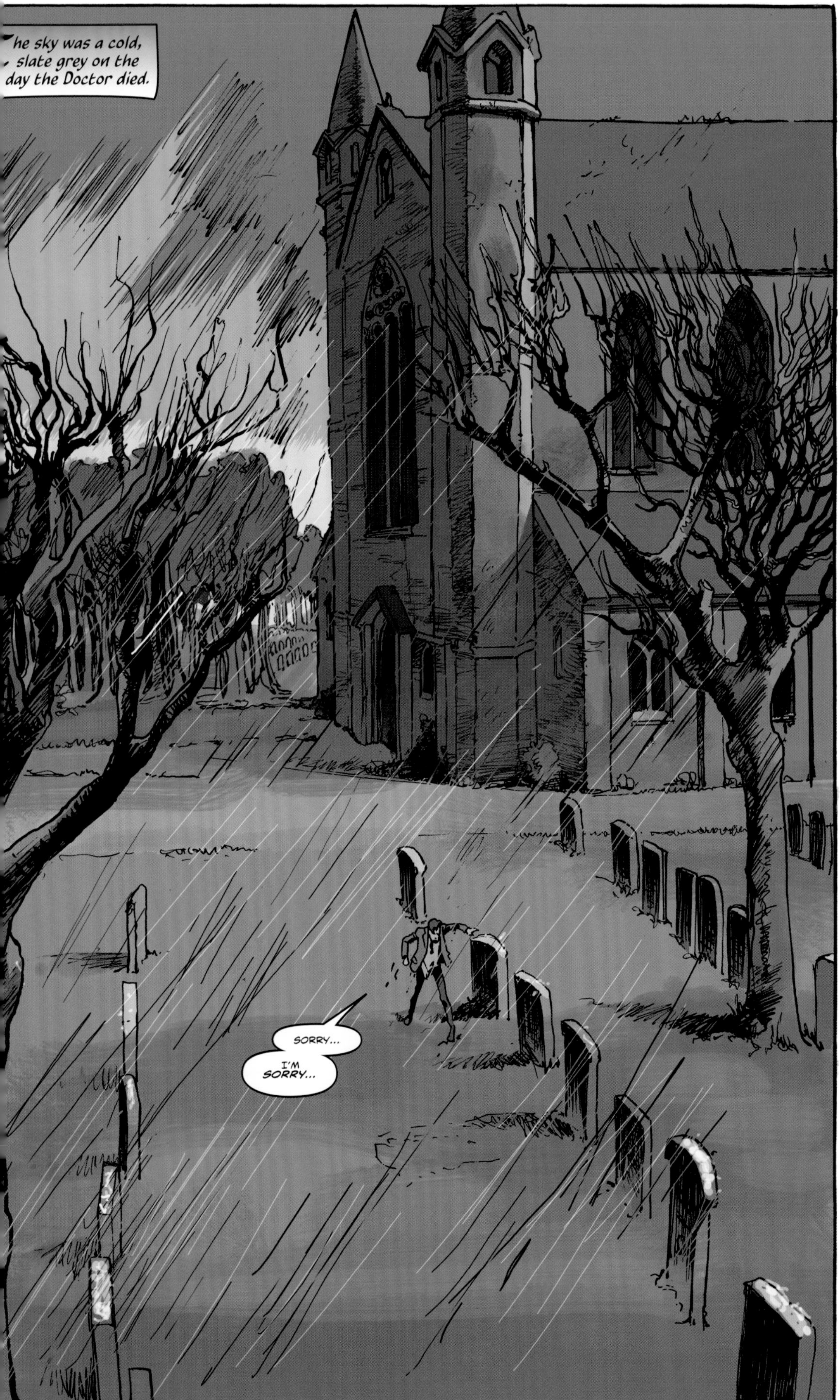
The sky was a cold, slate grey on the day the Doctor died.
SORRY...
I'M SORRY...

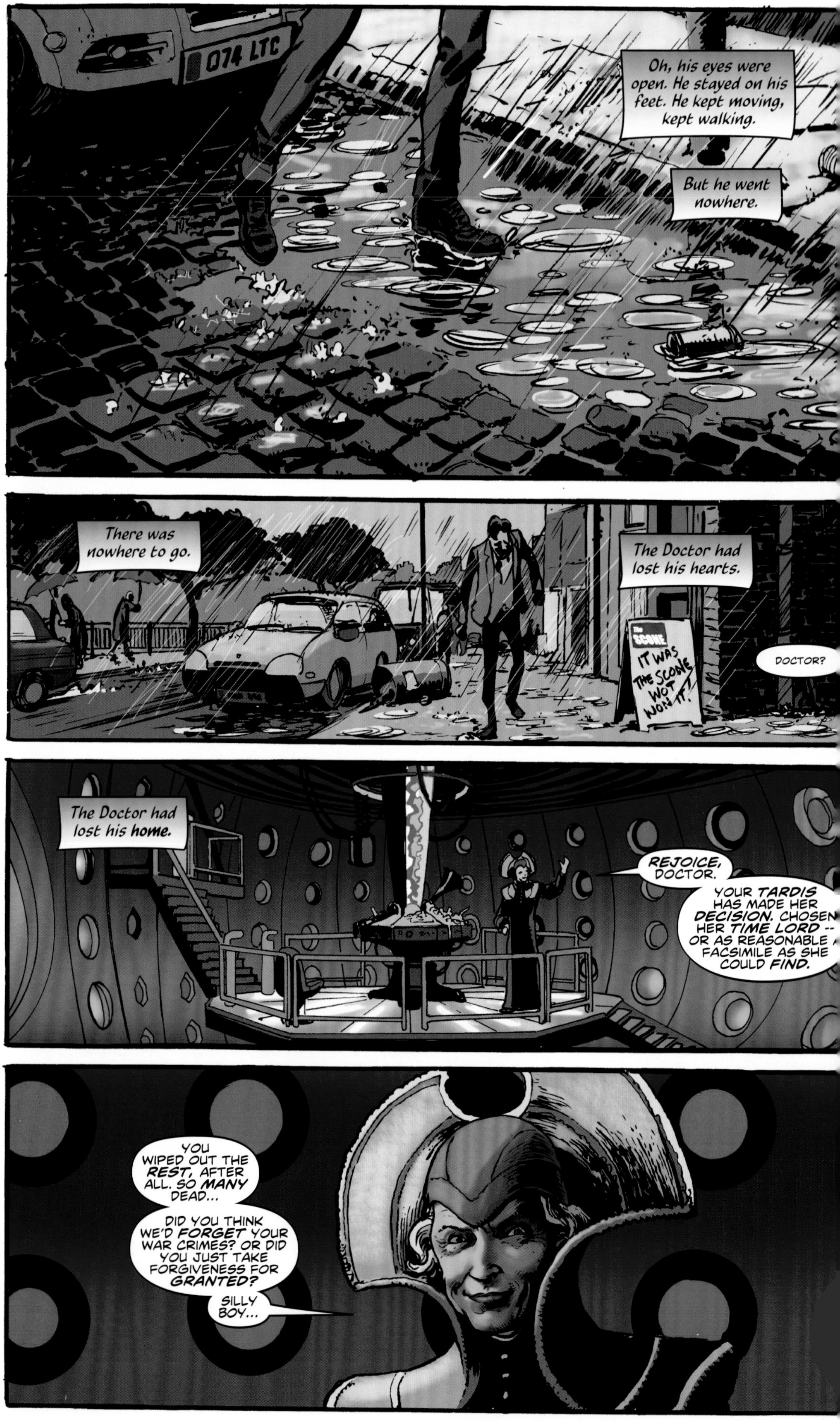
O74 LTC
Oh, his eyes were open. He stayed on his feet. He kept moving, kept walking.
But he went nowhere.
There was nowhere to go.
The Doctor had lost his hearts.
THE SCONE
IT WAS THE SCONE WOT WON IT!
DOCTOR?
The Doctor had lost his **home.**
REJOICE, DOCTOR.
YOUR ***TARDIS*** HAS MADE HER ***DECISION.*** CHOSEN HER ***TIME LORD*** -- OR AS REASONABLE A FACSIMILE AS SHE COULD ***FIND.***
YOU WIPED OUT THE ***REST,*** AFTER ALL. SO ***MANY*** DEAD...
DID YOU THINK WE'D ***FORGET*** YOUR WAR CRIMES? OR DID YOU JUST TAKE FORGIVENESS FOR ***GRANTED?***
SILLY BOY...

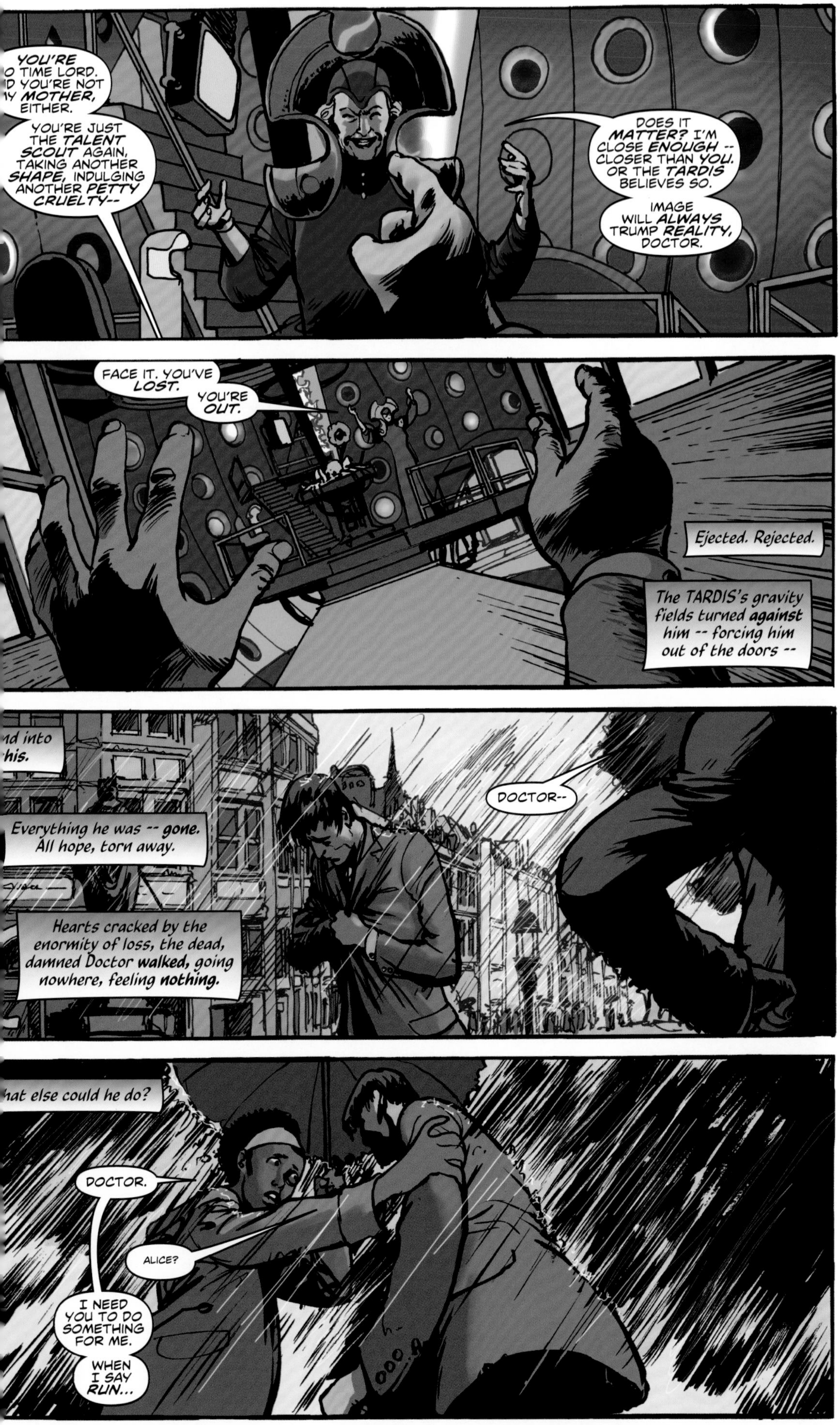
YOU'RE
O TIME LORD.
D YOU'RE NOT
Y MOTHER,
EITHER.
YOU'RE JUST THE TALENT SCOUT AGAIN, TAKING ANOTHER SHAPE, INDULGING ANOTHER PETTY CRUELTY--
DOES IT MATTER? I'M CLOSE ENOUGH -- CLOSER THAN YOU. OR THE TARDIS BELIEVES SO.
IMAGE WILL ALWAYS TRUMP REALITY, DOCTOR.
FACE IT. YOU'VE LOST.
YOU'RE OUT.
Ejected. Rejected.
The TARDIS's gravity fields turned against him -- forcing him out of the doors --
nd into
his.
DOCTOR--
Everything he was -- gone. All hope, torn away.
Hearts cracked by the enormity of loss, the dead, damned Doctor walked, going nowhere, feeling nothing.
hat else could he do?
DOCTOR.
ALICE?
I NEED YOU TO DO SOMETHING FOR ME.
WHEN I SAY RUN...

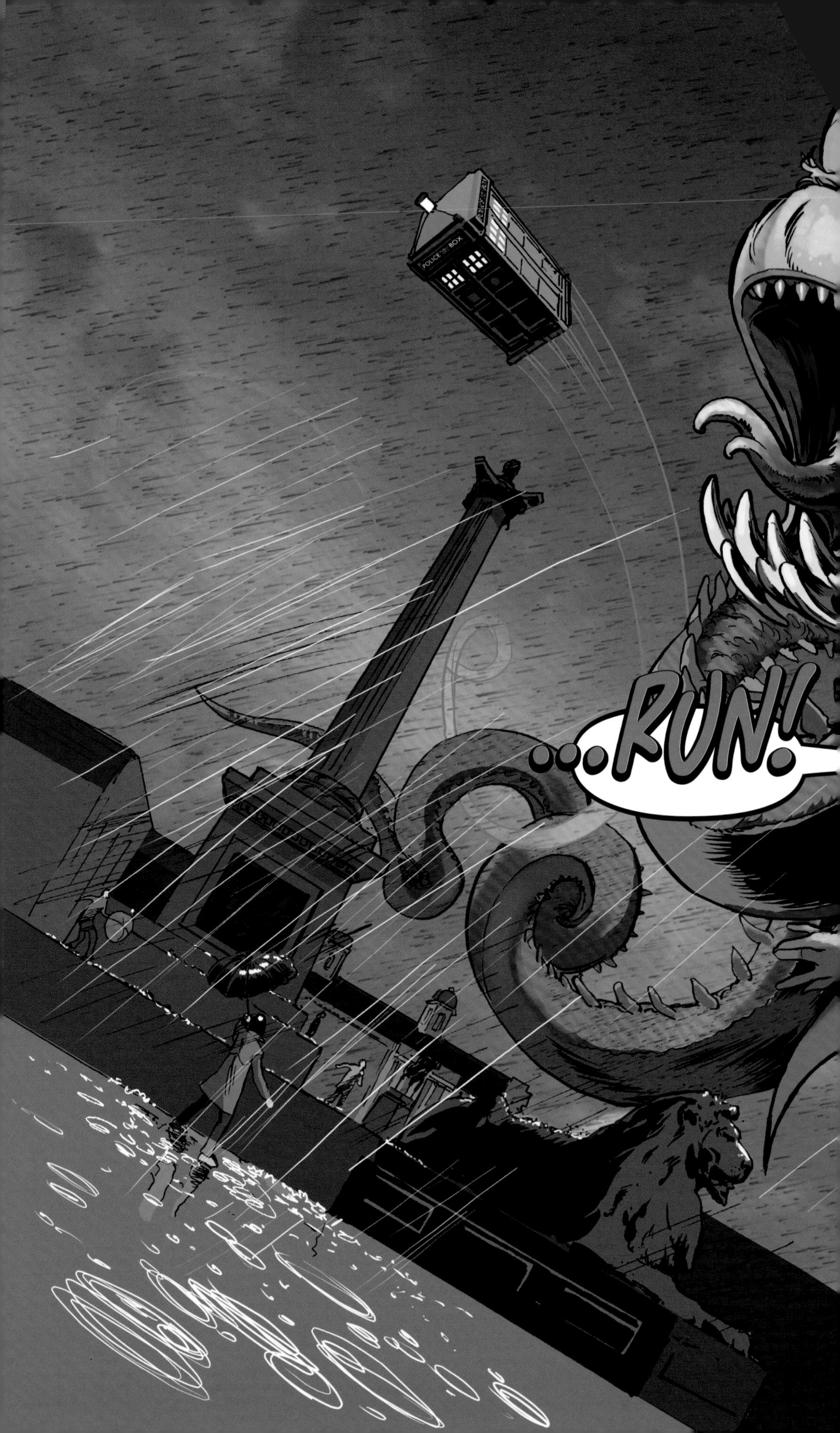

POLICE BOX
...RUN!

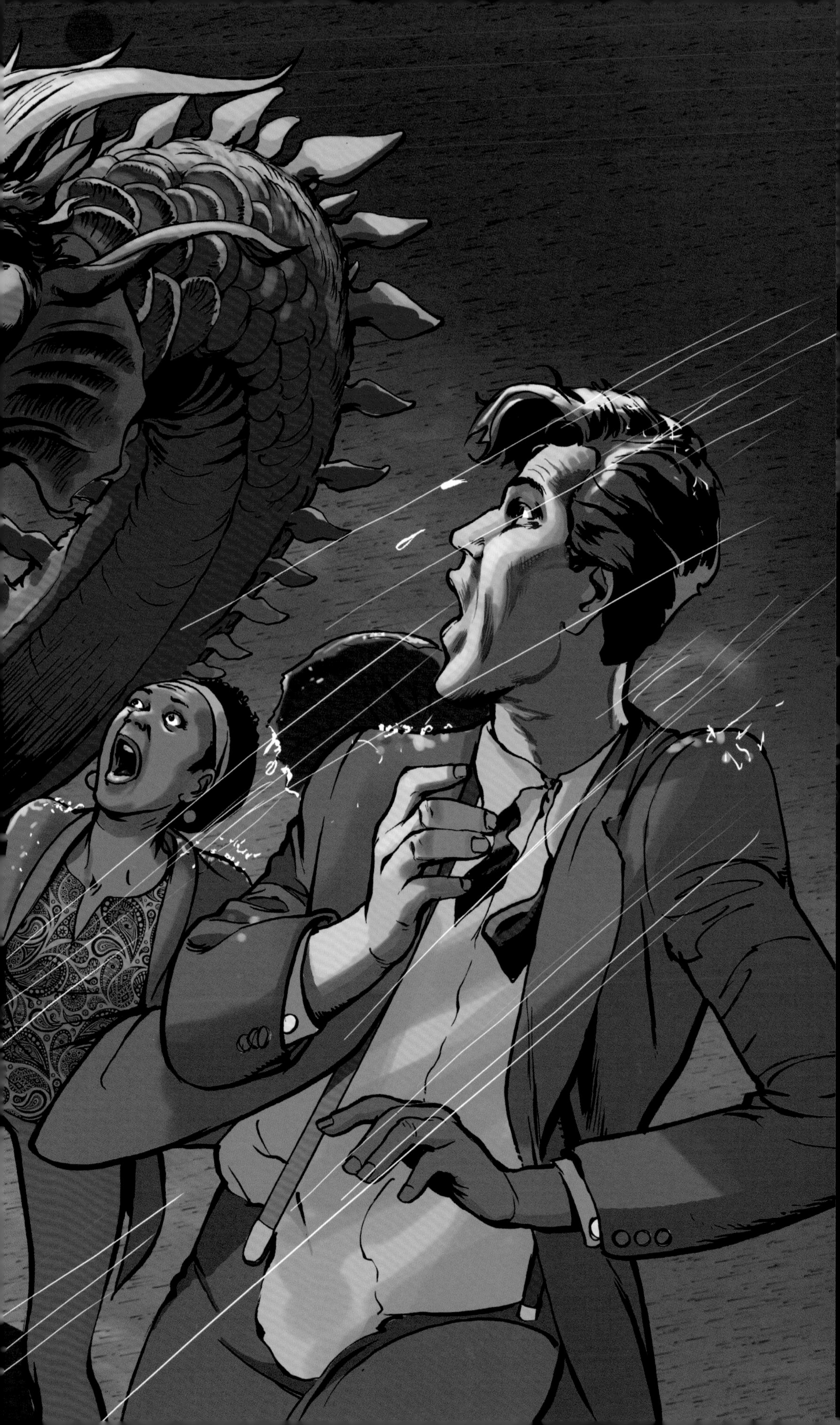

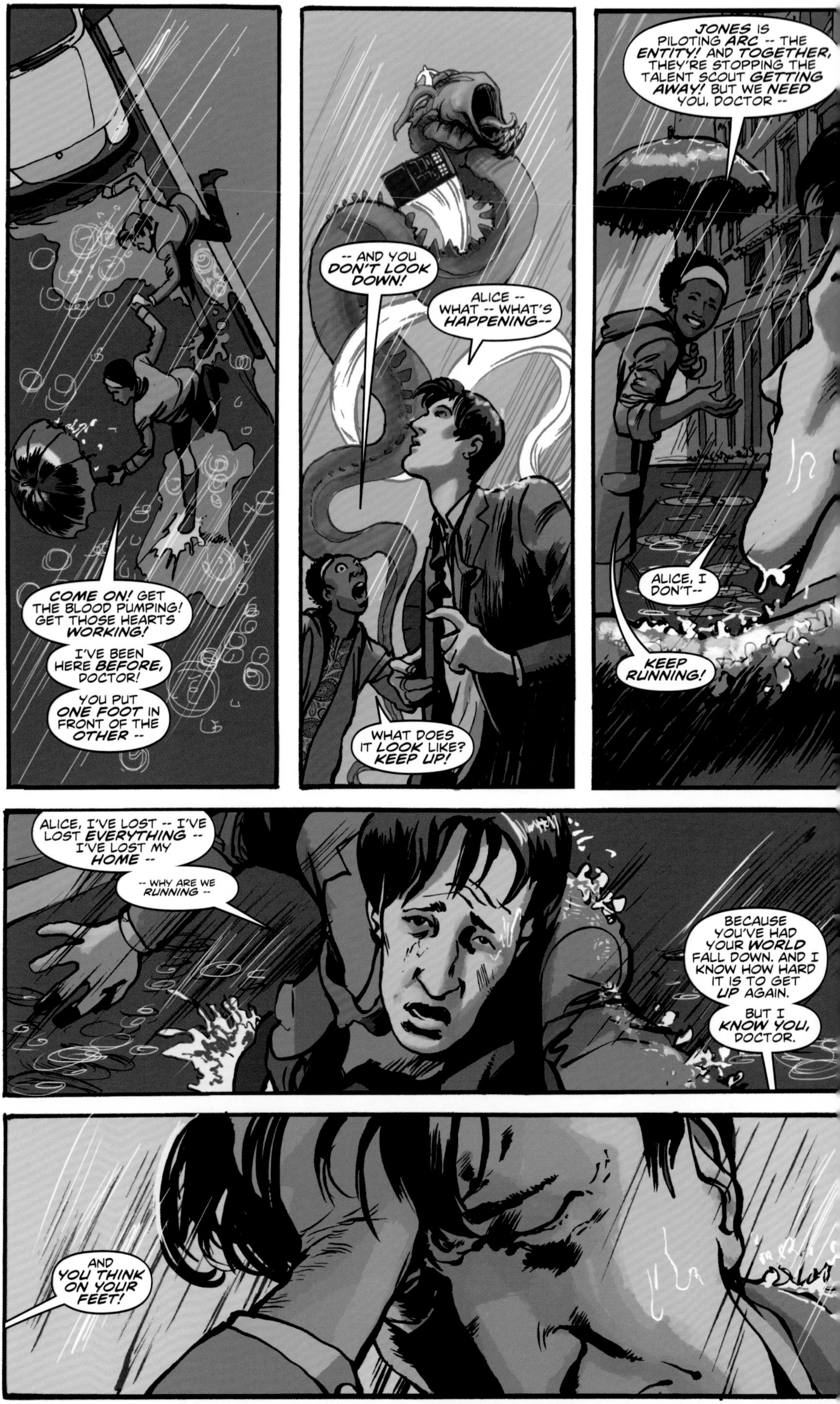
COME ON! GET THE BLOOD PUMPING! GET THOSE HEARTS WORKING!
I'VE BEEN HERE BEFORE, DOCTOR!
YOU PUT ONE FOOT IN FRONT OF THE OTHER --
-- AND YOU DON'T LOOK DOWN!
ALICE -- WHAT -- WHAT'S HAPPENING--
WHAT DOES IT LOOK LIKE? KEEP UP!
JONES IS PILOTING ARC -- THE ENTITY! AND TOGETHER, THEY'RE STOPPING THE TALENT SCOUT GETTING AWAY! BUT WE NEED YOU, DOCTOR --
ALICE, I DON'T--
KEEP RUNNING!
ALICE, I'VE LOST -- I'VE LOST EVERYTHING -- I'VE LOST MY HOME --
-- WHY ARE WE RUNNING --
BECAUSE YOU'VE HAD YOUR WORLD FALL DOWN. AND I KNOW HOW HARD IT IS TO GET UP AGAIN.
BUT I KNOW YOU, DOCTOR.
AND YOU THINK ON YOUR FEET!

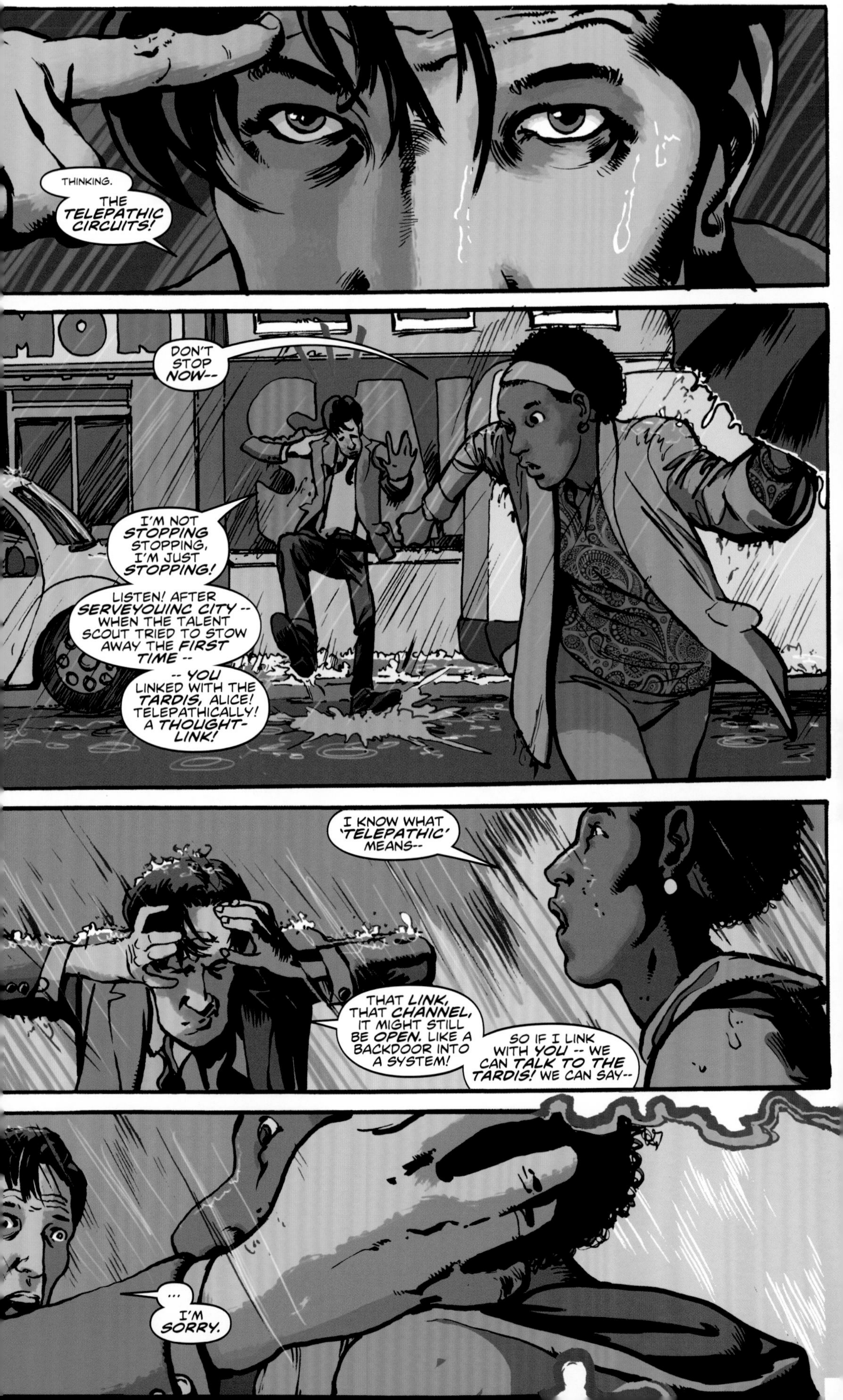
THINKING.
THE TELEPATHIC CIRCUITS!
DON'T STOP NOW--
I'M NOT STOPPING STOPPING, I'M JUST STOPPING!
LISTEN! AFTER SERVEYOUINC CITY -- WHEN THE TALENT SCOUT TRIED TO STOW AWAY THE FIRST TIME --
-- YOU LINKED WITH THE TARDIS, ALICE! TELEPATHICALLY! A THOUGHT-LINK!
I KNOW WHAT 'TELEPATHIC' MEANS--
THAT LINK, THAT CHANNEL, IT MIGHT STILL BE OPEN. LIKE A BACKDOOR INTO A SYSTEM!
SO IF I LINK WITH YOU -- WE CAN TALK TO THE TARDIS! WE CAN SAY--
...
I'M SORRY.

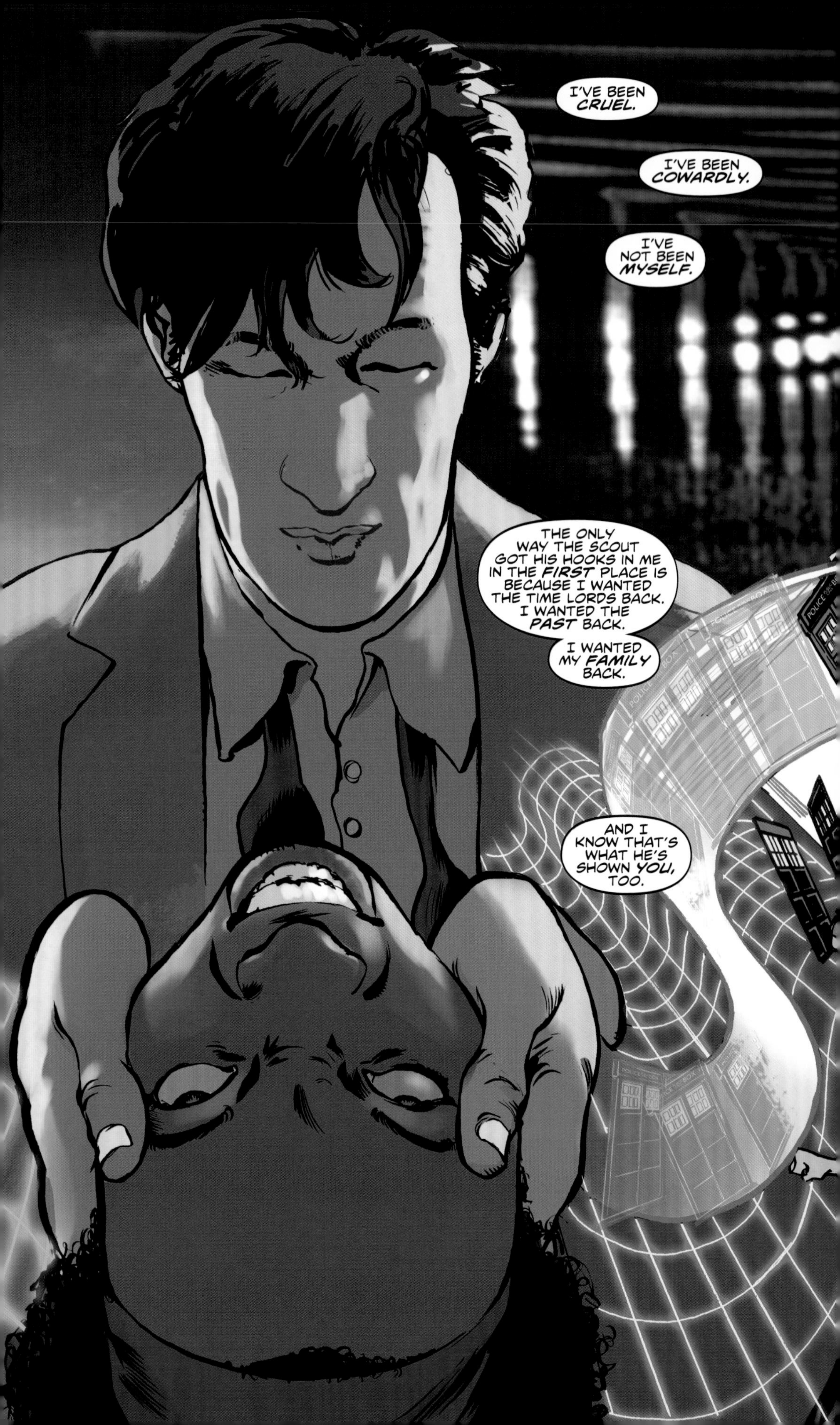
I'VE BEEN CRUEL.
I'VE BEEN COWARDLY.
I'VE NOT BEEN MYSELF.
THE ONLY WAY THE SCOUT GOT HIS HOOKS IN ME IN THE FIRST PLACE IS BECAUSE I WANTED THE TIME LORDS BACK. I WANTED THE PAST BACK.
I WANTED MY FAMILY BACK.
AND I KNOW THAT'S WHAT HE'S SHOWN YOU, TOO.

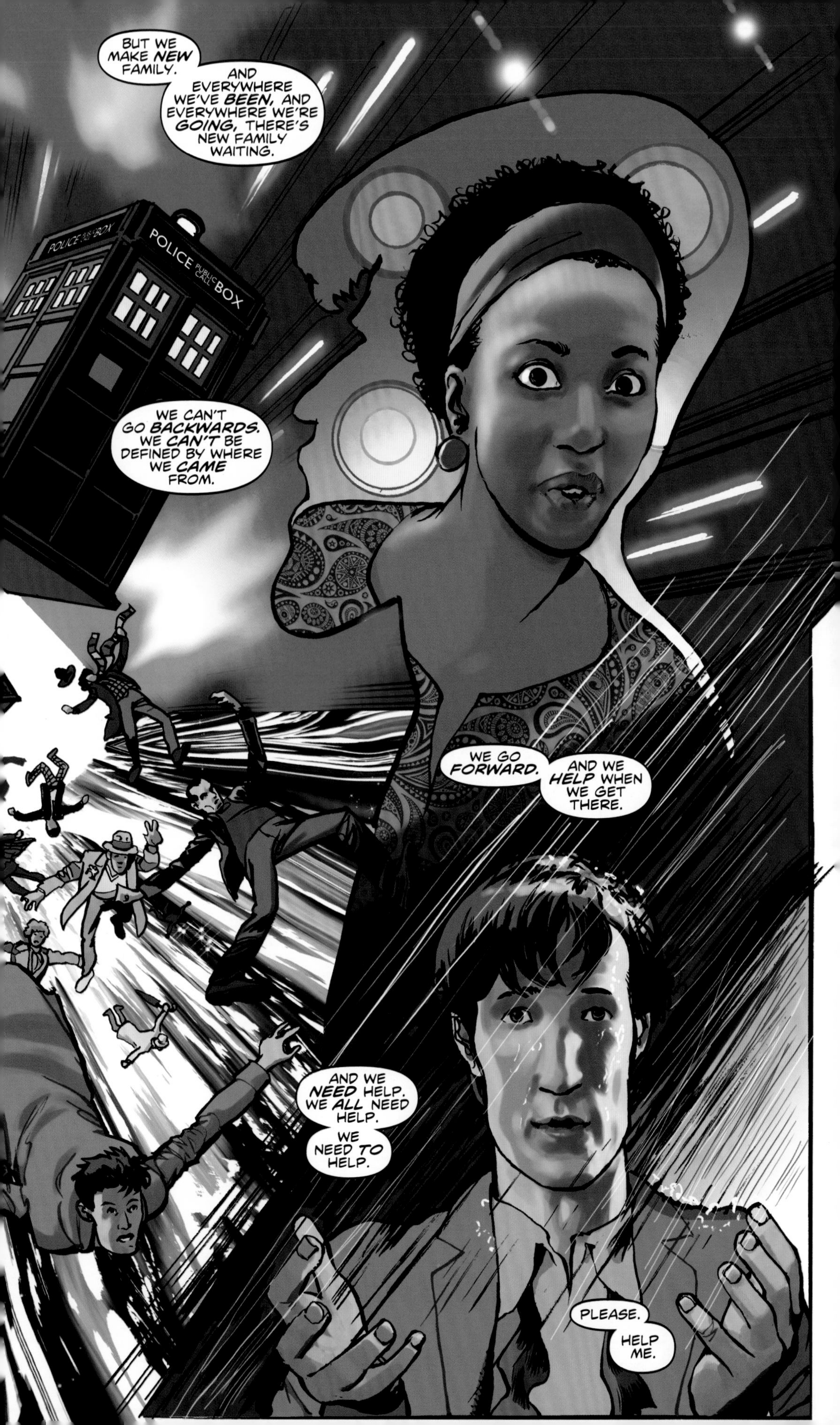
BUT WE MAKE NEW FAMILY.
AND EVERYWHERE WE'VE BEEN, AND EVERYWHERE WE'RE GOING, THERE'S NEW FAMILY WAITING.
POLICE PUBLIC CALL BOX
WE CAN'T GO BACKWARDS. WE CAN'T BE DEFINED BY WHERE WE CAME FROM.
WE GO FORWARD.
AND WE HELP WHEN WE GET THERE.
AND WE NEED HELP. WE ALL NEED HELP.
WE NEED TO HELP.
PLEASE.
HELP ME.

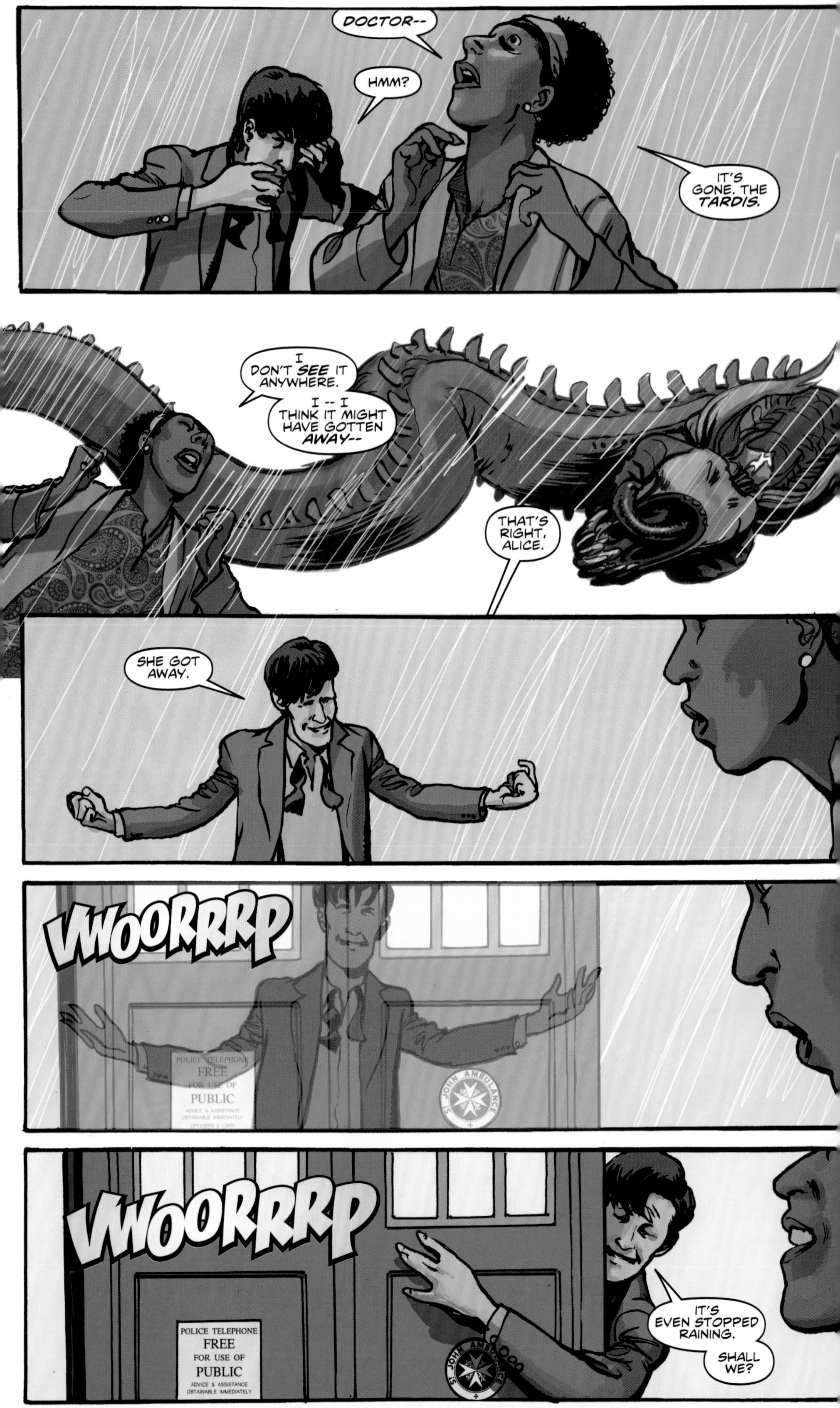
DOCTOR--
HMM?
IT'S GONE. THE TARDIS.
I DON'T SEE IT ANYWHERE.
I -- I THINK IT MIGHT HAVE GOTTEN AWAY--
THAT'S RIGHT, ALICE.
SHE GOT AWAY.
VWOORRRP
POLICE TELEPHONE FREE FOR USE OF PUBLIC
ST. JOHN AMBULANCE
VWOORRRP
POLICE TELEPHONE FREE FOR USE OF PUBLIC ADVICE & ASSISTANCE OBTAINABLE IMMEDIATELY
IT'S EVEN STOPPED RAINING.
SHALL WE?

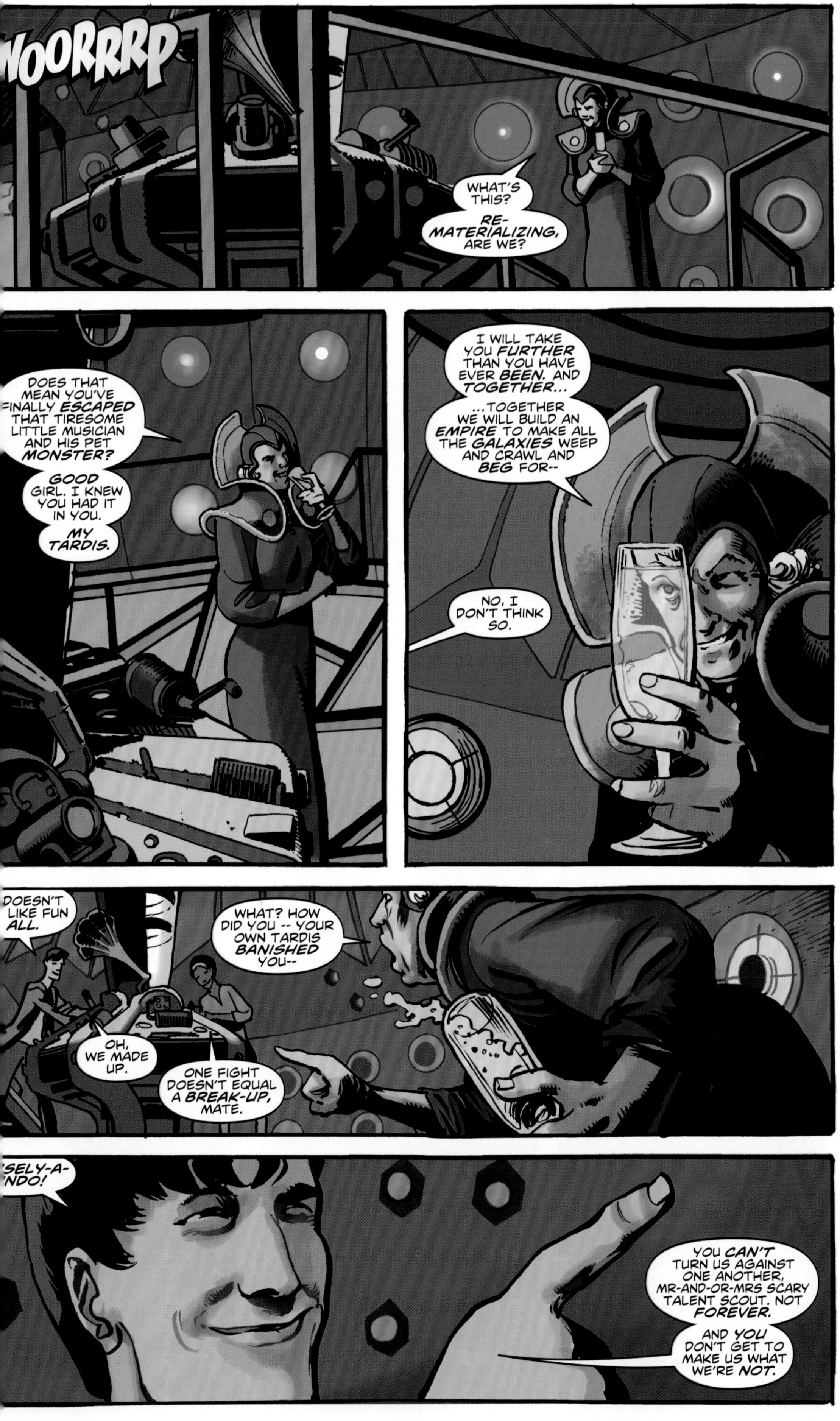
WOORRRP
WHAT'S THIS? RE-MATERIALIZING, ARE WE?
DOES THAT MEAN YOU'VE FINALLY ESCAPED THAT TIRESOME LITTLE MUSICIAN AND HIS PET MONSTER?
GOOD GIRL. I KNEW YOU HAD IT IN YOU.
MY TARDIS.
I WILL TAKE YOU FURTHER THAN YOU HAVE EVER BEEN. AND TOGETHER...
...TOGETHER WE WILL BUILD AN EMPIRE TO MAKE ALL THE GALAXIES WEEP AND CRAWL AND BEG FOR--
NO, I DON'T THINK SO.
DOESN'T LIKE FUN ALL.
WHAT? HOW DID YOU -- YOUR OWN TARDIS BANISHED YOU--
OH, WE MADE UP.
ONE FIGHT DOESN'T EQUAL A BREAK-UP, MATE.
SELY-A-NDO!
YOU CAN'T TURN US AGAINST ONE ANOTHER, MR-AND-OR-MRS SCARY TALENT SCOUT. NOT FOREVER.
AND YOU DON'T GET TO MAKE US WHAT WE'RE NOT.

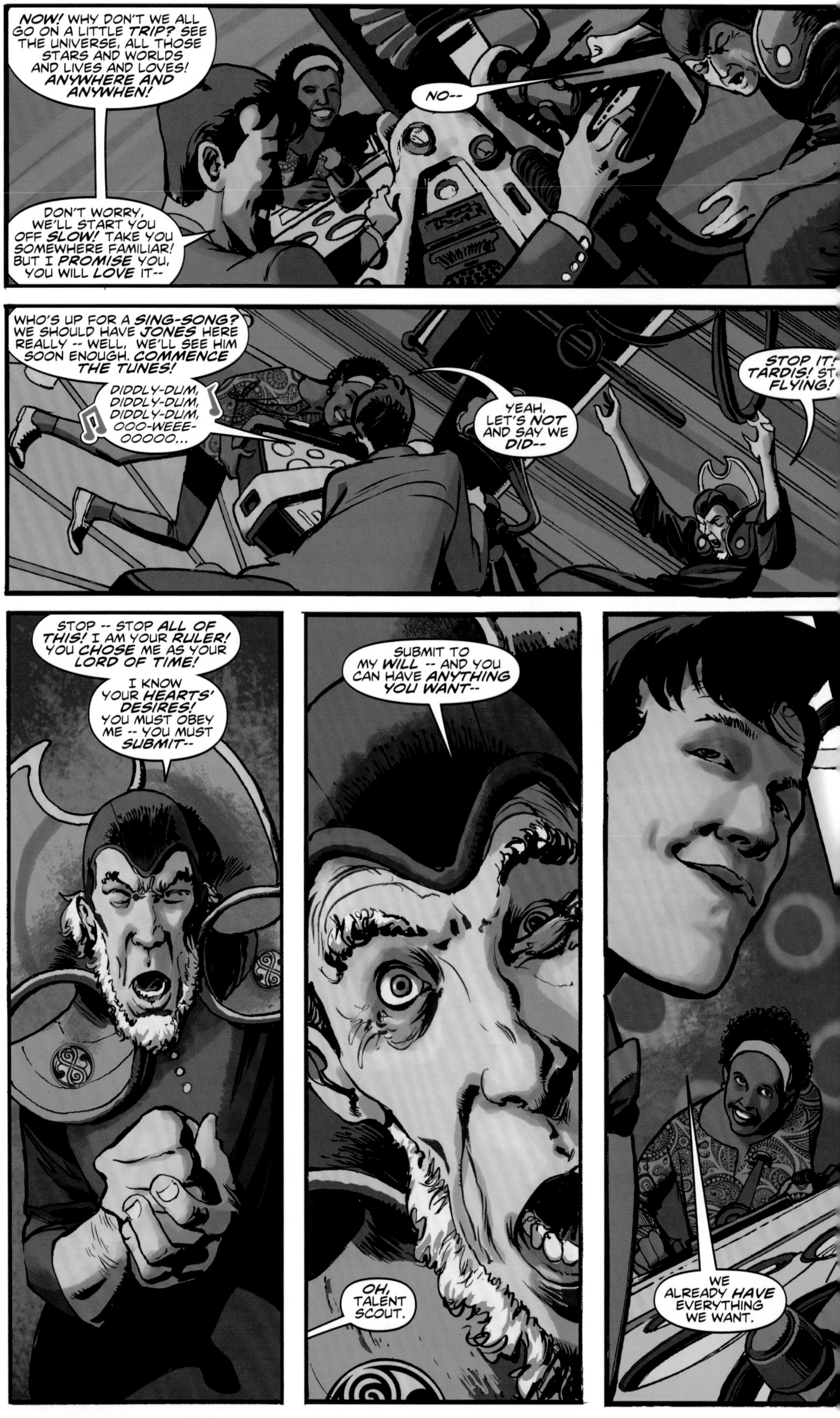
NOW! WHY DON'T WE ALL GO ON A LITTLE TRIP? SEE THE UNIVERSE, ALL THOSE STARS AND WORLDS AND LIVES AND LOVES! ANYWHERE AND ANYWHEN!
NO--
DON'T WORRY, WE'LL START YOU OFF SLOW! TAKE YOU SOMEWHERE FAMILIAR! BUT I PROMISE YOU, YOU WILL LOVE IT--
WHO'S UP FOR A SING-SONG? WE SHOULD HAVE JONES HERE REALLY -- WELL, WE'LL SEE HIM SOON ENOUGH. COMMENCE THE TUNES!
DIDDLY-DUM, DIDDLY-DUM, DIDDLY-DUM, OOO-WEEE-OOOOO...
YEAH, LET'S NOT AND SAY WE DID--
STOP IT! TARDIS! ST FLYING!
STOP -- STOP ALL OF THIS! I AM YOUR RULER! YOU CHOSE ME AS YOUR LORD OF TIME!
I KNOW YOUR HEARTS' DESIRES! YOU MUST OBEY ME -- YOU MUST SUBMIT--
SUBMIT TO MY WILL -- AND YOU CAN HAVE ANYTHING YOU WANT--
OH, TALENT SCOUT.
WE ALREADY HAVE EVERYTHING WE WANT.

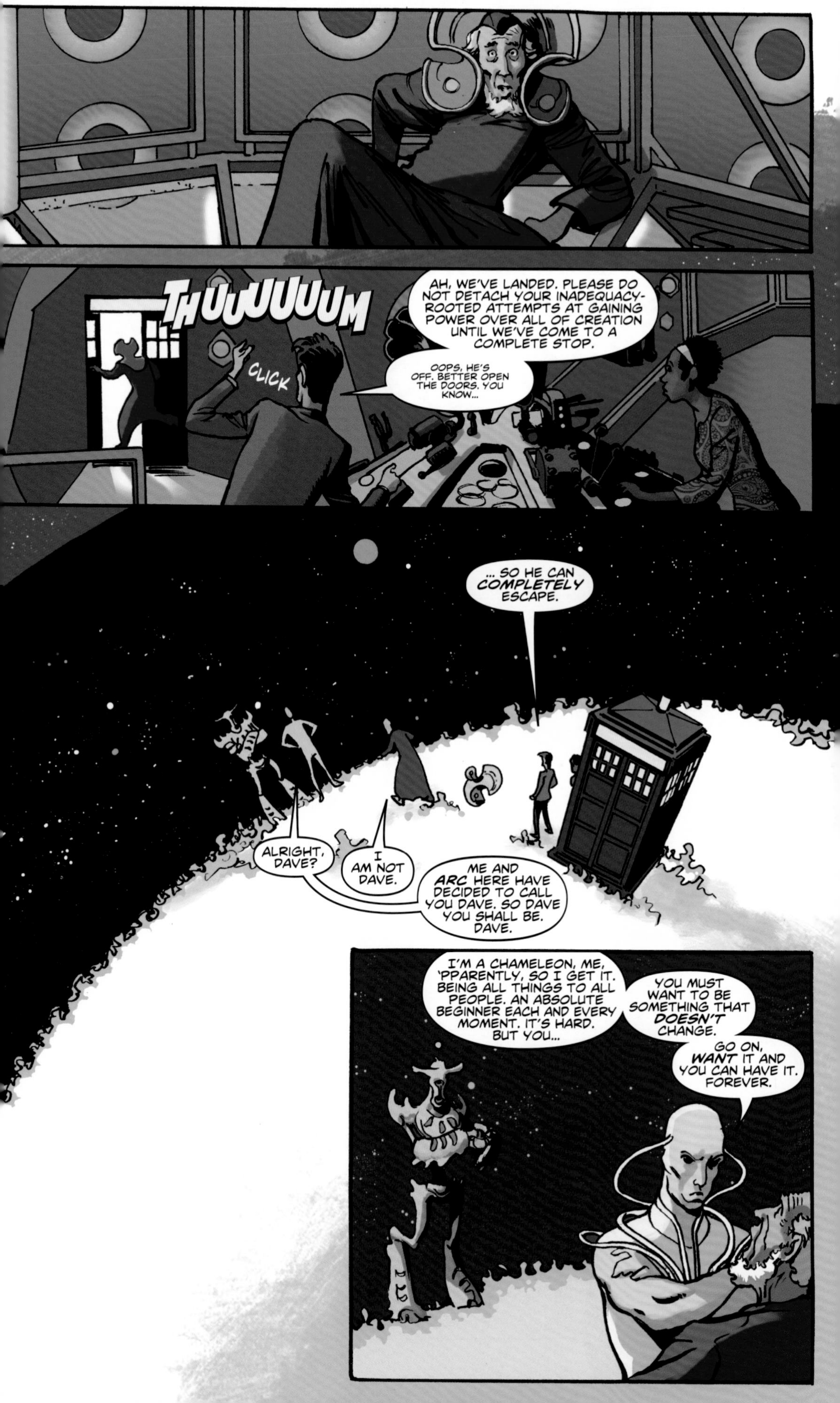
THUUUUUUM
AH, WE'VE LANDED. PLEASE DO NOT DETACH YOUR INADEQUACY-ROOTED ATTEMPTS AT GAINING POWER OVER ALL OF CREATION UNTIL WE'VE COME TO A COMPLETE STOP.
CLICK
OOPS, HE'S OFF. BETTER OPEN THE DOORS. YOU KNOW...
... SO HE CAN COMPLETELY ESCAPE.
ALRIGHT, DAVE?
I AM NOT DAVE.
ME AND ARC HERE HAVE DECIDED TO CALL YOU DAVE. SO DAVE YOU SHALL BE. DAVE.
I'M A CHAMELEON, ME, 'PPARENTLY, SO I GET IT. BEING ALL THINGS TO ALL PEOPLE. AN ABSOLUTE BEGINNER EACH AND EVERY MOMENT. IT'S HARD. BUT YOU...
YOU MUST WANT TO BE SOMETHING THAT DOESN'T CHANGE.
GO ON, WANT IT AND YOU CAN HAVE IT. FOREVER.

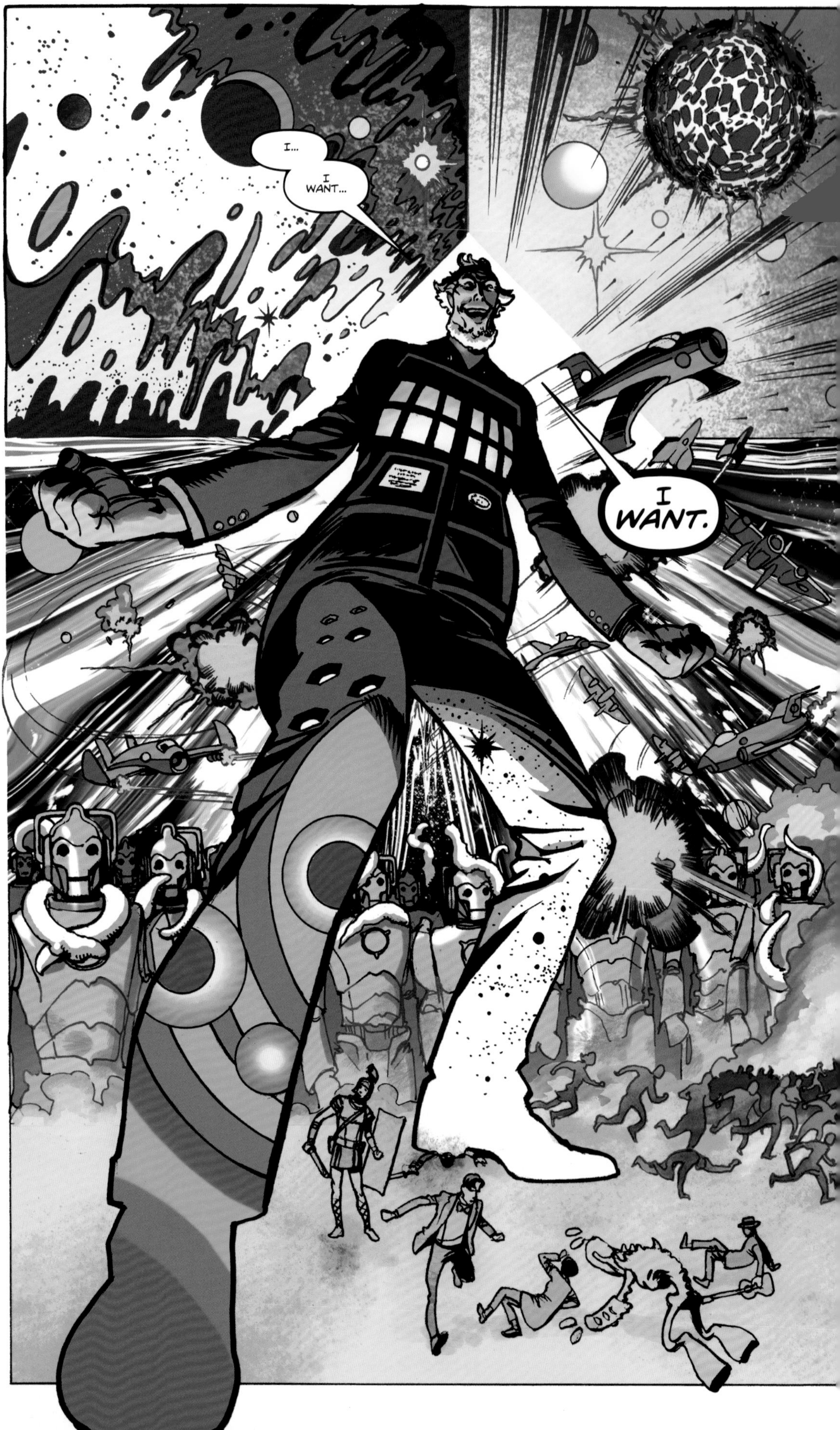
I...
I WANT...
I WANT.

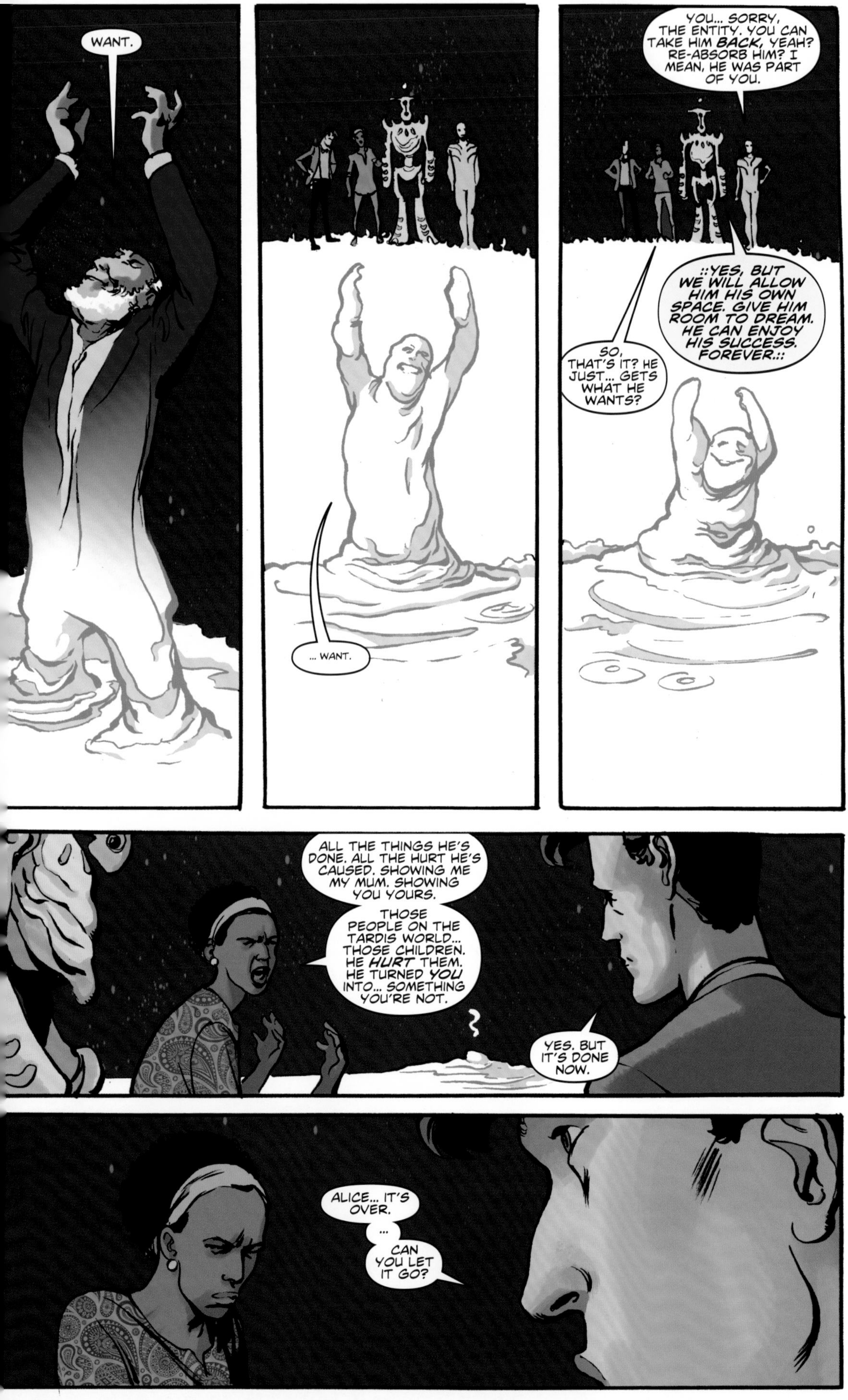
WANT.
... WANT.
YOU... SORRY, THE ENTITY. YOU CAN TAKE HIM BACK, YEAH? RE-ABSORB HIM? I MEAN, HE WAS PART OF YOU.
::YES, BUT WE WILL ALLOW HIM HIS OWN SPACE. GIVE HIM ROOM TO DREAM. HE CAN ENJOY HIS SUCCESS. FOREVER.::
SO, THAT'S IT? HE JUST... GETS WHAT HE WANTS?
ALL THE THINGS HE'S DONE. ALL THE HURT HE'S CAUSED. SHOWING ME MY MUM. SHOWING YOU YOURS.
THOSE PEOPLE ON THE TARDIS WORLD... THOSE CHILDREN. HE HURT THEM. HE TURNED YOU INTO... SOMETHING YOU'RE NOT.
YES. BUT IT'S DONE NOW.
ALICE... IT'S OVER.
...
CAN YOU LET IT GO?

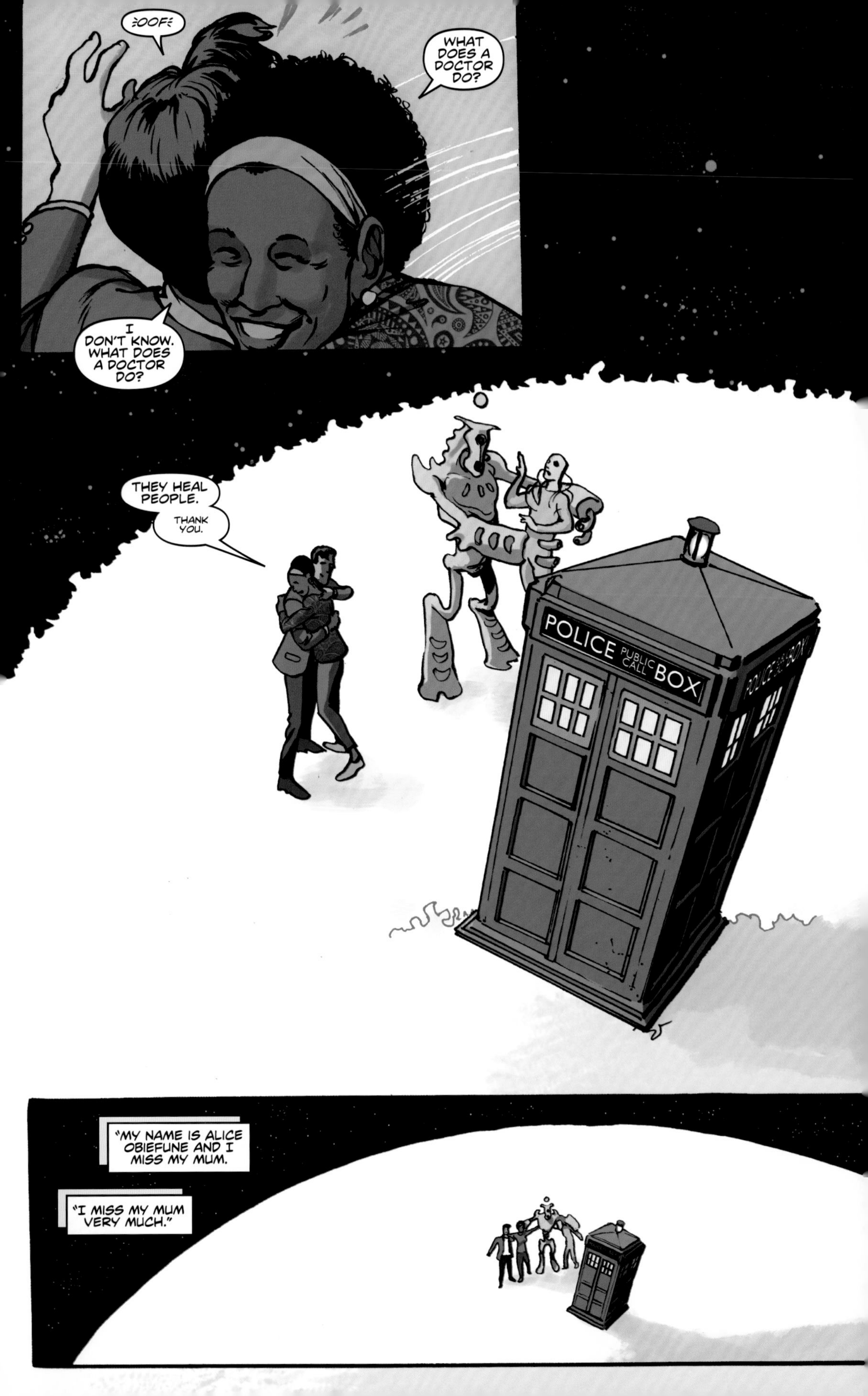
OOF
WHAT DOES A DOCTOR DO?
I DON'T KNOW. WHAT DOES A DOCTOR DO?
THEY HEAL PEOPLE.
THANK YOU.
POLICE PUBLIC CALL BOX
"MY NAME IS ALICE OBIEFUNE AND I MISS MY MUM.
"I MISS MY MUM VERY MUCH."

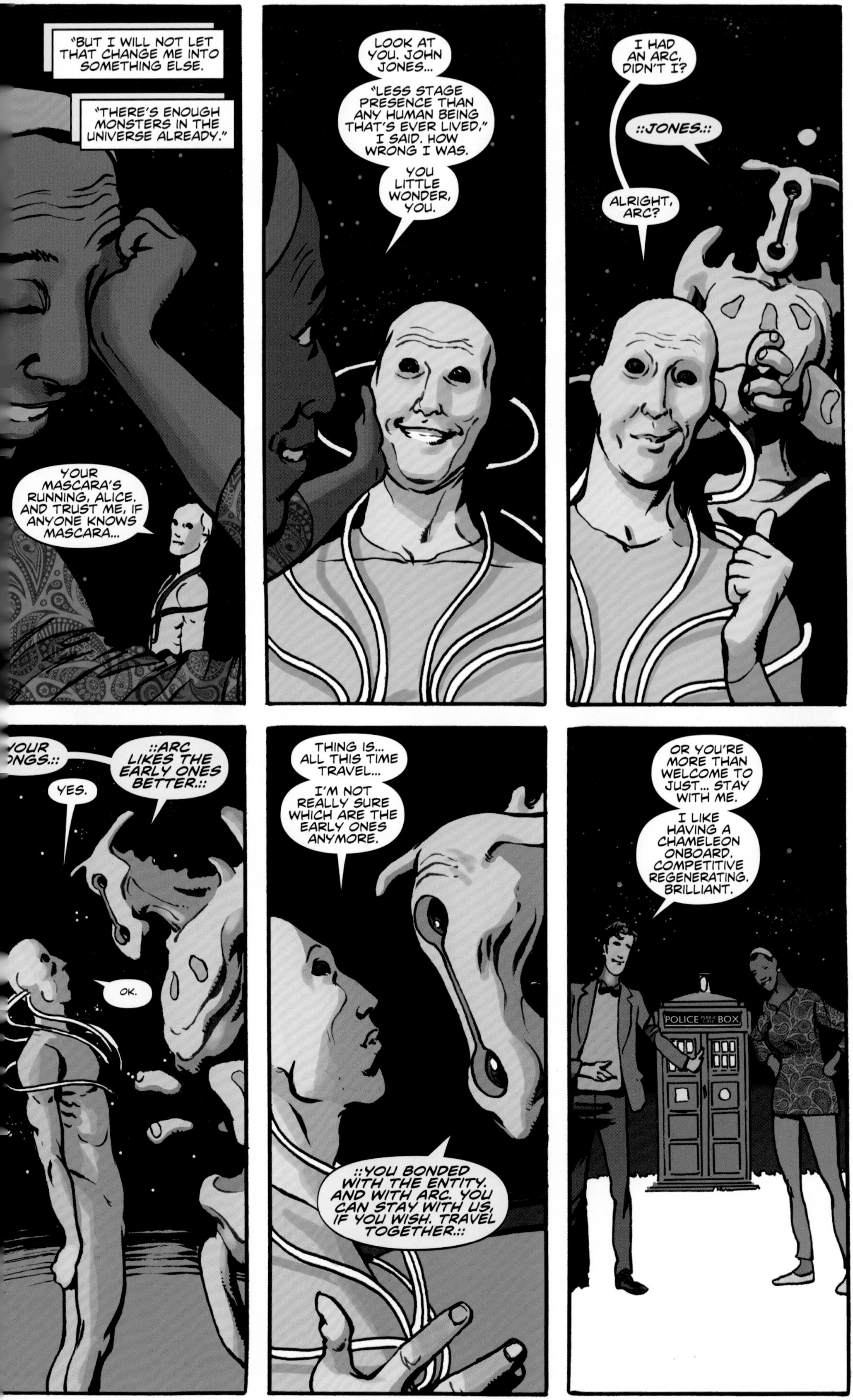
"BUT I WILL NOT LET THAT CHANGE ME INTO SOMETHING ELSE.
"THERE'S ENOUGH MONSTERS IN THE UNIVERSE ALREADY."
YOUR MASCARA'S RUNNING, ALICE. AND TRUST ME, IF ANYONE KNOWS MASCARA...
LOOK AT YOU. JOHN JONES...
"LESS STAGE PRESENCE THAN ANY HUMAN BEING THAT'S EVER LIVED," I SAID. HOW WRONG I WAS.
YOU LITTLE WONDER, YOU.
I HAD AN ARC, DIDN'T I?
::JONES.::
ALRIGHT, ARC?
::ARC LIKES THE EARLY ONES BETTER.::
YES.
OK.
THING IS... ALL THIS TIME TRAVEL...
I'M NOT REALLY SURE WHICH ARE THE EARLY ONES ANYMORE.
::YOU BONDED WITH THE ENTITY. AND WITH ARC. YOU CAN STAY WITH US, IF YOU WISH. TRAVEL TOGETHER.::
OR YOU'RE MORE THAN WELCOME TO JUST... STAY WITH ME.
I LIKE HAVING A CHAMELEON ONBOARD. COMPETITIVE REGENERATING. BRILLIANT.
POLICE BOX

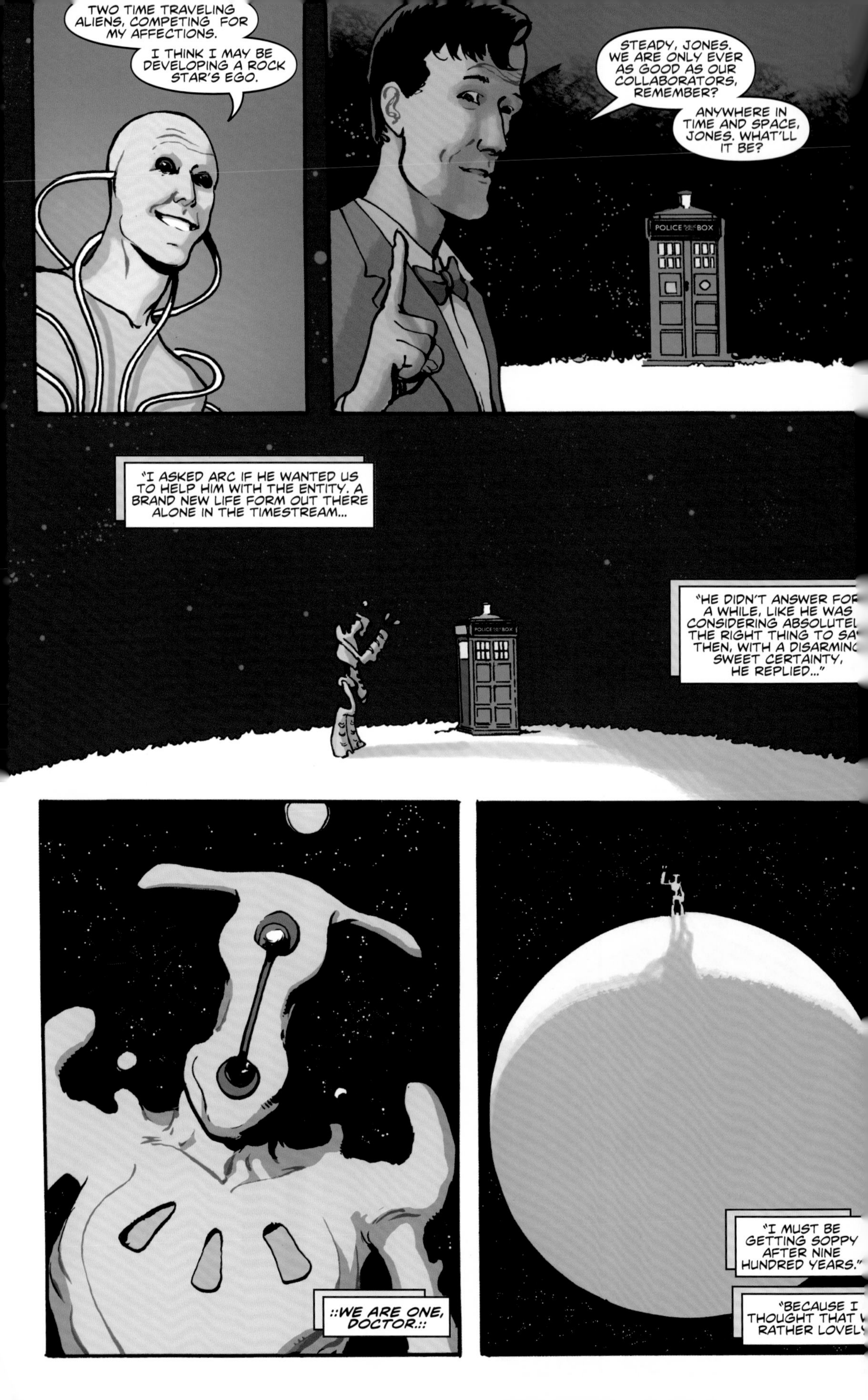
TWO TIME TRAVELING ALIENS, COMPETING FOR MY AFFECTIONS.
I THINK I MAY BE DEVELOPING A ROCK STAR'S EGO.
STEADY, JONES. WE ARE ONLY EVER AS GOOD AS OUR COLLABORATORS, REMEMBER?
ANYWHERE IN TIME AND SPACE, JONES. WHAT'LL IT BE?
POLICE BOX
"I ASKED ARC IF HE WANTED US TO HELP HIM WITH THE ENTITY. A BRAND NEW LIFE FORM OUT THERE ALONE IN THE TIMESTREAM...
"HE DIDN'T ANSWER FO
A WHILE, LIKE HE WAS
CONSIDERING ABSOLUTEL
THE RIGHT THING TO SA
THEN, WITH A DISARMIN
SWEET CERTAINTY,
HE REPLIED..."
::WE ARE ONE, DOCTOR.::
"I MUST BE GETTING SOPPY AFTER NINE HUNDRED YEARS."
"BECAUSE I
THOUGHT THAT
RATHER LOVEL

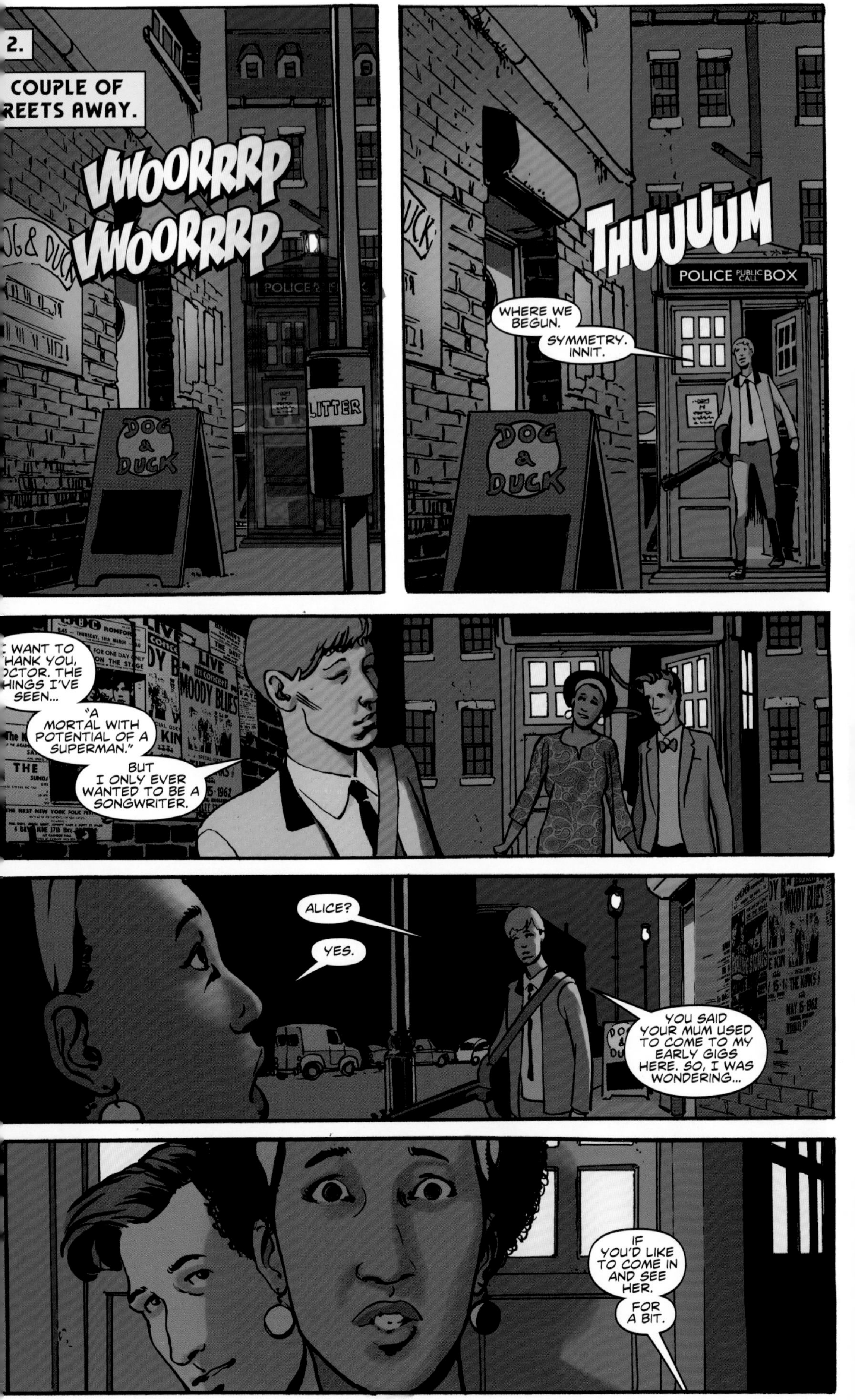
2.
COUPLE OF
REETS AWAY.
VWOORRRP VWOORRRP
DOG & DUCK
POLICE
LITTER
DOG & DUCK
THUUUUM
POLICE PUBLIC CALL BOX
WHERE WE BEGUN.
SYMMETRY. INNIT.
DOG & DUCK
I WANT TO THANK YOU, DOCTOR. THE THINGS I'VE SEEN...
"A MORTAL WITH POTENTIAL OF A SUPERMAN."
BUT I ONLY EVER WANTED TO BE A SONGWRITER.
MOODY BLUES
ALICE?
YES.
YOU SAID YOUR MUM USED TO COME TO MY EARLY GIGS HERE. SO, I WAS WONDERING...
MOODY BLUES
IF YOU'D LIKE TO COME IN AND SEE HER.
FOR A BIT.

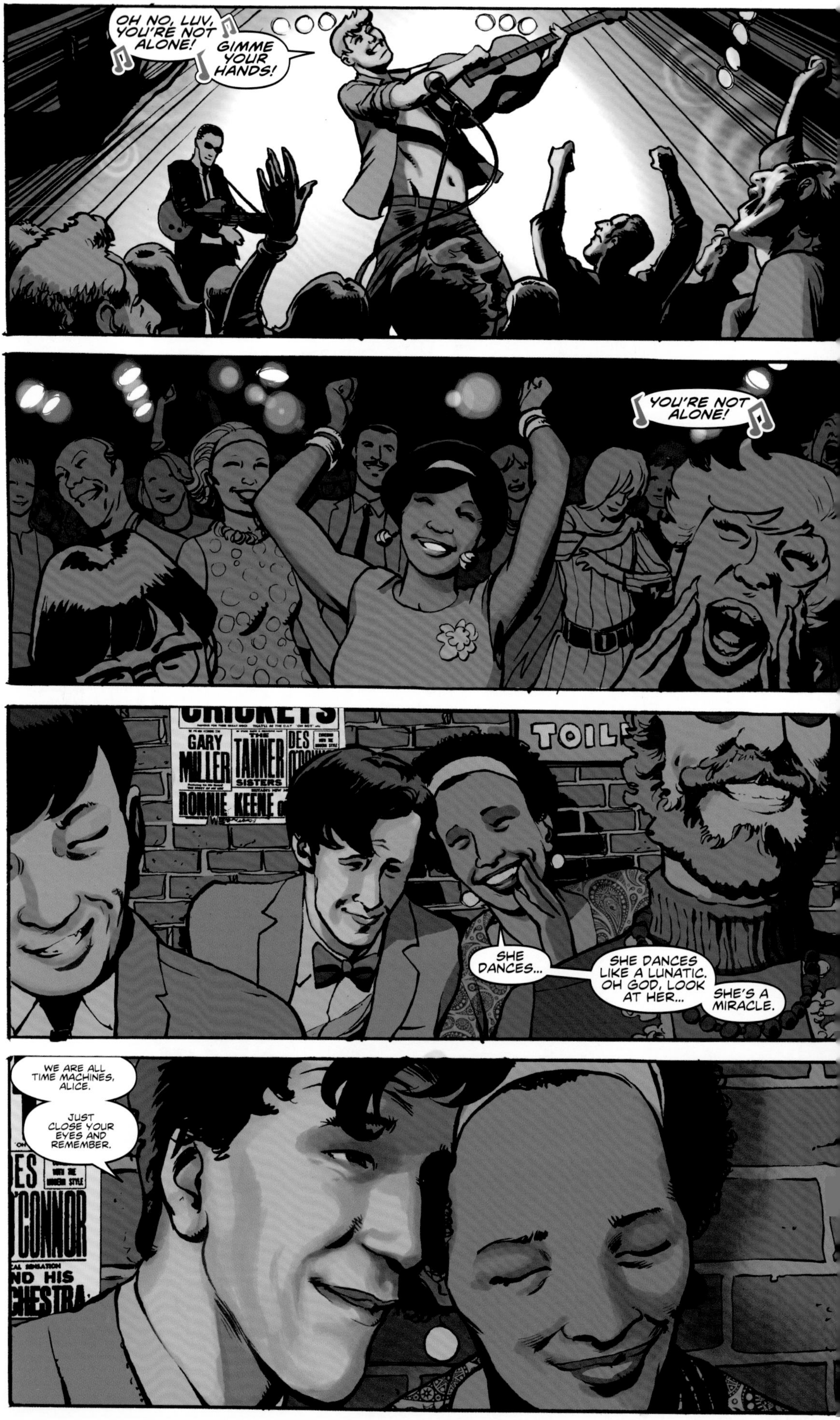
OH NO, LUV, YOU'RE NOT ALONE!
GIMME YOUR HANDS!
YOU'RE NOT ALONE!
CRICKETS
GARY MILLER
THE TANNER SISTERS
DES
RONNIE KEENE
TOIL
SHE DANCES...
SHE DANCES LIKE A LUNATIC. OH GOD, LOOK AT HER...
SHE'S A MIRACLE.
WE ARE ALL TIME MACHINES, ALICE.
JUST CLOSE YOUR EYES AND REMEMBER.
WITH THE MODERN STYLE
'CONNOR
ND HIS
CHESTRA

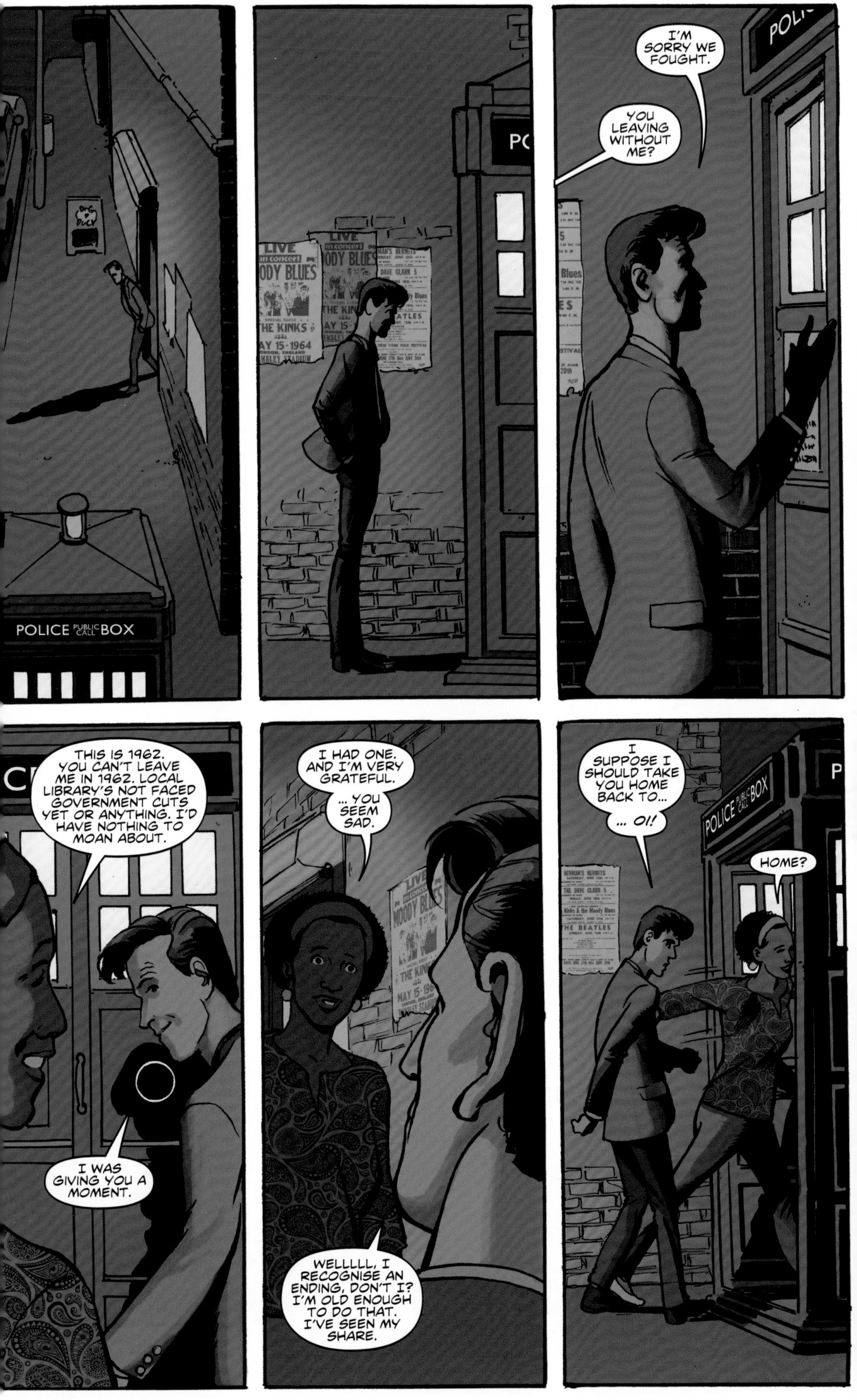
POLICE PUBLIC CALL BOX
I'M SORRY WE FOUGHT.
YOU LEAVING WITHOUT ME?
THIS IS 1962. YOU CAN'T LEAVE ME IN 1962. LOCAL LIBRARY'S NOT FACED GOVERNMENT CUTS YET OR ANYTHING. I'D HAVE NOTHING TO MOAN ABOUT.
I WAS GIVING YOU A MOMENT.
I HAD ONE. AND I'M VERY GRATEFUL.
... YOU SEEM SAD.
WELLLLLL, I RECOGNISE AN ENDING, DON'T I? I'M OLD ENOUGH TO DO THAT. I'VE SEEN MY SHARE.
I SUPPOSE I SHOULD TAKE YOU HOME BACK TO...
... OI!
HOME?
POLICE PUBLIC CALL BOX

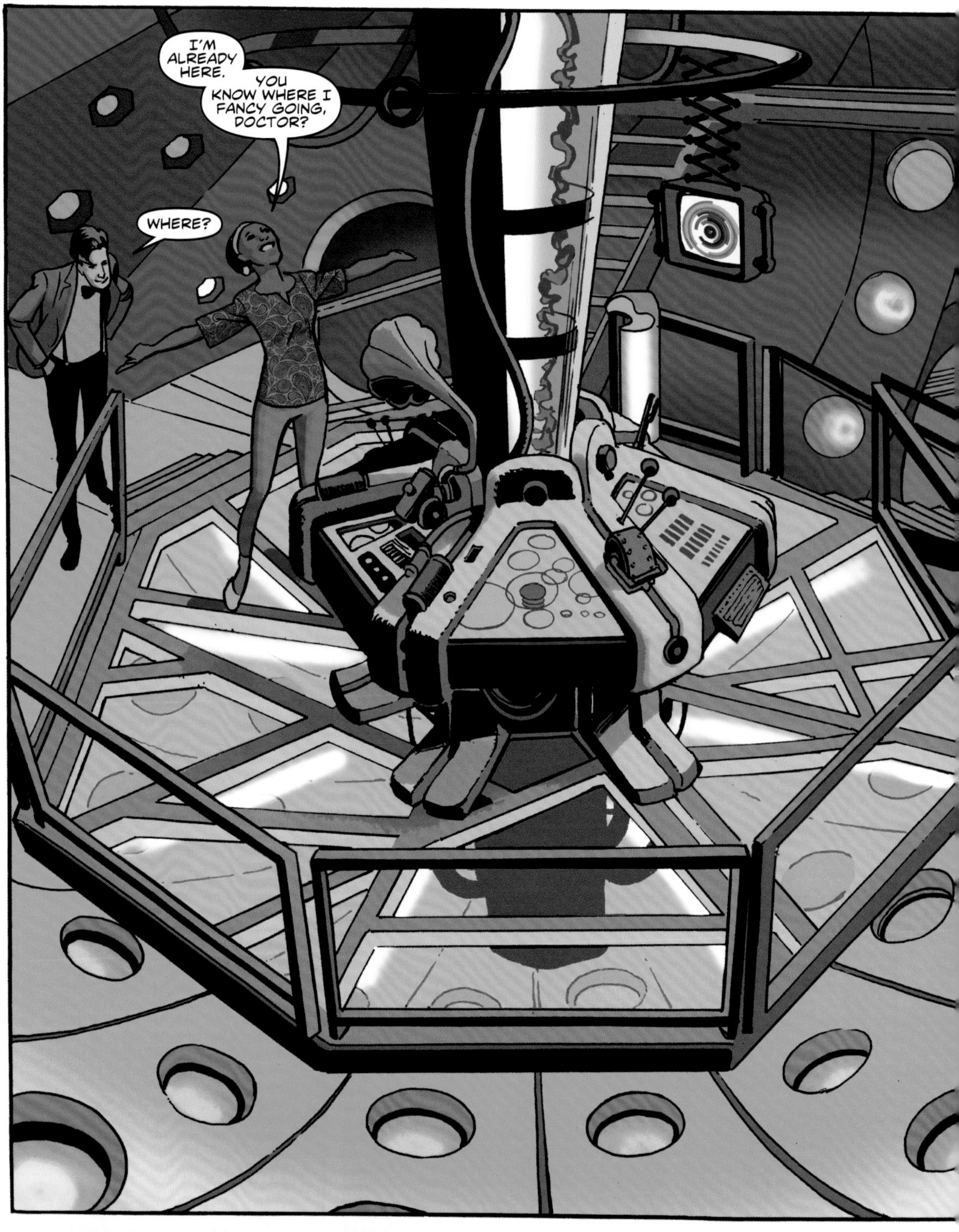
I'M ALREADY HERE.
YOU KNOW WHERE I FANCY GOING, DOCTOR?
WHERE?

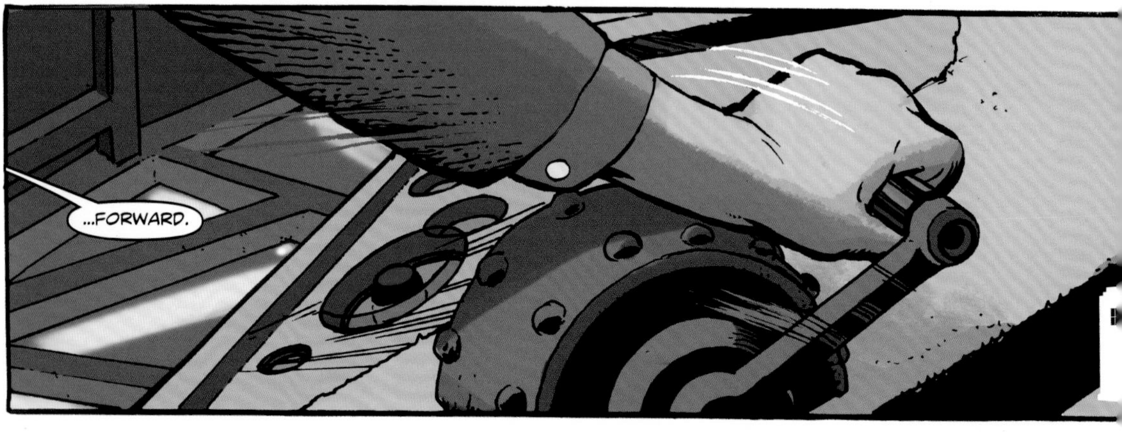
...FORWARD.

CHAPTER 15
THE COMFORT OF THE GOOD PART 2

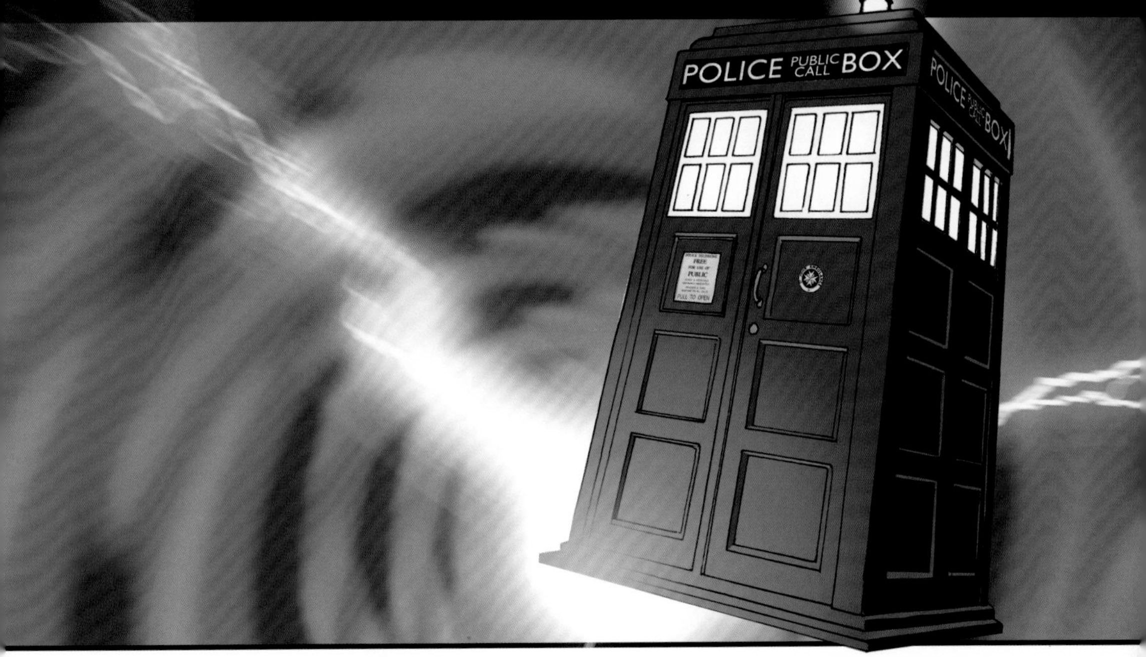
POLICE PUBLIC CALL BOX
POLICE PUBLIC CALL BOX
PULL TO OPEN

WRITERS
AL EWING & ROB WILLIAMS

ARTIST
SIMON FRASER

COLORIST
GARY CALDWELL

LETTERER
RICHARD STARKINGS AND COMICRAFT'S JIMMY BETANCOURT

DOCTOR WHO
THE ELEVENTH DOCTOR

COVER GALLERY

11A

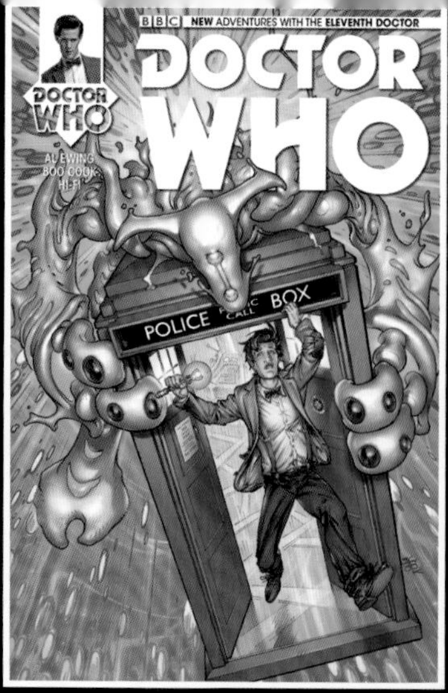

BBC NEW ADVENTURES WITH THE ELEVENTH DOCTOR
DOCTOR WHO
AL EWING
BOO COOK
HI-FI
POLICE PUBLIC CALL BOX

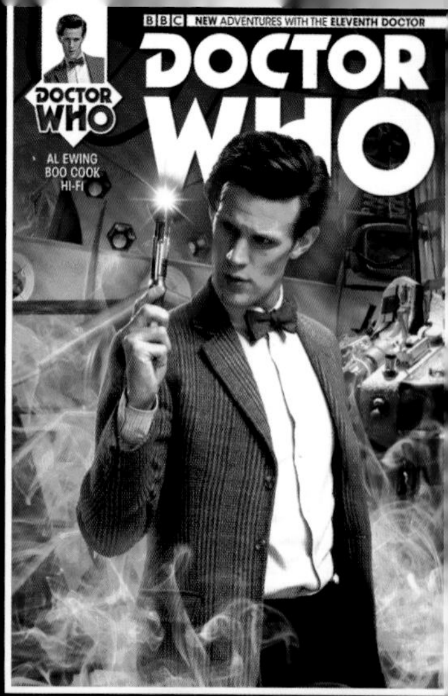

BBC NEW ADVENTURES WITH THE ELEVENTH DOCTOR
DOCTOR WHO
AL EWING
BOO COOK
HI-FI

11B

12A

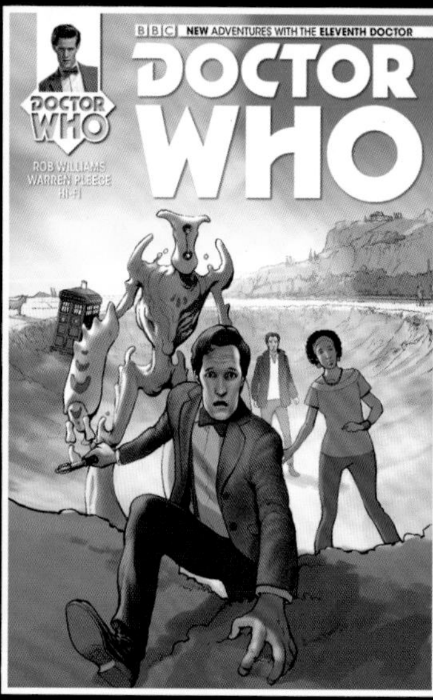

BBC NEW ADVENTURES WITH THE ELEVENTH DOCTOR
DOCTOR WHO
ROB WILLIAMS
WARREN PLEECE
HI-FI

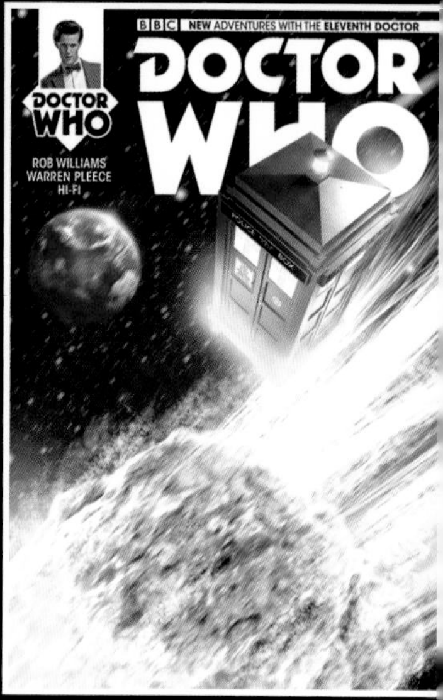

BBC NEW ADVENTURES WITH THE ELEVENTH DOCTOR
DOCTOR WHO
ROB WILLIAMS
WARREN PLEECE
HI-FI

12B

13A

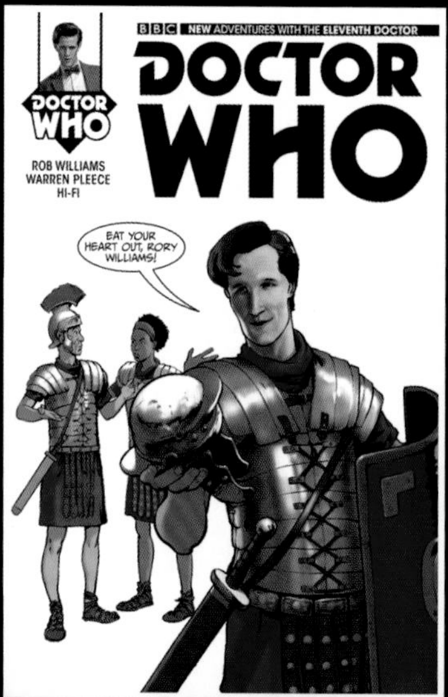

BBC NEW ADVENTURES WITH THE ELEVENTH DOCTOR
DOCTOR WHO
ROB WILLIAMS
WARREN PLEECE
HI-FI
EAT YOUR HEART OUT, RORY WILLIAMS!

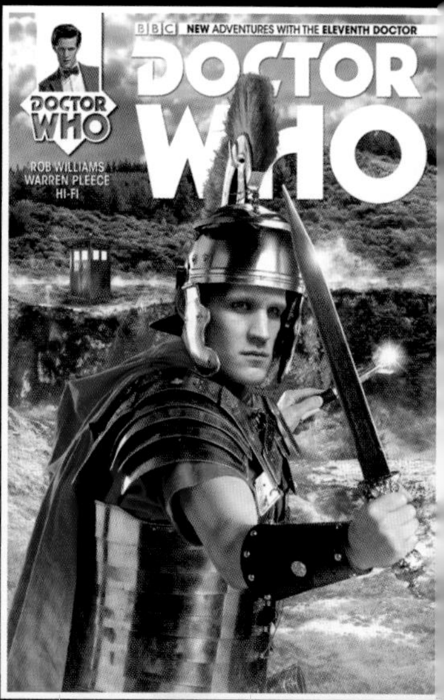

BBC NEW ADVENTURES WITH THE ELEVENTH DOCTOR
DOCTOR WHO
ROB WILLIAMS
WARREN PLEECE
HI-FI

13B

#13 A: Simon Fraser
#13 B: AJ

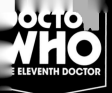

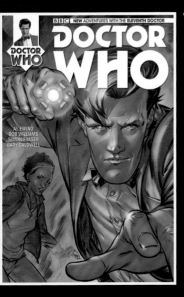

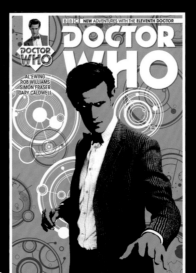

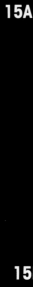

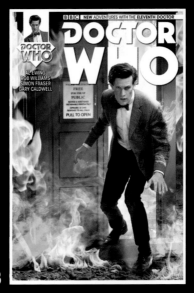

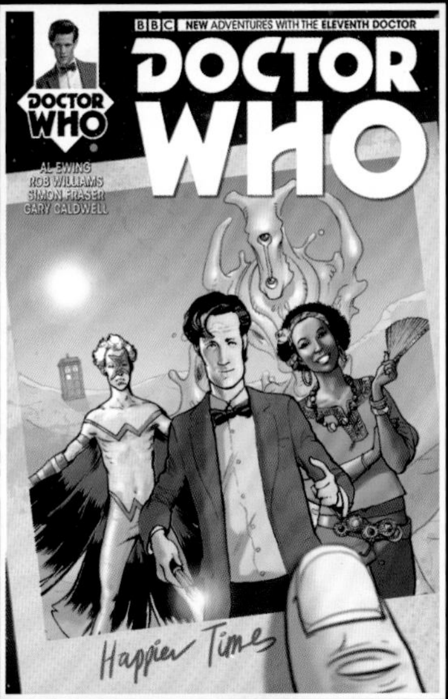

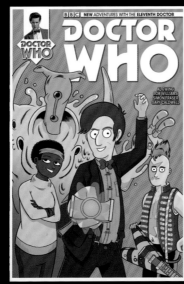

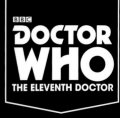

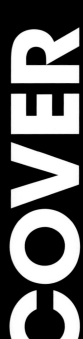

COVER GALLERY

14A

BBC NEW ADVENTURES WITH THE ELEVENTH DOCTOR
DOCTOR WHO
AL EWING
ROB WILLIAMS
SIMON FRASER
GARY CALDWELL

14B

BBC NEW ADVENTURES WITH THE ELEVENTH DOCTOR
DOCTOR WHO
AL EWING
ROB WILLIAMS
SIMON FRASER
GARY CALDWELL

15A

BBC NEW ADVENTURES WITH THE ELEVENTH DOCTOR
DOCTOR WHO
AL EWING
ROB WILLIAMS
SIMON FRASER
GARY CALDWELL
Happier Times

15B

BBC NEW ADVENTURES WITH THE ELEVENTH DOCTOR
DOCTOR WHO
AL EWING
ROB WILLIAMS
SIMON FRASER
GARY CALDWELL
FREE
PUBLIC
PULL TO OPEN

BBC NEW ADVENTURES WITH THE ELEVENTH DOCTOR
DOCTOR WHO
AL EWING
ROB WILLIAMS
SIMON FRASER
GARY CALDWELL

15C

#14 A: Boo Cook
#14 B: AJ/Rob Farmer
#15 A: Fraser/Cook/AJ
#15 B: AJ
#15 C: Marc Ellerby

COMPLETE YOUR COLLECTION! ELEVENTH DOCTOR VOL. 1 AND 2 AVAILABLE NOW!

DOCTOR WHO: THE ELEVENTH DOCTOR
VOL. 1: AFTER LIFE

BBC NEW ADVENTURES WITH THE ELEVENTH DOCTOR
DOCTOR WHO
AFTER LIFE
AL EWING • ROB WILLIAMS • SIMON FRASER • BOO COOK
GARY CALDWELL • HI-FI

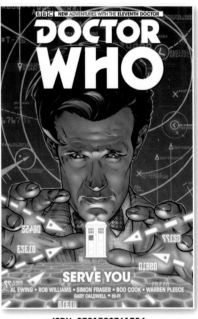

ISBN: 9781782761747
ON SALE NOW - $19.99 / $22.95 CAN / £10.99
(UK EDITION ISBN: 9781782763857)

DOCTOR WHO: THE ELEVENTH DOCTOR
VOL. 2: SERVE YOU

BBC NEW ADVENTURES WITH THE ELEVENTH DOCTOR
DOCTOR WHO
SERVE YOU
AL EWING • ROB WILLIAMS • SIMON FRASER • BOO COOK • WARREN PLEECE
GARY CALDWELL • HI-FI

ISBN: 9781782761754
ON SALE NOW - $19.99 / $25.99 CAN / £10.99
(UK EDITION ISBN: 9781782766582)

COMING SOON! DOCTOR WHO: THE NINTH DOCTOR VOL. 1: WEAPONS OF PAST DESTRUCTION

COLLECTS DOCTOR WHO: THE NINTH DOCTOR MINISERIES #1-#5
COMING SOON $19.99 / $25.99 CAN / £10.99

ISBN: 9781782763369
UK EDITION ISBN: 9781785851056

BBC NEW ADVENTURES WITH THE NINTH DOCTOR
DOCTOR WHO
WEAPONS OF PAST DESTRUCTION
CAVAN SCOTT • BLAIR SHEDD

AVAILABLE IN ALL GOOD COMIC STORES, BOOK STORES, AND DIGITAL PROVIDERS!

BBC